COMPLETE LEGAL GUIDE TO SPECIAL EDUCATION SERVICES

COMPLETE LEGAL GUIDE TO SPECIAL EDUCATION SERVICES

A Handbook for Administrators, Counselors, and Supervisors

Allan G. Osborne, Jr., Ed.D.

PARKER PUBLISHING COMPANY
West Nyack, New York 10995

Library of Congress Cataloging-in-Publication Data

Osborne, Allan G.
    Complete legal guide to special education services: a handbook
for administrators, counselors, and supervisors/Allan G. Osborne.

     p.   cm.
    Includes bibliographies and index.
    ISBN 0-13-162025-8
    1. Special education—Law and legislation—United States.
   2. Handicapped children—Education—Law and legislation—
United States.   I. Title.
KF4210.083 1988
344.73′0791—dc19
[347.304791]   88-17579
                                         CIP

ISBN 0-13-162025-8

PARKER PUBLISHING COMPANY
BUSINESS & PROFESSIONAL DIVISION
A division of Simon & Schuster
West Nyack, New York 10995

Printed in the United States of America

A Dedication

To my wife Debbie; an elementary school teacher who has always had a place in her classroom for special-needs students

and

to my parents Allan and Ruth Osborne; humanitarians who have dedicated their lives to helping those who are less fortunate.

About the Author

Allan G. Osborne, Jr., received a B.A. in psychology from the University of Massachusetts at Boston, an M.Ed. in special education from Fitchburg (MA) State College, and an Ed.D. in educational administration and supervision from Boston College. He specializes in the study of law and public policy in special education.

Dr. Osborne has fourteen years of experience as a teacher and administrator in special education. He is currently on the special education staff at the Quincy (MA) Public Schools and a member of the special education faculty at Bridgewater (MA) State College. He is also a consultant and researcher on law and public policy in special education with Sigma Squared Associates of Millis, Massachusetts.

Dr. Osborne has lectured and written extensively in the area of special education law. He has published numerous articles in special education, school law, and administrative journals and is a nationally recognized expert on special education law.

The author is a member of the Council for Exceptional Children, Phi Delta Kappa, and the National Organization on Legal Problems of Education. He serves as a field reviewer for *Exceptional Children* and is on the Authors Committee of the *Education Law Reporter*.

About This Book

"What exactly is an appropriate education?"

"When are school systems required to provide expensive services as psychotherapy?"

"Do special education students have a separate code of discipline?"

"At what point should a handicapped student be placed in a private school?"

These are questions that have often been asked by school administrators since the Education for All Handicapped Children Act, P.L. 94-142, was passed by Congress and signed into law by President Gerald Ford in 1975. The act, which became effective on October 1, 1977, provides that school systems are to assure all children a free appropriate public education and related services designed to meet their specific and unique needs. That act has had a greater impact on the operation of our public schools than any other piece of legislation.

Although the act has been implemented for a little more than a decade, it has become a major source of litigation in the federal and state courts, causing a great deal of concern among public school administrators. The act and the consequent litigation have drastically altered the scope and purpose of the public schools and have added new responsibilities and duties to the shoulders of school administrators. Although few administrators would argue with the intent of the law, most are not fully aware of all of the law's specific requirements and are often very apprehensive.

Critical decisions must be made daily concerning the development and implementation of programs for handicapped students and the allocation of scarce resources to those programs. To make these decisions, administrators need to consider the legal requirements involved in providing an appropriate program of special education and related services. The administrator needs to have knowledge of what is and is not required and an understanding of all pertinent legal issues. Unfortunately, as with many laws, the act itself does not always provide clear guidance. Administrators must look toward court decisions for additional insight before making these critical decisions.

Complete Legal Guide to Special Education Services provides comprehensive and detailed information about how the courts have interpreted the act. Legal trends and developing legal principles in providing special education and related services are extracted from the case law. These emerging concepts develop a set of guidelines that can be used by school administrators to make decisions. In today's public schools, administrators at all levels, from the superintendent down to the evaluation team chairperson, must have comprehensive information about what is and is not legally appropriate. This book provides that information in a clear, easily readable style.

This book has been designed to provide you with detailed information and guidelines that will help you make legally correct decisions regarding special education programs and special education students. It is not intended to replace the advice of the school district's attorney. However, by providing you with a better understanding of the legal issues involved in the provision of special education services, it will help you make decisions that will withstand legal challenges. An administrator who understands the legal implications and principles involved in various situations will make legally correct decisions and will thus avoid costly litigation. The book is organized by topics in such a way that it can serve as a ready reference for consultation regarding specific situations.

No school administrator can escape the special education web. In addition to special education personnel, building-level and central office administrators are also very much involved in special education programming. Building principals often supervise special education programs and personnel and are often involved in student placement decisions. Central office administrators must also consider how special education will affect and be affected by systemwide issues such as general policy, budget, personnel deployment, curriculum, and physical plant allocation. The special education administrator, of course, has direct responsibility for the total operation of the special education program.

Complete Legal Guide to Special Education Services has been organized to provide you with a comprehensive reference guide to the legal problems that will arise daily in the public schools. At the end of each chapter, you will find a comprehensive summary of the important cases that have come before the courts. This will allow you to compare a given situation to a case that has already been litigated. Also, the ready-to-use forms and checklists in each chapter will provide you with a quick reference and with some working tools for actual application of the law. These forms will help you document the decision-making process and may prove to be invaluable if any decisions are appealed to a due process hearing.

Chapter One provides an historical perspective of the special education movement. It begins with the exclusion of handicapped children from the public schools in the early part of our country's history and concludes with the implementation of the Education for All Handicapped Children Act. It also discusses the development of special education schools and classes for the handicapped, the effects of the civil rights movement on special education, and the landmark *PARC* and *Mills* cases.

Chapter Two outlines the specific rights of access to public special education programs and the right to an education in the least restrictive environment that handicapped children now have. It also defines the legal components of an appropriate education and discusses how you can determine if any given program is legally appropriate.

Chapter Three details the situations and circumstances under which a school district must provide and pay for an educational placement in a private day or residential school. Guidelines are provided to help you determine whether a public school placement would be adequate or whether a private school placement is necessary in any given situation.

Traditionally, the school year in most states lasts for 180 days. However, in certain situations school districts are required to provide handicapped students with educational programs that exceed the standard 180 days. Chapter Four discusses the circumstances under which this must be done and provides you with guidelines to help make the determination as to whether or not an extended school year is required for any particular handicapped child.

One provision of the act is its elaborate due process requirements. Due process must be provided any time a school district proposes to change a handicapped student's program. School districts often make adjustments to their educational programs, and due process is not necessarily required every time an adjustment is made to a handicapped child's program. Precisely what constitutes a change in placement requiring due process is outlined in Chapter Five. Also, the parents of handicapped children have often removed their children from the public schools and enrolled them in private facilities and have later sought to have the school district assume the costs. The circumstances under which the school district may be required to do so are also outlined in this chapter.

The act also requires school districts to provide handicapped students with certain related or supportive services to help them benefit from their special education programs. Chapter Six discusses the related services mandate and provides guidelines as to what services are required and how you can determine when the school district is required to provide services such as psychotherapy, recreation programs, and health services.

Disciplining handicapped students has been particularly troublesome for school administrators. School officials need to maintain order, but handicapped students also have the right to receive an education in the least restrictive environment. Chapter Seven provides you with guidance about how a balance can be struck between the rights of handicapped children under the act and your ever-present duty to maintain order and discipline in the school. The specific steps that need to be taken to discipline a handicapped student without violating the law are clearly outlined.

Chapter Eight discusses other issues that are also related to the handicapped student's legal right to special education and related services. Topics in this chapter include issues such as participation in basic skills or minimum competency testing, native language evaluations, student record requirements, and the provision of special education services to students attending parochial schools.

Chapter Nine provides a summary of the issues presented and draws some conclusions about what school districts are and are not required to do under the Education for All Handicapped Children Act. Further guidelines for administrators are also provided.

In short, *Complete Legal Guide to Special Education Services* provides today's school administrator with detailed information and guidance, substantiated by actual court cases, about how the law is to be implemented.

Allan G. Osborne, Jr.

Acknowledgments

An undertaking such as this cannot be successful without the support, encouragement, and counsel of many friends and colleagues. I am fortunate in that far too many people fall into this category than I am able to mention. So to all my past and present colleagues, I extend an all-inclusive, heartfelt "thank you."

I especially wish, however, to extend my sincere appreciation to the following for their many major contributions: Dr. Donald T. Donley, Dr. Lester E. Przewlocki, and Dr. Philip DiMattia of Boston College; Mr. Paul Primavera, Ms. Annette Packard, and Mr. Don Smith of the Bellingham (MA) public schools; and Mr. Louis Tozzi, Dr. Carol Lee Griffin, Mr. Morrie Hibbard, Mr. Richard DeCristofaro, Mr. Philip Connolly, and Mr. Theodore Curley of the Quincy (MA) public schools.

My appreciation to my family for a lifetime of moral support and encouragement can never be adequately expressed. However, I wish to extend a most sincere thank you to my parents Allan G. and Ruth L. Osborne for encouraging me to pursue my education, and especially to my wife, colleague, and friend, Debbie, without whom this would not have been possible.

Contents

Chapter 2

HOW IS AN APPROPRIATE EDUCATION DEFINED? **17**

Chapter 3

WHEN ARE PRIVATE DAY AND RESIDENTIAL PLACEMENTS REQUIRED? **59**

Chapter 4

WHEN IS IT NECESSARY TO PROVIDE SERVICES BEYOND THE TRADITIONAL SCHOOL YEAR? **88**

Chapter 5

WHAT MUST BE DONE TO CHANGE A HANDICAPPED STUDENT'S PLACEMENT? **103**

Chapter 6

WHAT ARE RELATED SERVICES
AND WHEN MUST THEY BE PROVIDED? **130**

Chapter 7

WHAT ARE THE SPECIAL REQUIREMENTS FOR DISCIPLINING HANDICAPPED STUDENTS? **156**

Chapter 8

WHAT ARE THE REQUIREMENTS FOR TESTING, RECORD KEEPING, AND PROVIDING SERVICES TO PAROCHIAL SCHOOL STUDENTS? **177**

Chapter 9

HOW DOES THE HANDICAPPED LAW AFFECT EDUCATIONAL POLICY AND DECISION MAKING?   **198**

APPENDICES

Chapter 1

HOW DID WE GET TO WHERE WE ARE TODAY?

> *This is a noble and humanitarian end in which the Commonwealth of Pennsylvania has chosen to join. Today, with the following Order, this group of citizens will have new hope in their quest for a life of dignity and self-sufficiency.*
>
> **District Judge Masterson**
> **P.A.R.C. v. Pennsylvania**
> **343 F.Supp. 279 at 302 (1972)**

Special education has evolved from being a private family concern in the seventeenth century to being a public concern today. When public schools first came into being in colonial America, the handicapped, or those who were "unable to profit from education," were virtually excluded. Any education or training received by handicapped students was the result of family concern and efforts for their well-being.

In the nineteenth century, special schools and classes for the blind, deaf, and physically disabled began to emerge. Toward the end of that century and the beginning of the next century, classes for the mentally retarded were developed. Unfortunately, these programs were segregated from the mainstream, and those who taught them were poorly trained.

EXCLUSION OF THE HANDICAPPED BEGINS

In 1893 the Supreme Judicial Court of Massachusetts upheld the exclusion of a mentally retarded student from the public schools in *Watson* v. *City of Cam-*

bridge. The student had earlier been excluded because he was too "weak minded" to profit from instruction. School records also indicated that he was troublesome and was unable to care for himself physically. The court ruled that the school committee, by law, had general charge of the schools and refused to interfere with their judgment. However, the court went on to state that if acts of disorder interfered with the operation of the school, whether committed voluntarily or because of imbecility, the school committee should be able to exclude the offender without being overruled by a jury that had no expertise to deal with educational matters.

In 1919 the Wisconsin Supreme Court also upheld the exclusion of a handicapped student in *State* v. *Antigo*. In this case a student with a form of paralysis was excluded after having attended the public schools through fifth grade. The student had normal intelligence, but his condition caused him to drool and make facial contortions, and his speech was affected. School officials claimed that his physical appearance nauseated teachers and other students, his disability required an undue amount of the teacher's time, and he had a negative impact on the discipline and progress of the school.

School officials had suggested that he attend the day school for deaf students and those with defective speech. The student refused and was supported by his parents. However, the superintendent and school board refused to reinstate him in the public schools' regular program. The court upheld the exclusion, stating that the child's right to attend the public schools could not be insisted upon when his presence there was harmful to the best interests of the school. The court further stated that if his presence was detrimental to the best interests of the school, the school board had an obligation to exclude him.

Compulsory Attendance and Exclusion of the Handicapped

In *Board of Education* v. *Goldman* the Court of Appeals of Cuyahoga County, Ohio, in 1934 upheld the authority of school officials to exclude certain students, but ordered that the child in question be allowed to attend school because the proper legal steps for exclusion had not been followed. In its opinion, the court recognized the dilemma between compulsory attendance requirements (and an entitlement to attend) and exclusionary provisions.

Ohio statute mandated that children between the ages of 6 and 18 attend school; however, the State Department of Education was given the power to prescribe standards to determine if certain children were incapable of profiting from continued instruction. The school board of Cleveland Heights had adopted a rule excluding any student with an I.Q. score below 50. A student with I.Q. scores ranging from 45 to 61 was subsequently excluded. The court concluded that the Ohio statute gave the state Department of Education the authority to exclude certain students. Since local officials, and not the state, had made the final determination, the student was admitted.

The Right to Attend School

Although the court in *Goldman* ruled that the state Department of Education had the statutory authority to exclude certain students from the public schools, it stated that students have a right to attend school and that they need to do so. The court further noted that education was considered to be so essential that between certain ages, it was compulsory.

Several other states such as New York, Maine, and Oregon also had statutes that specifically authorized school officials to exclude handicapped students. The New York law stated that the schools could exclude students who were so "feeble-minded" that they would not benefit from instruction.

THE INFLUENCE OF THE CIVIL RIGHTS MOVEMENT ON SPECIAL EDUCATION

The twentieth century, especially since World War II, has ushered in the greatest advancements in the field. These changes have not come easily; rather, they have come about because of a combination of improved professional knowledge, social advancements, and legal mandates initiated by concerned parents, educators, and citizens.

To a very large extent, the civil rights movement provided the initial stimulation for the special education movement. Many of the rights established for minorities were subsequently accorded to handicapped students. In *Brown* v. *Board of Education,* the landmark school desegregation case, the U.S. Supreme Court unknowingly laid the foundation for future right to education cases on behalf of handicapped children. Writing for the majority, Mr. Chief Justice Warren said that education was the most important governmental function. He noted that an education was necessary for citizens to exercise their most basic civic responsibilities. The Chief Justice further stated that "In these days, it is doubtful that any child may reasonably be expected to succeed in life if he is denied the opportunity of an education. Such an opportunity, where the State has undertaken to provide it, is a right that must be made available to all on equal terms" (P. 493).

Chief Justice Warren's full statement was often quoted directly or paraphrased in later handicapped education cases. This is not surprising because many similarities exist between the plaintiffs in civil rights cases and handicapped children in special education cases. In each situation the students were denied the basic right to an equal educational opportunity.

The Other Minority

In subsequent years the handicapped became known as "the other minority" as special educators and parents demanded that the handicapped be accorded the same rights to an equal educational opportunity as had been gained by racial and ethnic minorities.

THE EQUAL EDUCATIONAL OPPORTUNITY MOVEMENT MAKES HEADWAY

During the late 1960s and early 1970s, several cases came before the federal courts seeking an equal educational opportunity for the poor, for language minorities, and for racial minorities. Although not all these suits were successful, the movement helped to further the cause of the handicapped. As with the *Brown* case the legal principles and much of the language that came out of these cases had direct implications for the plight of the handicapped students.

Tracking Ruled Discriminatory

The U.S. District Court for the District of Columbia in 1967 ruled that the tracking system as used by the District of Columbia school system was discriminatory in that it afforded certain classes of students an unequal educational opportunity. The District of Columbia was ordered to abolish the track system, as a result of the ruling in *Hobson* v. *Hansen*.

Students had been placed in these tracks, or curriculum levels, as early as elementary school based on the school's assessment of their ability. That assessment relied heavily on the use of nationally normed standardized aptitude tests. Testimony at trial indicated that these tests may have been appropriate for white middle-class students, but they could give inaccurate and misleading results when used with other classes of students. Using these tests with poor minority students often resulted in their being placed according to environmental and psychological factors rather than according to innate ability. Unfortunately, once placed, it was difficult for a student to ever move out of the assigned track.

The court found substantial evidence that indicated that the District lacked the ability to determine accurately the innate learning abilities of a majority of its students. Their placement in lower tracks was, thus, not justified. The tracking system, as used by the District, deprived certain classes of students of their constitutional right to an equal educational opportunity in that students in the lower tracks received a limited curriculum. The tracking system further denied students an equal educational opportunity by failing to provide compensatory education to the disadvantaged child that would help bring him or her back into the mainstream of public education.

Culturally Biased Testing Forbidden

The courts faced the issue of placement of students on the basis of culturally biased testing on two other occasions. In *Diana* v. *State Board of Education,* a

Spanish-speaking student was placed in a class for the mentally retarded on the basis of an I.Q. test administered in English. The court ordered reevaluation in Spanish. The issue was similar in *Larry P.* v. *Wilson Riles* except that the plaintiff in this case was black. The court ordered the schools to use tests that were not racially biased.

Remedial English Becomes a Requirement

The U.S. Supreme Court in 1974 reversed the lower courts' rulings in regard to compensatory education programs for non-English–speaking students. A class action suit had been filed on behalf of Chinese students in the San Francisco school system who did not speak English and were not being provided with English language instruction. The district court denied the students relief, and the appeals court affirmed. The Supreme Court, however, reversed, finding that the failure to provide remedial English language instruction to non-English–speaking students was a violation of Section 601 of the Civil Rights Act of 1964. The Court found that the lack of remedial instruction denied the students a meaningful opportunity to participate in public education. In its decision, the Court quoted applicable regulations of the Department of Health, Education, and Welfare that state that

> Where inability to speak and understand the English language excludes national origin minority children from effective participation in educational programs offered by a school district, the district must take affirmative steps to rectify the language deficiency in order to open its instructional programs to these students. (35 Fed. Reg. 11595)

Since the San Francisco school system was a recipient of federal funds, it was bound by this regulation. The plaintiffs had also claimed that the lack of remedial instruction also violated the equal protection clause of the Fourteenth Amendment; however, the Supreme Court did not rule on this constitutional question.

The Issue of Equal Expenditure and Equal Education

A number of cases have come before the courts claiming that the poor were discriminated against in that the quality of education provided was based on the wealth of the district. In most of these cases, the use of the property tax to finance education, resulting in great disparities in educational expenditures among a state's school districts, was contested. The differences in expenditure levels, it was claimed, resulted in differences in quality of education. In the federal courts, the claims were made on the basis of the equal protection clause of the Fourteenth Amendment. In the state courts, the claims were based on similar clauses of the state constitutions.

The Supreme Court decided the matter in regard to the federal constitution in 1973 in the landmark *San Antonio* v. *Rodriguez* case. In reversing the lower court, the Supreme Court found that the poor were not a suspect class and that education was not a fundamental right. Mr. Justice Powell, in writing for the majority, stated that at least where wealth was concerned, the Equal Protection Clause did not require absolute equality.

The Court Defines a Suspect Class

The *Rodriquez* court did, however, delineate the criteria for what would constitute a suspect class. The Court stated that a suspect class is one "saddled with such disabilities, or subjected to such a history of purposeful unequal treatment, or relegated to such a position of political powerlessness as to command extraordinary protection from the majoritarian political process" (P. 28).

The "Strict Scrutiny Test"

Several courts later considered the idea of the handicapped being a suspect class. Categorization as a suspect class requires that the court use the strict scrutiny test. This is important because the plaintiffs generally win when they are entitled to strict scrutiny. It is much more difficult, however, when the court uses the rational basis test to determine whether or not a difference in treatment is justified.

On the basis of state constitutional provisions, several state courts of last resort have ruled on issues similar to those brought out in *Rodriquez*. For example, the California Supreme Court in 1971 found that state's school finance system to be in violation of the equal protection of the law provisions of the California Constitution in the well-known *Serrano* v. *Priest* case. The court employed the strict scrutiny test in reaching its conclusion. Overall, the state courts are fairly evenly split on the issue. How a given state would interpret its equal protection clause in regard to expenditures may affect its interpretation in regard to the handicapped.

THE P.A.R.C. AND MILLS ERA: EQUAL EDUCATIONAL OPPORTUNITY FOR THE HANDICAPPED

As the equal educational opportunity cases in the previous section were being decided, advocates for the handicapped were bringing similar cases before the courts on their behalf. Although all these cases were decided by lower federal courts or state courts, many are considered landmark cases in that they brought about substantial legal advancements in the area of equal educational opportunity for the handicapped.

Mentally Retarded Students Entitled to Education

One of the first decisions in favor of the handicapped, *Wolf* v. *Utah*, was handed down by the Third Judicial District Court of Salt Lake County, Utah, in 1969. Suit had been filed on behalf of two mentally retarded children who had been denied admission to the public schools. The children had been enrolled in a day care center at their parents' expense.

The Utah Constitution provided that the public school system should be open to all children in the state. The Utah Supreme Court had previously interpreted that provision broadly. Utah law further provided that public education would be provided at taxpayers' expense for all children between the ages of 6 and 21 who had not completed high school.

The court in this case declared that mentally retarded children were entitled to a free public education under the state constitution. The opinion of the court is remarkably similar to portions of the *Brown* opinion.

Right to Education for the Handicapped Established

In 1972 federal district courts in Pennsylvania and the District of Columbia decided a pair of cases that, taken together, have had a profound effect on the education of handicapped children in this country. In addition to influencing subsequent court opinions, these decisions formed the basis of later legislation for handicapped education. *Pennsylvania Association for Retarded Children* v. *Commonwealth of Pennsylvania* and *Mills* v. *Board of Education* established that handicapped children were entitled to receive a free, appropriate public education under the Equal Protection Clause of the U.S. Constitution.

State Obligated to Educate Mentally Retarded Children

A class action suit was brought before the court in Pennsylvania by the Pennsylvania Association for Retarded Children (P.A.R.C.) and thirteen parents of retarded children on behalf of all mentally retarded persons between the ages of 6 and 21 who had been excluded from a program of education and training in the public schools. The exclusions were based on four state statutes that relieved the state Board of Education of any obligation to educate a child certified as uneducable and untrainable by a school psychologist, allowed a postponement of admission of any child who had not attained a mental age of 5 years, excused a child from compulsory attendance who had been found unable to profit from education, and defined compulsory school age as 8 to 17 and was used to exclude retarded children not between those ages. The plaintiffs sought a declaratory judgment that the statutes were unconstitutional and a preliminary and permanent injunction against the enforcement of statutes.

The case was settled by a stipulation and consent agreement between the parties that was approved by the court. The stipulation stated that no mentally retarded child, or child thought to be mentally retarded, could be assigned to a special education program or be excluded from the public schools without due process. The consent agreement stated that the Commonwealth had an obligation to provide each mentally retarded child with a free public education and training program appropriate to the child's capacity.

Right to Education Extended to Other Handicapped Children

The *Mills* case extended the right to a free public education to other classes of exceptional children. The *Mills* court also ruled that lack of funds was not an appropriate defense for failure to provide an appropriate education to handicapped students.

The *Mills* suit was also a class action brought on behalf of seven children who had been excluded from the public schools after having been classified as behavioral problems, mentally retarded, emotionally disturbed, and hyperactive. The plaintiffs sought a declaration of rights and an enjoinment ordering the District of Columbia to provide publicly supported education to all exceptional children either within the public schools or at any alternative placement at public expense. It was estimated that eighteen thousand out of twenty-two thousand exceptional children were not receiving special education services.

The defendants admitted that they had the responsibility to provide a publicly supported education to meet the needs of all children in the District and that they had failed to do so. However, they claimed it was impossible to afford the plaintiffs the relief sought due to a lack of funds. The defendants also admitted that they had not provided the plaintiffs with due process procedures prior to their exclusion.

The court found that the defendants were required by the U.S. Constitution, the District of Columbia Code, and their own regulations to provide a publicly supported education to all children, including those classified as exceptional. The court ruled that the District must expend its available funds equitably so that all students would receive a publicly supported education consistent with their needs and abilities. If sufficient funds were not available, then existing funds would have to be distributed in such a manner that no child was entirely excluded, and the inadequacies could not be allowed to bear more heavily on the exceptional child than on the normal child. The District was ordered to also provide due process safeguards before any child was excluded from the public schools, reassigned, or had special education services terminated. In its opinion, the court outlined elaborate due process procedures that were to be followed. These procedures later formed the foundation for the due process safeguards that were mandated in the handicapped education laws.

Education Must Be Free

In 1973 the Family Court of New York City in *In re Downey* ruled that requiring the parents of a handicapped child to contribute to the costs of the child's education violated the equal protection clauses of both the U.S. and New York constitutions. The plaintiffs' son had been attending an out-of-state school because the city of New York did not have an adequate public facility that could meet his instructional needs. The school he attended had been approved by the state Department of Education. The plaintiffs had sought reimbursement for the difference between actual tuition costs and the state aid received. In its opinion, the court stated that it was the child who was given the right to an education, not the parent, and that right should not be limited or abridged by the parents' willingness to pay.

Handicapped Entitled to Education Under State Constitution

In 1974 the North Dakota Supreme Court ruled that a handicapped child had a constitutional right to an education under the state constitution. The dispute in *In re G.H.* arose after the child's parents had moved out of state, leaving her behind at the residential school she had been attending. The school district that had been responsible for her tuition and the welfare department argued over which party was responsible for her educational expenses. In reaching the conclusion that the school district was liable, the court first determined that the child had the right to have her tuition paid, declaring that handicapped children were entitled to no less than unhandicapped children under the state's constitution. The court also suggested that handicapped children constituted a suspect class because their handicaps were characteristics that were determined solely by the accident of birth. The court felt that depriving the handicapped of a meaningful educational opportunity was a similar denial of equal protection as had been held to be unconstitutional in racial discrimination cases.

Adequacy of Programs Challenged

In 1975 a case dealing with the adequacy of an educational placement came before a federal district court in Pennsylvania. The plaintiffs in *Fialkowski* v. *Shapp* claimed that their sons, who had mental ages of 19 months and 15 months, were not getting an appropriate education in that they were being taught academic subjects instead of self-help skills. The defendants, relying on the *Rodriquez* case, argued that the plaintiffs had no claim because there was no fundamental right to an education. The court ruled that *Rodriquez* was not controlling and found that the plaintiffs' sons were not being given an adequate education because their program was not giving them the tools they would need in life. The plaintiffs had argued that retarded children were a suspect class and the court felt that their argument had appeal. Reviewing the Supreme Court's criteria for a suspect class outlined in *Rodriquez*, the court stated that such a test could include retarded children. However, the court saw no need to resolve the issue in this case. A federal district court in Pennsylvania in 1976 heard a class action suit filed on behalf of children with specific learning disabilities who, the plaintiffs claimed, had been deprived of an education appropriate to their specialized needs. The complaint in *Frederick L.* v. *Thomas* alleged that children with specific learning disabilities who were not receiving instruction suited to their needs were being discriminated against in that "normal" children were receiving a free public education appropriate to their needs, that mentally retarded children were being provided with a free public education suited to their needs, and that some children with specific learning disabilities were receiving special instruction. Therefore, the plaintiffs claimed, specific learning disabled children who were not receiving an education designed to overcome their handicaps were being denied an equal educational opportunity. The court determined that the plaintiffs were not being provided with appropriate educational services in violation of Pennsylvania special education statutes and regulations. The Third Circuit Court of Appeals upheld the decision.

Classification of Handicapped Students Upheld

Also in 1976, a federal district court in Ohio ruled that a system that classified children according to their capacity to profit from instruction for placement purposes, and a system of training the mentally retarded that was discretionary in its availability, with greater emphasis being placed on those with the greatest intellectual capacity, were constitutional. The plaintiffs had claimed that the Ohio statutes classified students according to their I.Q. scores and that those with lower I.Q. scores were not granted the same rights and privileges as were those with I.Q. scores in the average range. The retarded were thus denied equal protection in that they were not provided educational opportunities on the same basis as the nonretarded.

The court found in *Cuyahoga County* v. *Essex* that Ohio statutes did not classify students according to their I.Q. scores but, rather, classified them according to their ability to profit from instruction. Using the rational basis test, the court declared that a system that recognized that some children would benefit only from special education and that others would not benefit from the public education system at all was not discriminatory. The court thus upheld the practice of educating some students in a segregated environment and excluding others. The court also ruled that the practice of placing the greatest emphasis, in terms of available funds, on training programs for those with a higher capacity, which resulted in the exclusion of some, was not unconstitutional.

The court did, however, find that Ohio's due process procedures for the assessment and placement of students in special education classes was deficient. The deficiency existed because the Ohio regulations did not require school authorities to provide notice, afford opportunity for reviewing of evidence, grant the right to introduce new evidence, and guarantee that the superintendent would receive all relevant information before rendering a decision.

The *Cuyahoga* decision is one of the few modern judicial opinions that have approved the exclusion of a category of mentally retarded children. It appears to have resulted because of the selection of the rational basis test and the misconception that certain retarded children could not benefit from instruction. In rendering its decision, the court apparently paid little attention to the equal educational opportunity for the handicapped opinions that had already been issued by other federal district courts. It is interesting to note that this decision was rendered after the passage of the Education for All Handicapped Children Act, but before its implementation.

Due Process Required Prior to Special Education Placement

Again in 1976 an exclusion and due process case came before a federal district court. Suit was brought in West Virginia on behalf of a student with spina bifida who had been excluded from regular public school classes even though she was mentally competent to attend them. The student in *Hairston* v. *Drosick* was excluded without prior written notice or other procedural safeguards. The school district offered three alternatives: she could (1) attend the regular program if her mother went to the school during the day to attend to her, (2) be given home instruction, or (3) be placed in a special class.

The court ruled that the exclusion of a minimally handicapped student from the public schools' regular classroom without a legitimate educational reason violated Section 504 of the Rehabilitation Act of 1973. The court also ruled that the exclusion of a child from the regular classroom and placement in a special education program without prior written notice, the opportunity to be heard, and other procedural safeguards violated the due process clause of the Fourteenth Amendment.

Education Must Be at Public Expense

A district court in Wisconsin ordered school districts in that state to provide an appropriate education at public expense to educable mentally retarded children. Not to do so, ruled the court, would be a violation of the Equal Protection Clause of the Fourteenth Amendment.

Panitch v. *Wisconsin* originated in 1972; however, proceedings were delayed since state legislation that would satisfy the plaintiffs' demands for a free public education were to go into effect in 1973. The stay was vacated when the court determined in 1977 that defendants' delay in implementing the state law had been inordinate. The court stated that the long delay was a sufficient indication of intentional discrimination in violation of the equal protection clause. The defendants were ordered to provide promptly the plaintiff class with an appropriate education at public expense.

Constitutional Right to a Free Appropriate Public Education

The foregoing cases established that handicapped children have a constitutional right to receive a free appropriate public education. However, since the U.S. Supreme Court has never rendered an opinion on the matter, it is not as firmly established as it might be. With the advent of federal legislation mandating special education programs for the handicapped, the question became somewhat moot. This is unfortunate because an interpretation that the Constitution mandates a free appropriate public education is preferable to having that right granted only by legislation that is subject to repeal.

LEGISLATIVE MANDATES

Although P.L. 94-142 is the best known and most far-reaching handicapped education law, it is not the only legislation granting specific educational rights to the handicapped. It is, however, the crown jewel in a series of federal laws for the handicapped. Several states had also passed legislation of their own along a similar vein prior to the passage of P.L. 94-142.

Section 504, The Rehabilitation Act

The Rehabilitation Act of 1973, Section 504, declared that

> No otherwise qualified handicapped individual in the United States . . . shall, solely by reason of his handicap, be excluded from the participation in, be denied the benefit of, or be subjected to discrimination under any program or activity receiving federal financial assistance. (29 U.S.C. § 794)

Section 504 was the first civil rights legislation that specifically guaranteed the rights of the handicapped. The provisions that the handicapped could not be discriminated against in programs receiving federal funds were similar to nondiscrmination provisions that had previously been granted on the basis of race and sex.

P.L. 93-380, Education of the Handicapped Amendment

The Education of the Handicapped Amendment of 1974, P.L. 93-380 (20 U.S.C. § 1221.1), reaffirmed that the goal of equal educational opportunity was a high priority of the United States and declared that it would be a national policy to provide all citizens with an education that would help them meet their full potential. P.L. 93-380 also provided funds for the education of handicapped students under Title IV-B, outlined due process procedures, and provided for education of the handicapped in the least restrictive environment. P.L. 93-380 was an amendment to the Elementary and Secondary Education Act. The ESEA, and its several amendments had previously provided funding for various programs for disadvantaged and handicapped children. In addition to providing funds to assist the states financially in developing and improving special education programs, the ESEA also created the Bureau of Education for the Handicapped and established the National Advisory Council on Handicapped Children.

P.L. 94-142, Education for All Handicapped Children Act

The Education for All Handicapped Children Act (EHCA) of 1975, P.L. 94-142 (20 U.S.C. § 1401 et seq.), was not an independent act; rather, it was an amendment to P.L. 93-380. One of the major differences is that P.L. 94-142 is permanent legislation, whereas P.L. 93-380 required periodic reauthorization. P.L. 94-142 retained the provisions for due process and education in the least restrictive environment while mandating a free appropriate public education for all handi-capped children. The new law directed that an Individualized Educational Program (IEP) be developed in conference with the parents for each handicapped child needing special education and related services. The law was very specific about how the IEP was to be developed and what was to be contained therein. Specifically, the IEP must include statements concerning the child's current performance level, annual goals, specific special education and related services, extent to which the child will participate in regular education, dates that the program will begin and end, and evaluation procedures. The law also contained a funding formula that allows all school districts to qualify for funds. Districts receiving funds are subject to fairly rigid auditing and management requirements.

THE ROLE OF THE COURTS

One of the major features of the EHCA is its elaborate due process mecha-nism. The EHCA provides for parental input throughout the process in such a way that the handicapped student's parent or guardian becomes a vital component of the school district's evaluation team.

The EHCA's due process mechanism also provides a means for parents to appeal any school district decisions regarding the evaluation and placement of a handicapped student. Initially the parents can appeal any decision through an administrative hearing process. If either the parents or the school district is dissatis-fied with the results of the administrative appeals, they may file legal action in either the state or federal courts.

The EHCA provides the courts with some fairly specific instructions as to their role in the process, but generally grants the courts wide latitude. The following excerpt from the act indicates the role of the judiciary in the interpretation and enforcement of the EHCA:

> the court shall receive the records of the administrative proceed-ings, shall hear additional evidence at the request of a party, and, basing its decision on the preponderance of the evidence, shall grant such relief as the court determines is appropriate. (20 U.S.C. § 1415 (e)(2)(c))

REFERENCES

Beattie v. *Board of Education,* 169 Wis. 231 (1919).
Board of Education v. *Goldman,* 47 Oh.App. 417 (1934).
Brown v. *Board of Education,* 347 U.S. 483 (1954).
Colorado A.R.C. v. *State of Colorado,* C.A. No. C-4620 (1973).
Cuyahoga County A.R.C. v. *Essex,* 411 F.Supp. 46 (1976).
Diana v. *State Board of Education,* Civ. No. C-70-37 RFP (1970 and 1973).

Fialkowski v. *Shapp,* 405 F.Supp. 946 (1975).

Frederick L. v. *Thomas,* 408 F.Supp. 832 (1976); 419 F.Supp. 960 (1976); aff'd 557 F.2d 373 (1977).

Hairston v. *Drosick,* 423 F.Supp. 180 (1976).

Hobson v. *Hansen,* 269 F.Supp. 401 (1967); aff'd 408 F.2d 175 (1969).

In re Downey, 72 Misc.2d 772 (1973).

In re G.H., 218 N.W.2d 441 (1974).

Larry P. v. *Wilson Riles,* 343 F.Supp. 1306; aff'd 502 F.2d 963 (1974).

Lau v. *Nichols,* 414 U.S. 563 (1974).

Mills v. *Board of Education,* 348 F.Supp. 866 (1972).

Panitch v. *Wisconsin,* 444 F.Supp. 320 (1977).

Pennsylvania A.R.C. v. *Commonwealth of Pennsylvania,* 343 F.Supp. 279 (1972).

San Antonio v. *Rodriquez,* 411 U.S. 1 (1973).

Serrano v. *Priest,* 5 Cal.3d 584 (1971).

State ex. rel. Beattie v. *Board of Education of Antigo,* 169 Wis. 231 (1919).

Watson v. *City of Cambridge,* 157 Mass. 561 (1893).

Wolf v. *State of Utah,* Civ. No. 182646 (1969).

Figure 1-1

LEADING CASES

Watson v. *City of Cambridge,* 157 Mass. 561 (1893)

The school committee has the right to exclude students that it determines are unfit.

Beattie v. *Board of Education,* 169 Wis. 231 (1919)

A child does not have the right to attend school if his presence therein is harmful to the best interests of the school.

Wolf v. *State of Utah,* Civ. No. 182646 (1969)

Mentally retarded children are entitled to receive a free public education.

P.A.R.C. v. *Pennsylvania,* 343 F.Supp. 279 (1972)

A stipulation and consent agreement was approved by the court that provided for the education and training of mentally retarded children within the state.

Mills v. *Board of Education,* 348 F.Supp. 866 (1972)

Ordered the District of Columbia to provide education for all exceptional children within their jurisdiction. Also outlined elaborate due process safeguards that are to be provided to exceptional children.

Figure 1-2

HISTORY OF FEDERAL LEGISLATION

P.L. 89-313 (1965)

Provided federal financial assistance to state-operated programs for the handicapped.

P.L. 89-750 (1966)

Provided funds to states to expand programs for handicapped children.

P.L. 90-247 (1968)

Further expanded programs for handicapped children.

P.L. 90-538 (1968)

Established experimental preschool and early childhood programs for the handicapped.

P.L. 93-112 (1973) Section 504

Civil rights legislation that specifically guaranteed that the handicapped could not be discriminated against in programs receiving federal financial assistance.

P.L. 93-380 (1974)

Provided a major increase in funding for programs for the handicapped. Also provided due process safeguards for the handicapped with assurances of a free appropriate public education in the least restrictive environment.

P.L. 94-142 (1975)

Amended P.L. 93-380 to provide more financial assistance and to strengthen the rights granted to handicapped children. Most important, P.L. 94-142 had no expiration date and was therefore permanent legislation.

Chapter 2

HOW IS AN APPROPRIATE EDUCATION DEFINED?

The law does not require that the handicapped student shall receive the best possible education, but assures that the efforts to educate will be effective and that the education shall be adequate and appropriate.

Senior District Judge Murray
Norris* v. *Massachusetts
529 F. Supp. 759 at 767 (1981)

One of the major provisions of the Education for All Handicapped Children Act (EHCA), commonly known as the mainstreaming mandate, is that handicapped children are to be given an appropriate education in the least restrictive environment.

The EHCA's regulations state that

Each public agency shall insure:
(1) That to the maximum extent appropriate, handicapped children, including children in public or private institutions or other care facilities, are educated with children who are not handicapped, and
(2) That special classes, separate schooling or other removal of handicapped children from the regular educational environment occurs only when the nature or severity of the handicap is such that education in regular classes with the use of supplementary aids and services cannot be achieved satisfactorily. (34 C.F.R. § 300.550(b))

SPECIFIC RIGHTS OF ACCESS TO REGULAR PROGRAMS

It is clear from these regulations that students cannot be removed from the regular classroom or the public school setting unless that removal is necessary to provide the student with an appropriate education. Section 504 has similar regulations that also make it clear that a handicapped person has the right of access to regular educational programs if such programs are appropriate with the addition of supplementary aids and services.

Exclusion from Public Schools Not Allowed

An early case, *Howard S.* v. *Friendswood Independent School District,* dealt specifically with the exclusion of a student from the public schools. The student had a long history of special needs education as a result of his having minimal brain damage, learning disabilities, and severe emotional difficulties. He was fairly successful until he entered high school, where he developed behavior problems. These difficulties were treated as discipline problems, and the special education department was not informed about them. He experienced similar difficulties at home and began seeing a child psychiatrist. His difficulties culminated in a suicide attempt and consequent hospitalization. After his release from the hospital, he was placed in a private school and the public school district officially dropped him from its rosters. His mother later met with school officials to advise them of his status and requested that a meeting be held to determine if an appropriate program could be developed for the student. At that meeting the school district declined to provide any special education services since the student had "moved."

The court, on the basis of Section 504, determined that the student was being denied a free appropriate public education and that the school district had failed to provide one since he entered high school. The school district was ordered to conduct a comprehensive evaluation of the student, develop an Individualized Educational Program (IEP) for him, and provide the appropriate services. The court relied on Section 504 in its ruling since the EHCA was not yet in force at the time the student had been excluded.

Segregation of Students without Appropriate Treatment Violates Their Rights

Another early case dealt with the segregation of students who had emotional handicaps that resulted in acting out and aggressive behaviors. The students involved in *Lora* v. *Board of Education of the City of New York* had been placed in special day schools. These schools had a high percentage of minority students, and the students claimed that the schools were intentionally segregated, that the facilities provided inadequate instruction, and that their placements in these schools were initiated and carried out without the prior provision of the due process procedures guaranteed by federal law.

The court noted that under federal law, placement of children out of the mainstream required due process protections and ruled that the placement of students in facilities segregated from the mainstream, without the provision of appropriate educational and therapeutic treatment, was a violation of their constitutional rights. The court held that the students had a right to adequate treatment, proper classification, the opportunity to contest a placement, and periodic reassessment of the appropriateness of that placement. The parties were ordered to work out an agreement that would provide the students with an appropriate remedy.

Hepatitis Carriers Can't Be Excluded

In another New York case, *New York State A.R.C.* v. *Carey,* mentally retarded children who were known carriers of hepatitis B were excluded from the public schools. Most of the excluded children were former residents of a state facility for the mentally retarded and were attending the public schools under the terms of a consent decree. The district court had held that the exclusion violated that consent decree as well as Section 504, the EHCA, state law, and the Fourteenth Amendment. The Board of Education then developed a plan to place the children affected in nine separate classes throughout the city; however, the court also invalidated that plan.

The Court of Appeals for the Second Circuit, in affirming the district court, held that the exclusion violated Section 504 in that the children were excluded from regular public school programs solely by reason of their handicaps. Only mentally retarded hepatitis B carriers were excluded, and no effort was made to identify and exclude nonretarded carriers. The courts also noted that the Board of Education had been unable to substantiate that the excluded children posed a health hazard.

In another case involving a Down's syndrome child who was a carrier of infectious hepatitis type B, *Community High School* v. *Denz,* an Illinois court held that the child was entitled to be educated in a mainstream setting. The student was educationally capable of attending a special education class; however, she was placed on homebound instruction because of her medical condition. After two years, it was requested that her placement be changed so that she could interact with other children. That request was denied and an appeal was filed. Testimony at the hearing indicated that with proper prophylactic procedures, the health danger could be sufficiently minimized. The hearing officer ruled that the student should be placed in a mainstream setting. The trial court and the appellate court upheld that ruling, finding that the school system's refusal to allow the student to be mainstreamed clearly infringed on her rights under the EHCA and state law since the preponderance of the evidence indicated that mainstreaming could be accomplished with a relatively low risk of transmission of hepatitis.

Mainstreaming of Severely Handicapped Students Ordered

In 1981 a state appeals court upheld the finding of an administrative hearing panel that a severely handicapped student had not been placed in the least restrictive environment. The student in *Mallory* v. *Drake* had originally been enrolled in the public schools but was transferred to a state school following an evaluation. Her parents became dissatisfied with the state school placement and requested that she be returned to the public schools. State authorities refused that request, feeling that the state school was the most appropriate placement. The parents then withdrew her from the state school and initiated due process proceedings. The administrative hearing panel found that the state had failed to demonstrate that the state school was the least restrictive environment and ordered that the student be placed in a special education class in a public school setting where she would have access to social interaction and modeling of less handicapped children. That decision was upheld by the trial court.

On appeal, the state claimed that the hearing panel's order was ambiguous, in violation of state statute, and impossible to implement since the student's former public school could not accommodate her. The appeals court dismissed all these claims and upheld the hearing panel's decision. The court emphasized that the order did not require that the student be placed in her former public school, but rather, a placement could be made in a neighboring school district that had an appropriate program.

The Court of Appeals for the Sixth Circuit in *Roncker* v. *Walter* held that what may appear to be a better placement could, in fact, be inappropriate due to its failure to provide for mainstreaming. The student here was a severely mentally retarded 9-year-old who required almost constant supervision because of his inability to recognize dangerous situations. After an evaluation, the school district decided to place him in a county school. County schools were exclusively for retarded children and provided no contact with nonhandicapped children. The student's parents refused to accept placement in the county school and requested a due process hearing. The hearing officer ruled that the school district had not proven that the proposed placement afforded the student with the maximum appropriate contact with nonhandicapped children and ordered that the student be placed in a special education class in a regular school setting. On appeal the state Board of Education found that the county school was appropriate, but that some provision should be made for contact with nonhandicapped students. During the pendency of the proceedings, the student had been placed in a special education class within the public schools. The district court found in favor of the school system, in part, because the student had made no significant progress in the public school setting.

The appeals court vacated and remanded the case back to the trial court. The appeals court noted that the EHCA did not require mainstreaming in every case but that it must be provided to the maximum extent appropriate. Since a placement that may seem better for academic reasons may be inappropriate due to its failure to provide for mainstreaming, the courts need to determine whether the services that make a particular placement better could also be provided in a less segregated setting. If they could, according to the court, placement in a segregated setting would be inappropriate. The appeals court also held that although a child's progress in an integrated setting is a relevant factor, courts should also consider whether the child could have been provided with additional services to improve his or her performance.

Placement in Neighborhood School Is Not Required

Also in 1981 a federal district court, in *Pinkerton* v. *Moye,* held that the least restrictive environment mandate did not require that a school district develop a program for a handicapped student at the school she would attend if she were not handicapped. The student in this case was diagnosed as having a learning disability with associated emotional difficulties. It was determined that her needs would best be met in a self-contained special education class. However, since such a class did not exist at her home school, it meant that she would have to transfer to another school within the district. Although the new school was only an additional 6 miles from the student's home, it required an additional half hour of travel due to transfers. The student's mother objected to this placement and demanded that a self-contained class be established at the home school. The school board refused and was upheld in administrative appeals. The regulations in question state that

> Unless a handicapped child's individualized education program requires some other arrangement, the child is [to be] educated in the school which he or she would attend if not handicapped . . . (34 C.F.R. § 300.52(c))

The court held that the school board had reached a reasonable accommodation by providing an appropriate program at another nearby school. That conclusion was supported by the facts that the proposed school was centrally located and only a small number of students in the district required such a placement. The court did, however, order the school board to provide better transportation arrangements. In weighing the EHCA's requirements against the fiscal and physical realities of a school system, the court stated that since educational funds were not unlimited, the various needs of the school district needed to be balanced. In this regard the court commented that excessive expenditures made to meet the needs of an individual handicapped child would reduce the funds available to educate other handicapped children.

In a 1983 case, *Troutman* v. *School District of Greenville County,* the district court held that a handicapped child did not have to be placed in the school closest to her home. The student was a blind second grader who had received special education services since entering school. This dispute arose when she was assigned to a school 11 miles from her home. The assignment was made to provide her with the special education services required by her IEP, specifically teachers trained to instruct visually impaired students and an orientation and mobility instructor. Her parents objected to the assignment, claiming that the EHCA required that a handicapped child attend the school she would have attended if not handicapped.

The court found that the EHCA required that a handicapped child be educated in the school the child would have attended if not handicapped, if possible and unless the IEP required that some other arrangements be made. In this case the court determined that the IEP required otherwise because the special education services needed by the student were only available at the assigned school. It was also not practical to offer these services in all the district's schools because of budgetary constraints. The court further indicated that the purpose of this regulation was to encourage mainstreaming and that since mainstreaming would be provided in the assigned school, the purpose of the regulation was being met.

The court in *Wilson* v. *Marana Unified School District* upheld the right of a school district to transfer a handicapped child to a school where the child would receive a more appropriate education. The student was a physically handicapped child who had difficulty learning to read because of her handicap. She had been instructed by a learning disabilities teacher, but after determining that her progress wasn't satisfactory, school officials proposed that she be transferred to a school that had a teacher of the physically handicapped. Her parents objected but were unsuccessful in their administrative and judicial appeals. The Ninth Circuit Court of Appeals found that school districts were not required to provide the best possible education to a handicapped child but were not prevented from providing a program that they consider to be more appropriate than that proposed by the parents. The appeals court upheld the school district's proposal after noting that it did not conflict with any state or federal law and did not thwart the EHCA's mainstreaming objective. In fact, the court found that the school's proposal complimented the act by providing a teacher specifically trained to deal with the student's handicaps.

More Restrictive Environment Is Allowed If Needed to Provide an Appropriate Education

Also in 1983 a federal district court upheld the principle that a student may be placed in a more restrictive environment if such a placement is needed to provide the student with an appropriate education. The student in *Johnston* v. *Ann Arbor Public Schools* was an 11-year-old with cerebral palsy. After an evaluation, it was proposed that she be placed in an educational center for physically handicapped students located in an elementary school other than the one she had been attending. Her mother objected, claiming the proposed placement violated the least restrictive environment mandate of the EHCA. The proposed placement was upheld in administrative appeals.

The district court, refusing to substitute its judgment for that of school officials, affirmed the hearing officer's decision. The court found that all proper procedures had been followed in making the placement decision and that the evidence indicated that it was likely to provide the student with an appropriate education. The court also found that evidence indicated that an appropriate education could not be provided in a less restrictive environment even with the addition of supplementary aids and services.

Services Must Be Provided to Age 21

The Tenth Circuit Court of Appeals held that a handicapped student is entitled to receive educational services until the age of 21 in *Helms* v. *Independent*

School District. The student, a trainable mentally handicapped child, had her special education services terminated by the school district prior to her reaching the age of 21. The reason given for the early termination was that she had received 12 years of schooling. The district court and the appeals court, however, found that nonhandicapped students who fail a grade or grades are allowed to repeat those grades and thus receive a cumulative total of more than 12 years of schooling. The court held that handicapped students were also entitled to receive more than the customary 12 years of education. Since evidence indicated that the student had been classified as a tenth grader at the end of her 12 years of school, the court ordered the school district to provide her with 2 more years of educational services. The Supreme Court of the United States let the decision stand by declining to review the case.

Access to Nonacademic Services and Activities

The EHCA regulations concerning the least restrictive environment also state that handicapped children are entitled to access to nonacademic and extracurricular services and activities. However, the specific wording of the regulation in question has been held to conflict with the U.S. Supreme Court's interpretation of Congress' intent in enacting the handicapped legislation.

> Specifically, the EHCA's regulations provide that:
> (a) Each public agency shall take steps to provide nonacademic and extracurricular services and activities in such a manner as is necessary to afford handicapped children an equal opportunity for participation in those services and activities.
> (b) Nonacademic and extracurricular services and activities may include counseling services, athletics, transportation, health services, recreational activities, special interest groups or clubs . . . (34 C.F.R. § 300.306)
> In providing or arranging for the provision of nonacademic and extracurricular services and activities, including meals, recess periods, and the services and activities set forth in [the regulations], each public agency shall insure that each handicapped child participates with non-handicapped children in these services and activities to the maximum extent appropriate to the needs of that child. (34 C.F.R. § 300.553)

The district court in *Rettig* v. *Kent City School District,* found that the school district had failed to provide after-school activities to a handicapped student on an equal basis with nonhandicapped students as called for in the regulations. That decision, however, was eventually overturned by the appeals court because it felt that the district court's decision conflicted with the U.S. Supreme Court's decision in *Rowley* (discussed later in this chapter) that school districts did not have to maximize the educational potential of handicapped students commensurate with the opportunities provided to nonhandicapped students. Under the appeals court ruling, which the Supreme Court has allowed to stand by declining certiorari, the "equal opportunity for participation" clause of the regulation cited above cannot be interpreted strictly.

However, this does not mean that school districts do not have to provide handicapped students with nonacademic and extracurricular services. Naturally, handicapped students cannot be denied the opportunity to participate in an activity that they would otherwise be eligible to participate in. Under Section 504 handicapped children cannot be denied the opportunity to participate in any activity or service only on the basis of their handicap if they meet all other requirements for participation. Also, they may be entitled to certain services and activities under the related services mandate the EHCA discussed in Chapter Six.

Application of EHCA to Other Public Facilities

Questions have also arisen as to whether the EHCA applies to children who attend or reside in public facilities other than the local public school districts. The EHCA makes it clear that its provisions apply to certain U.S. territories, Indian reservation schools, and correctional facilities but gives little guidance as to other facilities (20 U.S.C. § 1411).

In 1980 the District Court for the District of Columbia held that the EHCA also applied to government-operated schools overseas. In *Cox* v. *Brown* the court ordered the placement of two severely learning disabled children in private schools. The father of the two children was a civilian employee of the U.S. government on loan to the North Atlantic Treaty Organization. The children had been attending a Department of Defense–operated school. The students contended that the special education programs offered by the Department of Defense's dependent school system were insufficient to meet their special education needs. The court agreed and ordered the Department of Defense to provide and pay for private residential schooling in the United States.

The district court in *Green* v. *Johnson* ruled that incarcerated youth were entitled to the provision of special education services. A class action suit had been filed on behalf of inmates of several county houses of correction who were below the age of 22 and who had not yet received a high school diploma. Evidence submitted at the trial indicated that a large number of inmates in correctional facilities were below the age of 22, had not received a high school diploma, and had special educational needs. The court ruled that the plaintiff class was entitled to special education services under federal and state laws. Although their incarcerated status might require particular adjustments in the delivery of services, the court stated that it did not eliminate their entitlement under federal and state law.

In another 1981 case, a district court held that the EHCA's provisions extended to residents of state-operated facilities for the handicapped. A class action suit was filed in *A.R.C. of Colorado* v. *Frazier* on behalf of all handicapped children residing at a state home and training school. The education agencies in the district in which the state school was located and in which the parents of the children resided refused to provide the children with IEPs as required by the EHCA. The defendants argued that the EHCA did not apply to handicapped children receiving services in a state-operated program funded by federal legislation other than the EHCA.

The court ruled that the EHCA imposed upon the state an obligation to assure that all handicapped children were provided a free appropriate public education. The court held that this included those placed in state institutions, since all handicapped children within a state acquired the EHCA's entitlements once the state received funds under the act.

COMPONENTS OF AN APPROPRIATE EDUCATION

The regulations implementing the Education for All Handicapped Children Act define a free appropriate public education as

> [S]pecial education and related services which:
> (a) Are provided at public expense, under public supervision and direction, and without charge,
> (b) Meet the standards of the State educational agency . . . ,
> (c) Include preschool, elementary school, or secondary school education in the State involved, and
> (d) Are provided in conformity with an individualized education program which meets the requirements under [the act]. (34 C.F.R. § 300.4)

Special education is further defined as

> [S]pecially designed instruction . . . to meet the unique needs of a handicapped child, including classroom instruction, instruction in physical education, home instruction, and instruction in hospitals and institutions. . . . [and] includes speech pathology, or any other related service . . . [and] also includes vocational education . . . (34 C.F.R. § 300.14)

Although these regulations provide some guidance, much is left open for interpretation. We must, therefore, turn to the courts for further clarification of what constitutes an appropriate education.

IEP Must Be Individually Tailored

A 1980 case, *Laura M.* v. *Special School District,* illustrates the concepts that a special education program must be individually tailored to meet the specific needs of the handicapped student and must provide accommodations so that the student can have access to regular programs to be appropriate. The plaintiff was a high school student with an emotional disorder and a learning disability. An IEP was developed for her that called for a combination of special tutoring and placement in regular classes in the local high school. The student's parents rejected this proposed IEP, also rejected a modified IEP, and requested a due process hearing. The hearing officer ruled that the proposed IEP would be appropriate if it included provisions for monitoring and certain support services. The student's parents were not satisfied, however, and appealed. The state-level hearing examiner recommended that she be educated in a classroom with a larger than one-to-one teacher-to-pupil ratio, that a special education teacher be available for assistance, and that such education be carried out either in large special education classes or mainstream classes team-taught by regular and special education teachers. The Assistant State Commissioner of Education, however, ruled that the decision of the original hearing officer was adequate, with the following modifications: (1) review the student's situation prior to each trimester, (2) determine what accommodations would be required of classroom teachers, (3) have special education staff administer all tests, and (4) review her progress on a regular basis. Her parents then filed an action in the federal district court requesting that her IEP be declared inappropriate and that the decision of the state-level hearing examiner be reinstated.

In declaring the IEP to be inappropriate, the court determined that the evidence indicated that the student needed the opportunity to deal with her learning disability in as normal a setting as possible, clear instructions, immediate assistance and feedback, and a nurturing and structured environment. Since the proposed IEP failed to guarantee all these, the court ordered the school district to develop an IEP that would provide a review of her strengths and weaknesses prior to each trimester, a determination of what classroom accommodations must be made because of her handicap, the availability of constant monitoring and immediate help, administration of modified tests by special education staff, and weekly reviews of progress.

Another 1980 case, *Anderson* v. *Thompson,* also illustrates that the IEP must be designed to meet the specific needs of the handicapped student. The plaintiffs' daughter had attended a private special education facility for several years. Since she was eligible for only one more year at the private facility and since her parents wanted a less specialized environment for her, they requested that the public schools develop a program for her. She was evaluated and determined to have speech and language difficulties and other undifferentiated special needs. A diagnostic placement in a class for the educable mentally retarded was recommended. Her parents disagreed with this recommendation and appealed. An independent evaluation diagnosed her as having speech and language disabilities, learning disabilities, and emotional disturbance. Her parents failed to gain the desired program through administrative appeals and filed legal action in the district court. At the time of the trial, all parties agreed that the child had speech and language disabilities and learning disabilities and would best be served in the public schools' learning disabilities program. The dispute centered on whether or not she was emotionally disturbed and how the transition from the private school to the public school would be handled.

The court ruled that the evidence indicated that the child had an emotional disturbance and ordered that the IEP be modified to place a greater emphasis on goals and objectives in the areas of emotional and social skills. The court also ordered that the IEP incorporate a transition period where the child would attend the private facility half-time and the public schools half-time. Periodic assessments were to be made of her adjustment, and she was to commence full-time attendance in the public schools when deemed appropriate.

Appropriate Does Not Mean Best

The concept that an appropriate education does not mean the best possible education has been developed through a number of cases. The first of these, *Springdale School District* v. *Grace,* was decided by the Court of Appeals for the Eighth Circuit in 1981. The student in this case was a profoundly deaf child who had either been born deaf or had lost her hearing prior to developing speech. She was initially taught, with little success, by an oral instruction method. When her parents moved to Arkansas, she was enrolled in the Arkansas School for the Deaf where a total communications method was employed. The student made marked progress in that program. A few years later her parents moved to Springdale and enrolled her in a fourth grade class in the local public schools. The Springdale schools formulated an IEP for her that called for her to return to the Arkansas School for the Deaf. Her parents disagreed, preferring that she be educated in the local schools.

A hearing officer ruled that the student could receive an appropriate education in the local schools. The Department of Education affirmed, and she was provided with a full-time teacher of the deaf. The school system, however, filed a suit in the district court that ruled that, although the School for the Deaf would provide the best education, the local schools could provide an appropriate education, which is all that the EHCA required.

The appeals court, in affirming, stated that the EHCA did not require the state to provide the best education but instead required it to provide an appropriate education. The appeals court held that through the provision of extra services, the student would be offered an opportunity to achieve her full potential commensurate with the opportunity offered all other students in the school district. The court noted that its holding was further supported by the mainstreaming provisions of the EHCA.

The U.S. Supreme Court in a summary judgment vacated and remanded the case for further consideration in light of its decision in the *Rowley* case (discussed later). On remand the appeals court saw no reason to change its verdict. Again the court emphasized the mainstreaming mandate of the EHCA and noted that the Supreme Court in its *Rowley* decision made it clear that the act did not require states to make available the best possible option. The concept that an appropriate education is not necessarily the best possible education, but is one that provides the handicapped child with needed functional skills, was reiterated in *Rettig* v. *Kent City School District.* The student in this case was a 16-year-old who was autistic and mentally retarded. He was first educated in private schools but later transferred to the public schools. His parents were initially satisfied with his progress, but conflicts developed later over his instructional program and the instructional techniques used. The school system initiated several changes, including changes in staff and the location of his class, to satisfy his parents. His parents, however, still rejected a proposed IEP. The IEP was upheld in administrative appeals and court action followed.

In ruling that the proposed IEP was appropriate, the court stated that an appropriate education for a child as severely handicapped as the one in this case was one that would give him a reasonable chance to acquire the skills he needed to function outside an institution. The court indicated that this did not mean that the child deserved a perfect education, or even that the school system was required to provide any and all services that might be beneficial. It also did not mean that the school system was required to experiment with every new teaching technique that might be suggested. This decision was affirmed by the Sixth Circuit Court of Appeals.

Existence of a Better Program Does Not Make a Proposed Program Inappropriate

In *Buchholtz* v. *Iowa* the Supreme Court of Iowa ruled that the existence of a better program did not make a proposed program inappropriate. The student in this case was diagnosed as having learning disabilities and was placed in a learning disabilities class for the last ten weeks of the school year. That summer he was tutored by a learning disabilities teacher from a neighboring school district. The following September the student's father enrolled him in that district on a tuition basis feeling that it offered a better program. He then sought to have his home district pay the tuition for his son's placement in the neighboring district. The local district refused, and its decision was upheld by the state Board of Public Instruction.

The Iowa Supreme Court ruled that both the EHCA and Iowa law did not require the best program but, rather, required the provision of an education that was appropriate for the child's special needs. The standard, according to the court, was that a special education student should receive a level of education commensurate with that provided a nonspecial education student. The court did not define the term "commensurate" but indicated that a school district should strive to meet the needs of handicapped students with the same level of effort that it devoted to meeting the needs of nonhandicapped students. Whether this goal is met or not depends on a number of factors, including the nature of the handicap, and can only be determined on a case-by-case basis. The court ruled that the program offered by the home district was appropriate and that the fact that a better program may have existed did not render it inappropriate.

The U.S. Circuit Court of Appeals for the Sixth Circuit also declared that the existence of a better program did not make a proposed program inappropriate. A conflict developed in *Age* v. *Bullitt County Public Schools* between school officials and the parents of a hearing impaired student over the form of instruction used in the proposed placement. The student, whose hearing loss was assessed to be in the severe to profound range, had attended a school in another county that utilized the oral/aural method. The Bullitt County School System developed a program for the hearing impaired and proposed that the student attend it. His parents objected because, although he would still be taught through the oral method, other children in the class would be taught by the total communications method. The parents maintained that this was not appropriate since it exposed him to sign language, which they felt would hinder his oral development, and denied him the opportunity to interact with other children taught by the oral method.

Although the school's proposed IEP was upheld in administrative appeals, the district court held that it was inappropriate because of the lack of peer interaction. The school department later proposed a second program in which the student would be placed in a classroom with four other students, three of whom would be taught by the oral method. The student's parents again protested the use of two methods in the classroom; however, the district court approved the program since it contained the element of peer interaction.

The appeals court, in holding that the mere existence of a better program did not make the proposed program inappropriate, found that the proposed program was properly staffed and carefully developed, and that students in it progressed satisfactorily. The court, in noting that although a better program was available, stated that the school department had properly reconciled the student's need for a free, appropriate public education with the district's need to allocate scarce funds among as many handicapped children as possible.

Appropriate Peer Group Preferred

One of the issues in the *Age* case was the element of peer interaction. Providing a handicapped student with opportunities for peer interaction is not always possible but should be considered whenever possible. The court, in *Hines* v. *Pitt County Board of Education,* declared that a handicapped student should be placed with an appropriate peer group. The student involved in this case was a 10-year-old severely emotionally disturbed child. It was determined that the student required placement in a residential treatment facility; however, the particular facility recommended had a current enrollment of students between 11 and 17 years old. The student's parents appealed, and the hearing officer determined that this was not an appropriate placement, but a state review officer reversed.

Testimony at trial indicated that the student needed social interaction with children of approximately the same developmental level. Since the student was below average in general development, an appropriate peer group would consist of children between the ages of 8 and 10. It was also indicated that the student was likely to withdraw in a setting with older children. The court ruled that the population at the proposed facility did not provide an appropriate peer group and it was, thus, not an appropriate placement.

The district court in *County School Board* v. *Lower* found a proposed program to be inappropriate as it did not provide an appropriate peer group for a student who had imitative tendencies. The student was a 13-year-old multihandicapped child who had attended private day schools for several years. An evaluation team determined that the private school she had been attending was no longer appropriate and recommended that she attend a public school multihandicapped class. Her parents objected and enrolled her in a new private school. Both the proposed public school and the new private school were found to be inappropriate in administrative hearings.

The court found the public school class to be inappropriate as the other students in the class would not constitute an appropriate peer group. Since the student had imitative tendencies, an appropriate peer group was determined to be a necessary component of an appropriate placement. The evidence indicated that the student had been progressing at her new private school so that placement was determined to be appropriate.

Program Must Meet Student's Unique Needs

The EHCA's mainstreaming requirement and individualization were also issues in *Campbell* v. *Talladega County Board of Education*. The student in this case was a severely retarded 18-year-old who attended a facility for handicapped children that was located on the campus of a local high school. Although he had attended this facility for several years, his parents rejected a proposed IEP because they felt that this facility did not provide him with sufficient contact with nonhandicapped students. The proposed IEP was upheld in administrative hearings and court action followed. Testimony at trial indicated that the student had a mental age of $2\frac{1}{2}$, was nonverbal, and had poor fine-motor skills. He did, however, engage in some communication with others and had learned basic self-help skills. Further testimony indicated that he was capable of learning, but that the program he was in taught him virtually no functional skills, lacked individualization, and lacked detailed evaluation and record keeping.

The district court, in ruling that the proposed placement was inappropriate, noted that it did not provide the student with the skills he would need to develop the degree of self-sufficiency and independence he was capable of. Specifically, it did not provide him with instruction in functional and communication skills and did not place him into contact with nonhandicapped students to the maximum extent possible. The court ordered an IEP that would focus on functional daily living skills, vocational instruction, recreational activities, social interaction skills, and communication skills while providing increased contact with nonhandicapped children.

As is evidenced by several of the cases cited here, a handicapped child's placement must be suited to the child's unique needs. Questions may still remain, however, as to whether a particular placement is, or is not, suited to a particular child's unique needs. One court has suggested that the answer may be determined by whether or not the child is making meaningful progress toward the educational goals of that placement. In *Gladys J.* v. *Pearland Independent School District*, a dispute arose as to the proper placement of a multihandicapped adolescent. The student had been identified as trainable mentally retarded, but also became severely withdrawn. She was later diagnosed as also having organic childhood schizophrenia. Her parents requested a residential placement, but the school system offered only a day program with home support.

In ordering the residential placement, the court determined that a preponderance of the evidence indicated that the student had made no significant progress in her current day placement and that it was unlikely that she would make progress in any placement that did not provide a constant structured environment, a 24-hour-a-day behavior modification program, and an intensive language program. In framing the issue before it, the court stated that the question was reduced to whether the child's educational placement was suited to her unique needs and that the answer was determined by whether or not the child was making meaningful progress toward achievement of her educational goals. To determine whether meaningful or significant progress has occurred, the courts will rely on objective data, such as test scores, and the opinions of experts in the field, such as psychologists and educational diagnosticians.

IEP Must Be Developed According to the Needs of the Student

A Massachusetts case illustrates the point that an IEP must be developed according to the educational needs of the student rather than according to what resources the school has available. In *Norris* v. *Massachusetts Department of Education,* a learning disabled student, whose handicap caused him to perform poorly in school, feel inadequate, and become easily frustrated, had a placement consisting of at least 60 percent special education in elementary school. When he transferred to junior high school, the school department proposed a program that called for substantially less special education because a more intensive program was not available.

The court, in ordering a private day school placement, stated that the law did not require that the handicapped student should receive the best possible education but guaranteed that the efforts to educate the child would be effective and that the educational program would be adequate and appropriate. The court also noted that evidence indicated that the student had failed to show significant growth and that the gap between his achievement and that of his age group was not closing. Since the school system had indicated that a program of the intensity that the court deemed necessary was not available, private school placement was ordered.

Imperfections in an IEP Do Not Make It Inappropriate

In a case decided late in 1981, a district court ruled that an IEP that had imperfections was not necessarily inappropriate. The court also ruled that the cost of a program could be a factor in determining what was appropriate. The student in *Bales* v. *Clarke* was injured in an automobile accident and spent two years in a crippled children's home. After her release from the home, her father requested that the school system place her in a private school for severely handicapped children and provide a summer language therapy program. The school system recommended that she attend a regional special education program. While the case was proceeding through the administrative appeals process, the student attended the regional program. During the two years she attended that program, she made academic and emotional progress. One of her parents' objections to the regional program was that very few girls were enrolled in it.

The court, in upholding the regional program placement, agreed that it would be beneficial to have both sexes fairly represented, but ruled that the lack of one sex did not make the setting inappropriate. The court also noted that the existence of imperfections in an educational offering did not mean that the student was receiving an inappropriate education. In a tersely worded statement, the court declared that the student's parents were seeking an ideal education for their child but that parents of handicapped children did not have the right to expect an ideal education at public expense. The court also indicated that the cost of a program could not be overlooked because cost was very much a factor in determining the appropriateness of any educational program. However, the court did not provide any further guidelines concerning how cost could be factored in the determination of whether or not a particular program was appropriate.

The Rowley Standard: Appropriate Means Sufficient to Confer Educational Benefit

In June 1982 the U.S. Supreme Court handed down a decision in the first case to come before it under P.L. 94-142, *Board of Education of the Hendrick Hudson Central School District* v. *Rowley*. This case also concerned the services provided to a deaf student who had minimal residual hearing, but was an excellent lipreader. When she had entered school, she was placed in a regular kindergarten to determine what services she would need. Several members of the school's staff had previously taken a course in sign language, and a teletype machine was installed to communicate with her parents who were also deaf. At the end of the trial period it was determined that the student should remain in the regular classroom but that she should be provided with an FM hearing aid that would amplify words spoken by the teacher and other students. When she entered first grade an IEP was developed that called for regular class placement, the FM hearing aid, one hour of instruction per day from a tutor for the deaf, and three hours of speech therapy per week. Her parents agreed to the IEP, but additionally requested a sign language interpreter for all academic classes. Such an interpreter had been tried in kindergarten, but the interpreter reported that these services were not needed. The student's parents then requested a hearing.

The hearing officer upheld the school officials' decision, finding that the student was achieving educationally, academically, and socially without the interpeter. On appeal the state's Commissioner of Education affirmed. The district court reversed, however, finding that, although the student performed better than average, she understood considerably less of what went on in the classroom than if she were not deaf. In ruling that the proposed IEP was not appropriate, the court determined that an appropriate education was one that provided a handicapped child an opportunity to achieve her full potential commensurate with the opportunity provided to nonhandicapped children. The U.S. Court of Appeals for the Second Circuit affirmed.

The U.S. Supreme Court reversed, ruling that the lower courts erred when they held that the EHCA required a school district to maximize the potential of each handicapped student commensurate with the opportunity provided to nonhandicapped students. Mr. Justice Rehnquist, writing for the majority, stated that the education provided had to be sufficient to confer some educational benefit on the student:

> Insofar as a State is required to provide a handicapped child with a "free appropriate public education," we hold that it satisfies this requirement by providing personalized instruction with sufficient services to permit the child to benefit educationally from that instruction. Such instruction and services must be provided at public expense, must meet the State's educational standards, must approximate the grade levels used in the State's regular education, and must comport with the child's IEP. In addition, the IEP, and therefore the personalized instruction, should be formulated in accordance with the requirements of the Act and, if the child is being educated in the regular classrooms of the public education system, should be reasonably calculated to enable the child to achieve passing marks and advance from grade to grade. (3049)

Since the student performed better than the average student in her class, advanced easily from grade to grade, and received personalized instruction that was reasonably calculated to enable her to meet her educational needs, the Court ruled that a sign language interpreter was not required.

Mr. Justice Blackmun, in a concurring opinion, agreed in the result but felt that the question was whether the student's program, taken as a whole, offered her the opportunity to understand and participate in the classroom in a substantially equal fashion to that given her nonhandicapped classmates. In his opinion, that standard had been met.

Mr. Justice White, writing for a three-member minority, dissented, stating that providing a teacher with a loud voice would not meet the student's needs and would not satisfy the EHCA. Justice White favored the reasoning of the lower courts, feeling that a handicapped child should be given an equal opportunity to learn through the provision of a program that would eliminate the effects of the handicap as much as possible.

The *Rowley* decision, as would be expected, has generated a fair amount of debate and controversy. While it has been applauded for having affirmed the procedural provisions of the EHCA, advocates for the handicapped have expressed some disappointment in its strict interpretation. Some concern has also been expressed that the Court's opinion may be misinterpreted by the school districts to mean that they no longer have to provide related and supplementary services. At least one state educational agency has stated that the *Rowley* decision was not likely to have a major impact on special education in that state since their own comprehensive state law requirements were unaffected by the decision.

Post-Rowley: Maximization of Potential Not Required

Prior to the *Rowley* decision several courts had indicated that a student had to make significant progress for the IEP to be appropriate or that the level of services provided needed to be commensurate with those provided to nonhandicapped students. In *Rowley* the Supreme Court stated that this is not necessarily so and that the EHCA merely established a basic floor of opportunity for handicapped children. According to this interpretation an IEP is appropriate if some educational benefit is obtained by the student. The *Rowley* decision, of course, supersedes all previous lower court decisions to the contrary.

One month after the Supreme Court's decision, a state court in Wisconsin applied the *Rowley* standard in holding that a proposed IEP was appropriate. The dispute in *Frank* v. *Grover* also arose over the techniques used to educate a deaf student. The student, who had congenital bilateral deafness, was transferred from a private residential school for the hearing impaired to the public schools at the start of the ninth grade. The school district's evaluation team recommended that he be educated through a total communication technique. His parents disagreed, preferring an oral only method. A hearing officer found in favor of the parents, but was reversed by the state Superintendent of Public Instruction. Court action followed.

The Wisconsin court held that *Rowley* did not require a school district to provide an educational program that maximized the potential of the handicapped student but, rather, required a program that would result in some educational benefit. The court noted that the current action arose over an honest disagreement over methodology between the parties. The role of the court, however, was to determine if the school system had complied with the EHCA and if the proposed IEP was reasonably calculated to enable the student to receive educational benefits. Since the evidence indicated that the EHCA had been complied with and that the IEP was designed to provide the student with educational benefits, the court ruled that the *Rowley* standard had been met.

The district court in *Lang* v. *Braintree School Committee* also found *Rowley* persuasive in holding that a proposed IEP was appropriate. The student involved in this action had been diagnosed as mentally retarded, mentally ill, and epileptic and had attended a private day school for a number of years. When her parents moved to a new community, the local district developed an IEP that called for placement in the public schools. Her parents objected to that plan; however, it was upheld in administrative hearings and court action followed. Testimony during the administrative hearings indicated that the public school program was educationally sound.

The court, in applying the *Rowley* standard, stated that it would not interfere in a situation where the school district was providing an education that was of some benefit to the student and was utilizing a minimally acceptable approach. The court held that the public schools clearly offered a program that would benefit the student.

The Most Appropriate Program Is Not Required

In another 1982 case, the district court applied the *Rowley* standard retroactively in determining whether or not a child was entitled to compensatory services for what the parents claimed had been an inadequate program. The student in *Timms* v. *Metropolitan School District* was a mentally handicapped adolescent who had been institutionalized for many years. She had been receiving instruction for 1 hour per day provided by the local school district. Her parents requested that her instructional program be changed to a full day. The school district agreed to increase the program to 1½ hours per day, but declined to provide more than that, feeling that such an increase would cause her considerable frustration and increase self-abusive behaviors. The student's parents authorized the increase, but rejected the IEP. During the appeals process the student was enrolled in a full-day program. Her parents then sought compensatory education services to make up for what they felt was an inappropriate education.

The court determined that the student's program had been appropriate. Since no complaint had been raised concerning the content of the IEP or the procedures used to develop it, the court inferred that the EHCA's mandates were complied with. In determining whether or not the IEP had been reasonably calculated to enable the student to receive educational benefits, the court held that the school district's assessment should be given substantial weight because of their experience teaching the student. The court ruled that the IEP also satisfied the second prong of the *Rowley* standard and denied the request for compensatory education.

In an early 1983 case, *Hessler* v. *State Board of Education of Maryland,* the Fourth Circuit Court of Appeals in finding that a proposed public school placement was appropriate, held that the mere existence of a more appropriate program did not render any given program inappropriate. The *Rowley* standard, according to the court, provided that there was no duty to offer a handicapped student the best program money could buy. The dispute arose after the school district had proposed placement in a public school special education class. The student's parents rejected that recommendation because they felt that a private school placement was more appropriate and they claimed that the school district had a statutory duty to consider the private school. The district court had rejected that claim and the appeals court upheld.

Promotion Does Not Automatically Mean That a Program Is Appropriate

Early in 1983 a state court held that an educational program did not automatically meet the *Rowley* standard of appropriateness simply because the student had never failed a grade. The student in *In re Van Overreem* was an eighth grade learning disabled child with average intelligence. Even though the student had been receiving special education instruction in the public schools, he was achieving only at a fourth grade level. He was still promoted each year, however.

After a dispute over his educational program arose, an administrative hearing panel held that the student required a more restrictive program, such as a day school, to receive educational benefits. The school system appealed, contending that the review panel's decision would provide the student with a level of education that would assist him in reaching his maximum potential instead of the appropriate education defined by *Rowley*. The court held that the *Rowley* standard did not provide that every handicapped student who was promoted from grade to grade was automatically receiving an appropriate education. The court found that the evidence indicated that the student was not benefiting from his current educational program and upheld the hearing panel.

A Program Is Appropriate as Long as It Provides Some Benefit

The court in *Doe* v. *Lawson* approved the transfer of a severely multihandicapped child who suffered from severe retardation, blindness, and a profound hearing loss from a private facility to an educational collaborative program. The student had been enrolled in a day school at a private center for brain-injured children at public expense. The school district proposed that his placement be changed to a public school collaborative program, but his parents rejected that plan. The Massachusetts Bureau of Special Education Appeals found the proposed transfer to be appropriate whereupon the student's parents filed court action claiming that their son would not receive an appropriate education in the collaborative program.

In approving the transfer, the district court found the collaborative program to be properly staffed in accordance with state regulations. The court further found that although differences existed between the techniques used in the two programs, the preponderance of the evidence did not indicate that the collaborative program would not provide educational benefit. Since the program provided educational benefit, it was appropriate according to the EHCA so the court approved the school district's proposed transfer.

The district court in *Cothern* v. *Mallory,* using the *Rowley* standard, found a state school program to be appropriate. The student was a 7-year-old severely retarded child who had been evaluated and placed in a state school for the severely handicapped. However, after only 23 days his parents removed him and enrolled him in an out-of-state private facility. One year later they requested a review of the decision to place the student in the state school. At that review the state school was again recommended. The student's parents appealed, and the administrative hearing panel found the state school to be appropriate.

The district court, applying the *Rowley* standard, affirmed. The court determined that the evidence indicated that the state school was not only appropriate, but was better than the private school the student was attending. The evidence also indicated that the student had progressed at the state school before his removal.

IEP Must Be Viewed as a Whole

The issue in a Second Circuit Court of Appeals case, *Karl* v. *Board of Education of the Genesco Central School District,* was the appropriateness of a recommended staff-to-student ratio. The school district proposed an IEP for a 21-year-old educably mentally retarded student that called for a basic resource room academic program with mainstreaming in a commercial food preparation program. The food preparation class had a staff-to-student ratio of 1 to 12. The student's parents objected, preferring a ratio of 1 to 6. A hearing officer held that a ratio of 1 to 9 would be appropriate, but the state Commissioner of Education reversed, holding that the 1-to-12 ratio was sufficient. The district court, however, favored the 1-to-9 ratio recommended by the hearing officer.

On appeal, the Second Circuit Court reversed, finding that the proposed IEP met the requirements set forth in *Rowley* for an appropriate education. In so ruling, the court stated that an IEP was to be reviewed as a whole rather than by evaluating its individual components in isolation and that the educational benefits of the IEP must be determined by assessing the combination of offerings rather than the single components. The court found that none of the evidence indicated that the student would not receive educational benefits from the IEP in question. Even though evidence indicated that the student would benefit more from the smaller ratio, the court held that under *Rowley* that evidence was insufficient since it did not prove that school officials failed to develop an IEP that was reasonably calculated to provide educational benefits.

A Program Must Meet State Standards

The Ninth Circuit Court of Appeals held in *Students of the California School for the Blind* v. *Honig* that the state was required to conduct additional seismic testing on a proposed site for a new school. The students claimed that proper seismic testing in accordance with the California Education Code had not been completed. The appeals court held that although the EHCA did not specifically mandate seismic testing, it could be concluded that such testing was required since an appropriate education is defined, in part, as one that meets state education standards. Since California law requires seismic safety of schools, the court concluded that a seismically unsafe school would not meet the state education standards and thus could not be part of an appropriate education. The court also noted that several other courts in reimbursement cases considered physical safety to be a component of an appropriate education.

Separate Facilities Are Not Necessarily Inappropriate

A Missouri district court held that educating severely handicapped students in special schools was not inappropriate. In *St. Louis Developmental Disabilities*

Treatment Center Parents Association v. *Mallory,* the state's system of providing special education services to certain severely handicapped students in special schools and facilities was challenged. The special facilities in question were substantially separate schools attended only by handicapped children. The student's parents claimed that the placement of handicapped children in such facilities was inappropriate and in violation of the EHCA because the students would not progress as they would if they attended classes in a local public school setting.

The district court found that the evidence indicated that it is possible to provide an appropriate education in a separate facility. The court further found that interaction with nonhandicapped peers in a regular educational setting was not necessarily a prerequisite to an appropriate education. The court held that educating severely handicapped students in a separate facility was not per se a violation of the EHCA. The EHCA requires that each handicapped child be treated as an individual. The court found that this was being done and that the placement of these students in a separate facility occurred only after careful consideration of all alternatives.

IEP Must Address All of a Student's Needs

A California district court held that a class for the trainable mentally retarded was not an appropriate placement for a multihandicapped child with physical, cognitive, and language difficulties because it did not address all three of those areas. The student in *Russell* v. *Jefferson School District* began receiving special services when he was preschool age and had most recently been in a class for children with severe disorders of language. After both the student's parents and the school district agreed that this was not an appropriate placement, the school district proposed that the student attend a class for the trainable mentally retarded. The student's parents rejected that proposal and initiated due process proceedings. The hearing officer determined that the proposed TMR class was appropriate, and court action was filed.

The court disagreed, however, and held that the proposal was not appropriate. The court held that the IEP was inadequate because it did not address all three of the student's special education needs and did not contain a statement of the specific educational services that were to be provided. The court further found that the TMR class was not appropriate, as the other children in the class were physically larger and more active than was the student in question and could thus pose a physical danger to him. Furthermore, the court found that testimony indicated that the TMR class might not be able to meet his language needs. The case was remanded back to the school district with instructions that if it could not develop an IEP to meet the student's needs in any of its special education programs, it must provide a private placement.

State Standards Are Incorporated into the EHCA

In addition to the EHCA, each individual state has legislation of its own governing special education. Although the state laws may differ from the federal statute, they must be consistent with it. State standards, however, may be more stringent than the federal standards. In 1985 the federal appeals courts in the First and Third Circuits ruled that state laws that imposed a higher standard of appropriateness than the EHCA were valid.

In *Geis* v. *Board of Education* the Third Circuit Court upheld a district court ruling that New Jersey's special education statute imposed a higher standard of appropriateness than the EHCA and that this standard was incorporated into the federal law. The appeals court found that such incorporation of state standards was explicit in the EHCA and that federal courts were authorized to enforce such standards under their federal question jurisdiction.

The First Circuit Court in *David D.* v. *Dartmouth School Committee* also upheld a district court decision that relied on Massachusetts' higher standard of appropriateness to determine that a proposed IEP was not sufficient to meet the student's needs. According to the district court the state's standard required that an IEP should be designed to maximize a handicapped child's potential to be appropriate. The appeals court determined that Congress intended for the states to enact policies and procedures consistent with the federal law but that where a state has chosen to provide greater benefits to handicapped children, the courts are required to incorporate the state's standards into the EHCA when determining the appropriateness of the IEP. In reaching its decision, the court found that Congress did not intend to reduce state standards to the federal minimum. The U.S. Supreme Court has denied certiorari in the case and has thus allowed the First Circuit's decision to stand.

The cases cited here indicate that although the EHCA establishes a basic floor of opportunity for handicapped children, individual states, and even school districts, can establish policies that go beyond that basic floor. The EHCA does not establish a ceiling where substantive rights to an appropriate education are concerned. In states where the state statute has set a standard of appropriateness higher than the EHCA's, school districts must adhere to that standard in addition to meeting the substantive requirements of *Rowley.*

REFERENCES

Age v. *Bullitt County Public Schools,* 673 F.2d 141 (1982).
Anderson v. *Thompson,* 495 F.Supp. 1256 (1980).
Association for Retarded Citizens of Colorado v. *Frazier,* 517 F.Supp. 105 (1981).
Bales v. *Clarke,* 523 F.Supp. 1366 (1981).
Board of Education of Hendrick Hudson Central School District v. *Rowley,* 102 S.Ct. 3034 (1982).

Buchholtz v. *Iowa Department of Public Instruction,* 315 N.W.2d 789 (1982).

Campbell v. *Talladega County Board of Education,* 518 F.Supp. 47 (1981).

Community High School v. *Denz,* 463 N.E.2d 998 (1984).

Cothern v. *Mallory,* 565 F.Supp. 701 (1983).

County School Board v. *Lower,* 555 EHLR 130 (1983).

Cox v. *Brown,* 498 F.Supp. 823 (1980).

David D. v. *Dartmouth School Committee,* 775 F.2d 411 (1985).

Doe v. *Lawson,* 579 F.Supp. 1314 (1984).

Frank v. *Grover,* 554 EHLR 148 (1982).

Geis v. *Board of Education,* 774 F.2d 575 (1985).

Gladys J. v. *Pearland Independent School District,* 520 F.Supp. 869 (1981).

Green v. *Johnson,* 513 F.Supp. 965 (1981).

Hessler v. *State Board of Education of Maryland,* 700 F.2d 134 (1983).

Helms v. *Independent School District,* 750 F.2d 820 (1984).

Hines v. *Pitt County Board of Education,* 497 F.Supp. 403 (1980).

Howard S. v. *Friendswood Independent School District,* 454 F.Supp. 634 (1978).

In re Van Overreem, 555 EHLR 182 (1983).

Johnston v. *Ann Arbor Public Schools,* 569 F.Supp. 1502 (1983).

Karl v. *Board of Education of Genesco Central School District,* 736 F.2d 873 (1984).

Lang v. *Braintree School Committee,* 545 F.Supp. 1221 (1982).

Laura M. v. *Special School District,* 552 EHLR 152 (1980).

Lora v. *Board of Education of New York,* 456 F.Supp. 1221 (1978), 587 F.Supp. 1572 (1984).

Mallory v. *Drake,* 616 S.W.2d 124 (1981).

New York State Association for Retarded Children v. *Carey,* 612 F.2d 644 (1979).

Norris v. *Massachusetts Department of Education,* 529 F.Supp. 759 (1981).

Pinkerton v. *Moye,* 509 F.Supp. 107 (1981).

Rettig v. *Kent City School District,* 788 F.2d 328 (1986).

Roncker v. *Walter,* 700 F.2d 1058 (1983).

Russell v. *Jefferson School District,* 609 F.Supp. 605 (1985).

St. Louis Developmental Disabilities Center v. *Mallory,* 591 F.Supp. 1416 (1984).

Springdale School District v. *Grace,* 656 F.2d 300 (1981), vac'd and rem'd 102 S.Ct. 3504 (1982), 693 F.2d 41 (1982).

Stacey G. v. *Pasadena Independent School District,* 547 F.Supp. 61 (1982), partially vac'd and rem'd 695 F2d 949 (1983).

Students of California School for the Blind v. *Honig,* 736 F.2d 538 (1984).

Timms v. *Metropolitan School District,* 554 EHLR 361 (1982).

Troutman v. *School District of Greenville County,* 554 EHLR 487 (1983).

Wilson v. *Marana Unified School District,* 735 F.2d 1178 (1984).

Figure 2-1

LEADING CASES

Springdale School District v. *Grace,* 656 F.2d 300 (1981)

The EHCA does not require the state to provide the best possible education but, rather, only requires it to provide an appropriate education.

Age v. *Bullitt County Public Schools,* 673 F.2d 141 (1982)

The mere existence of a better program does not make a proposed program inappropriate.

Board of Education v. *Rowley,* 102 S.Ct. 3034 (1982)

An appropriate education is one that provides the student with personalized instruction such that it permits the child to benefit educationally and one that is formulated in accordance with the procedural requirements of the EHCA.

Roncker v. *Walter,* 700 F.2d 1058 (1983)

Mainstreaming is not required in every case, but it must be provided to the maximum extent appropriate.

Karl v. *Board of Education,* 736 F.2d 873 (1984)

In determining the appropriateness of an IEP, it must be reviewed as a whole rather than by evaluating its individual components in isolation.

Figure 2-2

COMPONENTS OF AN APPROPRIATE EDUCATION

1. *Specifically designed instruction*—personalized instruction designed to meet the specific unique needs of the handicapped child.

2. *Appropriate peer group*—the handicapped child should be educated, if possible, in a peer group that contains children of approximately the same age and developmental level, and with similar disabilities. Other members of the same sex are also desirable.

3. *Least restrictive environment* (mainstreaming)—the handicapped child should be educated with nonhandicapped children to the maximum extent feasible. However, mainstreaming should not be provided if a more restrictive environment is necessary to provide an appropriate education.

4. *Educational benefit*—the special services provided should be such that the child will make meaningful progress toward the goals of the IEP.

5. *Procedural requirements*—the educational program must be developed in accordance with the EHCA's procedural requirements.

6. *State requirements*—the educational program must also conform to any state educational standards.

7. *Support services*—related or supportive services must be provided if they are necessary for the student to benefit from the educational program.

8. *Public expense*—must be at no cost to the student or parents.

Figure 2-3

ACCESS FOR THE HANDICAPPED

1. The handicapped child is entitled to have access to regular programs, if appropriate. Special accommodations may be required if necessary for the student to gain meaningful access to regular programs.

2. The handicapped child should have access to nonacademic programs and extracurricular activities when appropriate.

3. Unless other arrangements are necessary to provide an appropriate education, the handicapped child is entitled to attend the school she would attend if she were not handicapped.

4. If necessary to provide an appropriate education, the handicapped child is entitled to have access to private day or residential schools.

5. Certain handicapped children are also entitled to have access to educational programs that extend beyond the traditional school year.

6. Handicapped children are entitled to have access to educational programs from the ages of 3 through 21 or until they earn a high school diploma.

7. Handicapped students are entitled to have access to certain related services (such as transportation, counseling, school health services) if such services are necessary for them to benefit from their special education.

Figure 2-4

LEAST RESTRICTIVE ENVIRONMENT

The following is one state's scheme for meeting the mainstreaming requirement:

502.0 *Program Prototypes*

502.1 Regular education program with modifications

502.2 Regular education program with no more than 25% time out

502.3 Regular education program with no more than 60% time out

502.4 Substantially separate program

502.5 Day school program

502.6 Residential school program

502.7 Home, hospital, regional adolescent program

502.8 Program for children ages three and four

502.9 Diagnostic program

From Chapter 766 Regulations, Massachusetts Department of Education (71B Mass. Gen. Laws §1 et seq.).

Figure 2-5

QUESTIONS ADMINISTRATORS OFTEN ASK ABOUT AN
APPROPRIATE EDUCATION

1. *Must a school system provide a handicapped student with the best possible education?*

No, school systems are only held to the standard of providing an adequate education. Typically school systems do not provide nonhandicapped students with the best possible education, and no higher standard is imposed when the student is handicapped.

2. *Do all handicapped students have to be educated in the mainstream?*

No, education in the mainstream would not be appropriate or even advisable for all students. However, any student who is capable and would benefit from mainstreaming must be provided with as much of it as is appropriate.

3. *What about lunch, recess, and nonacademic portions of the day—should handicapped students be mainstreamed in these areas?*

These are areas where handicapped students are typically mainstreamed. Again, if it would be to the child's benefit, school administrators should make every effort to mainstream a handicapped child in these areas.

4. *The term "appropriate" is hard to define—how can you tell when a program is legally appropriate?*

The Supreme Court has said that an appropriate program is one that was developed according to the law's proscriptions and is designed to provide some educational benefit. Even the existence of a better program would not render any given program inappropriate.

Figure 2-6

STEPS IN THE EVALUATION/PLACEMENT PROCESS

1. Student is referred for an evaluation by a teacher, principal, counselor, parents, or other knowledgeable person.

2. Parents are notified of the referral, are given the reasons for the referral, and are asked to consent to the evaluation.

3. The evaluation is conducted by a multidisciplinary team consisting of any combination of the following: school psychologist, school nurse or physician, current teacher(s), administrator, guidance counselor, special education teacher, speech and language therapist, parents, and any other pertinent parties.

4. A placement conference is held to discuss the results of the evaluation, make a determination as to whether special education services are needed, and develop an Individualized Educational Program if warranted.

5. A proposed IEP is sent to the parents. They may accept it, reject it, attempt to work out an alternative IEP, or postpone a decision while they seek an independent evaluation.

6a. If the IEP is accepted, it is implemented immediately.

6b. If the IEP is rejected, due process begins immediately.

6c. If an alternative plan is worked out, a new IEP is issued and implemented immediately on parents' acceptance.

6d. If an independent evaluation is sought, the child remains in the current placement until an IEP is finally developed and accepted.

7. The accepted IEP is reviewed annually, and the student is reevaluated every three years.

Figure 2-7

REFERRAL FOR SPECIAL EDUCATION EVALUATION

Date: _____

Student: _____ D.O.B. _____

Parent or Guardian: _____

Address: _____

Telephone: _____

School: _____ Grade: _____ Sex: _____

Teacher: _____ Native Language: _____

Reasons for Referral (Please be specific):

1. _____

_____

2. _____

_____

3. _____

_____

Please list the student's most recent standardized test scores:

Please indicate what attempts you have made to resolve the problem prior to making the referral:

Additional information:

Referral made by: _____ Position: _____

Referral received by: _____ Date: _____

Figure 2-8

LETTER TO PARENTS REGARDING REFERRAL FOR EVALUATION

Date: _____

Parent/Guardian: _____

Address: _____

_____

Dear _____ :

    Your child _____ has been referred for a special education evaluation by _____ for the following reasons: _____ _____ .

    Federal and state special education laws require that the school district obtain your written permission prior to conducting the recommended evaluation. So that we may evaluate your child I would appreciate your signing and returning the attached Permission to Evaluate form.

    The purpose of the evaluation is to determine if your child requires special education services to receive an appropriate education. The recommended evaluation will be conducted by a team of trained professionals retained for that purpose by the school district. You will be invited to become a member of the evaluation team.

    If it is determined that your child does require special education services, an Individualized Educational Program will be developed outlining those services. That program will not be implemented without your written approval.

    If you would like to meet with the evaluation team chairperson prior to granting approval for the recommended evaluation, please call this office and a meeting will be arranged.

    Please be advised that any information generated through this evaluation will be shared only with school district personnel who have a need for the information to teach your child properly. It will not be released to any third parties without your written consent.

                                       (Special Education
                                       Administrator's Signature)

Figure 2-9

PARENTAL PERMISSION TO EVALUATE FORM

Student: _____

School: _____ Grade: _____

The school district requests your permission to conduct a special education evaluation on the above child as described in the enclosed cover letter. It is recommended that the assessments indicated below be completed as part of that evaluation.

_____ Psychological testing/cognitive area

_____ Psychological testing/projective (personality)

_____ Achievement testing

_____ Perceptual testing

_____ Educational history

_____ Description of classroom performance

_____ Speech and language assessment

_____ Home visit assessment

_____ Medical examination

_____ Hearing screening

_____ Vision screening

* *

_____ I grant permission for the evaluation as recommended.

_____ I do not grant permission for the evaluation.

_____ I grant permission for the evaluation but object to the following assessments:

Signature: _____ Date: _____

Date received by special education office: _____

Figure 2-10

NOTICE TO PARENTS CONCERNING PROCEDURAL RIGHTS UNDER FEDERAL
AND STATE LAW
(Should accompany all communications with parents)

1. Your written consent to conduct the special education evaluation is voluntary and may be revoked at any time.

2. You may meet with the chairperson of the evaluation team at any time to discuss the reasons for the referral, the particular assessments to be conducted, or any other matters that may concern you.

3. You may bring any person of your choice (at your own expense) to any meetings in which your child's evaluation or placement will be discussed.

4. The special education evaluation must be conducted within thirty days of receipt of your written consent.

5. An Individualized Educational Program (IEP) must be developed within ten days of the placement conference if special education services are recommended. If special education services are not recommended, a written statement to that effect must be provided within ten days.

6. If an IEP is proposed, you may either accept or reject that plan.

7. If you accept the IEP, it is to be implemented immediately.

8. If you reject the IEP, you have the right to a hearing before an impartial hearing officer.

9. Prior to going to a hearing, you have the right to meet with the Administrator of Special Education to attempt to work out an acceptable IEP.

10. If you dispute the findings of the evaluation team or any of the individual assessments, you may seek an independent evaluation either at your own expense or at the school department's expense. If you wish to have the independent evaluation conducted at school department expense you must notify the Administrator of Special Education in writing, explaining what assessments are disputed and why they are disputed. You must receive written authorization from the Administrator of Special Education for the evaluation to be conducted at an approved facility.

11. You may request copies of all assessments conducted as part of the evaluation.

12. You may inspect any records generated as a result of the special education evaluation.

Figure 2-11

CHAIRPERSON'S CHECKLIST

Student: _____ Parent/Guardian: _____

Address: _____ Phone: _____

School: _____ Grade: _____ Teacher: _____

D.O.B. _____ C.A. _____ Native language: _____

This evaluation is an: _____ Initial _____ Reevaluation

Date of referral: _____ Date referral received: _____

Date parent notified of referral: _____

Date permission to evaluate received: _____

Date parent invited to TEAM conference: _____

Date of conference: _____ Date IEP sent to parents: _____

Date IEP signed: _____

Indicate below any additional contacts with parents or their representatives (phone calls, letters, meetings, etc.):

Indicate below reasons for any delays or postponements:

In-House Assessments:

Date	Assessment	Evaluator	Position

Outside Specialist Assessments:

Date	Assessment	Evaluator	Affiliation

Parents' medical insurance coverage: _____

Figure 2-12

EDUCATIONAL HISTORY

Student: _____ Date: _____

School: _____ Grade: _____

Briefly describe the student's current educational placement including any special or remedial services.

Summary of Educational Placements (listed in reverse chronological order):

Year	*Grade*	*School/City*	*Type Program*	*Comments*

Report prepared by: _____ Position: _____

Figure 2-13

CLASSROOM TEACHER ASSESSMENT

Student: _____ Date: _____ Grade: _____

Assessed by: _____ Position: _____

1. Please comment on the student's current grade-level achievement and general status in each of the following areas:

   Reading Skills (decoding and comprehension)

   Written Language

   Oral Language

   Ability to Follow Directions

   Spelling

   Math

   Fine Motor Skills

   Gross Motor Skills

   Other Subjects

2. Please comment on the student's performance in the following areas:

   Classroom Behavior

   Work Habits

   Attention

   Cooperation

   Peer Relationships

   Relationships with Adults

3. What, in your opinion, are the student's strengths?

4. What, in your opinion, are the student's weaknesses?

5. What teaching/learning style have you found to be most appropriate for the student in your classroom?

6. Does the student have any known physical handicaps, medical condition, or visual or auditory acuity deficits?

Figure 2-14

HOME VISIT ASSESSMENT

Student: _____ Date: _____

School: _____ Grade: _____

Date of visit: _____ Interview with: _____

Relationship to student: _____

Family Unit

	Name	Occupation	Age	Educational Level
Father				
Mother				
Siblings				

Summarize each of the following:

Student's Health History

Interactions with Other Family Members

Developmental History

Student's Interests

Other Information

Completed by: _____ Position: _____

Figure 2-15

NOTICE OF EVALUATION TEAM MEETING

Student: _____ Date: _____

Address: _____

Parent/Guardian: _____

Dear _____ :

　　　You are invited to attend and participate in an evaluation team meeting concerning your child. The meeting will be held as follows:

Date: _____ Time: _____

Location: _____

The purpose of the meeting is to discuss:

_____ An initial evaluation

_____ A reevaluation

_____ A review of progress

The following have been invited and are expected to be in attendance:

Name　　　　　　　　　　　　　　*Position*

You may bring any person of your choosing (at your own expense) to the meeting. However, we would appreciate advance notice if you intend to bring another party.

Please call this office if you cannot keep the above appointment.

　　　　　　　　　　　　(Signature of the Special Education
　　　　　　　　　　　　Administrator or Evaluation Team Chairperson)

Figure 2-16

LETTER ACCOMPANYING IEP

Date: _____

Parent/Guardian: _____

Address: _____

_____

Dear _____ :

   The special education evaluation has been completed on your child. The enclosed Individualized Education Program has been proposed by the evaluation team.
   The following options are available to you regarding your action on the IEP:

1. You may accept the plan as proposed.
2. You may reject the plan and request a due process hearing before an impartial hearing officer.
3. You may postpone action pending an independent evaluation either at your own expense or school district expense.
4. You may postpone action and meet with the special education administrator to attempt to work out an acceptable alternative plan.

   Please indicate your decision and sign and return one copy of the enclosed IEP. The other copy may be retained for your own records. If you have any questions or concerns please call this office.
   Please note that the services outlined in the IEP cannot be implemented until we receive your written permission to do so. Once you have accepted the IEP you still retain the right to reject it at a later date.

(Special Education Administrator's Signature)

Figure 2-17

ADMINISTRATOR'S CHECKLIST

Questions to ask in determining if a proposed program is appropriate:

1. Were all the EHCA and state law procedural requirements adhered to in formulating the IEP? _____

2. Does the IEP clearly spell out what services will be provided and what the goals of the program are? _____
   _____

3. Is the program designed to meet this student's individual unique needs? _____

4. Will the proposed program be carried out in the least restrictive environment possible? If not, why not?
   _____
   _____

5. Describe the efforts made to provide the child with as much contact as possible with nonhandicapped children.
   _____
   _____

6. Does the educational environment provide for interaction with an appropriate peer group? _____
   Describe the peer group. _____

7. Are any support services necessary? _____ Are they provided for in the IEP? ____

8. Is the proposed IEP reasonably calculated to bring about an educational benefit to the child? _____

9. Describe the child's access to all appropriate regular education programs.
   _____
   _____

Figure 2-18

PROCEDURAL SAFEGUARDS CHECKLIST

Date

1. The student's parents were fully informed of all aspects of the evaluation process.

2. Parental consent was obtained in writing to conduct the evaluation.

3. The parents were informed that consent is voluntary and may be revoked at any time.

4. The parents were informed of their right to inspect any records pertaining to the evaluation.

5. The parents were informed of their right to obtain an independent evaluation.

6. The parents were notified that the school district either planned to make an educational placement or did not plan to change the student's placement as a result of the evaluation.

7. Parental consent was obtained for the proposed placement.

8. Parents were notified of their right to request a due process hearing if they disagreed with the school district's proposal.

Chapter 3

WHEN ARE PRIVATE DAY AND RESIDENTIAL PLACEMENTS REQUIRED?

> *The requirement of a free appropriate education includes the guarantee that when a child is placed at a residential facility . . . , the placement must be free of cost to the child's parents.*
>
> **District Judge Marshall**
> *Parks* v. *Pavkovic*
> **536 F.Supp. 296 at 304 (1982)**

The placement of handicapped students in private day or residential schools has generated a tremendous amount of litigation since the implementation of the Education for All Handicapped Children Act (EHCA). School systems have been reluctant to place students in such programs, often feeling that less restrictive programs available within the school system were adequate; however, many parents have contended that such a placement was necessary because the public schools did not have an appropriate program.

CIRCUMSTANCES REQUIRING PRIVATE PLACEMENTS

The regulations implementing the EHCA specifically provide that

Each public agency shall insure that a continuum of alternative placements is available to meet the needs of handicapped children for special education and related services. (34 C.F.R. § 300.551(a))

and

> If placement in a public or private residential program is necessary to provide special education and related services to a handicapped child, the program, including non-medical care and room and board, must be at no cost to the parents of the child.
> *Comment.* This requirement applies to placements which are made by public agencies for educational purposes . . . (34 C.F.R. § 300.302)

Twenty-four-Hour Care and Instruction Are Needed

Early in 1979 the district court in *Ladson* v. *Board of Education of the District of Columbia* ordered the school district to provide a residential placement after it found that the student required 24-hour-a-day care. The student was an 11-year-old profoundly retarded Down's syndrome child. An evaluation team had unanimously recommended a residential placement following a determination that the student had a mental age of 18 months, was not toilet trained, could not speak, and had difficulty climbing stairs and that gains made were not followed through in the home. The school board, however, rejected this proposal and determined that the student's educational needs were being met in her current day school placement. On appeal a hearing officer found that the proposed residential school was inadequate but ordered the school department to propose an alternate residential placement. The school department refused to comply and court action followed.

In ordering the residential placement, the court found that the student's handicaps were severe and that she regressed because of inadequate follow-up in the home. After assessing the evidence, the court determined that the student required 24-hour-a-day care to meet the goals of her individualized education program.

The court found that residential placement was required when the student needed 24-hour-a-day instruction and treatment in *Gladys J.* v. *Pearland Independent School District.* The student in this case was a multihandicapped adolescent who had been enrolled in special education classes since the age of 6 after having been identified as trainable mentally retarded. After a time she became so severely withdrawn that her parents had her evaluated at a psychiatric hospital. There she was diagnosed as being a schizophrenic. She continued in a class for the mentally retarded until her behavior at home deteriorated and her parents placed her in a residential diagnostic facility for multihandicapped children. An assessment indicated that she had regressed intellectually and adaptively. She was again diagnosed as having organic childhood schizophrenia and a residential placement was recommended. Her parents requested such a placement from the school district, but the school district declined, offering instead a 6-hour day program with home support. The parents appealed, but were ultimately unsuccessful in the administrative hearing process.

The court, in ordering the school district to provide the residential placement, held that since the student had made no meaningful progress toward the attainment of her educational goals in the day program, that placement was not appropriate to her unique needs. The court found that she needed a constant structured environment, a 24-hour-per-day behavior modification program, and an intensive language program. This, the court determined, could not be provided in a 6-hour day program with home support. Residential placement was, thus, required.

The Supreme Court of Nebraska in *Adams Central School District* v. *Deist* ordered a residential placement for an autistic, mentally retarded student when it found that the evidence supported a hearing officer's determination that the student required such a placement. The student had attended a school for the trainable mentally retarded, but was involuntarily removed from that school when his behavior became disruptive and destructive. His parents placed him in a regional center for handicapped children and later in a psychiatric institute when the regional placement did not work out. After several months of meetings between school officials and the parents failed to produce an acceptable alternative placement, the parents began due process appeals. The hearing officer determined that the student required a residential placement after having heard testimony that the student required a 24-hour management program. The trial court reversed that decision; the state supreme court reinstated it, however. The U.S. Supreme Court has declined to review the decision.

In *Diamond* v. *McKenzie* the district court found that a residential placement was necessary to provide an appropriate education for a 17-year-old severely learning disabled and severely emotionally disturbed student when the school department failed to show that such a placement was not required. The student had attended a private day school for several years. The school department proposed that the student continue in a day placement at another facility. At a hearing called to determine an appropriate placement, the hearing officer noted that the school department failed to present any evidence or testimony that its proposed placement was appropriate and ordered it to consider a residential placement. The court further ordered that if the school district determined that a residential placement was not necessary, it provide a rationale for that decision. The school department later decided that a residential placement was not justified but failed to provide an explanation for its decision.

The student's mother had already placed him in a residential facility. Testimony at the trial indicated that the student needed a 24-hour structured program. Further evidence indicated that he had made progress since entering the facility. The court found this evidence persuasive, noting that the staff at the residential facility clearly had greater familiarity with the student than the public school officials. The residential program was determined to be appropriate.

Full-Time Instruction Is Required

The district court in *DeWalt* v. *Burkholder* weighed the pros and cons of a residential placement prior to approving it. In this case the residential placement was recommended by the school system and opposed by the parents. The student was a multihandicapped child who had a severe to profound hearing loss, borderline mental retardation, slight cerebral palsy, and seriously delayed social-emotional development. She began receiving educational services at the age of 3 and entered a day program for the hearing impaired when she was 5 years old. One year later, on the advice of a physician and other professionals, she was enrolled in a residential school for the deaf. After she attended that program for one year, her parents decided to withdraw her and tried to enroll her in the hearing impaired program in the public schools. School officials determined, after performing several evaluations, that an appropriate program did not exist within the public schools and that a residential school was the appropriate placement. The student's parents objected to this recommendation, but it was upheld in administrative appeals.

The court found that the preponderance of the evidence indicated that the student's primary problem was one of language, that it was unlikely that the language problem would be remediated in a day program, that it was more likely that the language problem could be solved in a 24-hour total immersion setting, and that a residential setting would probably only be temporary, after which the student would be able to enter the public schools. On the other hand, the court noted that a residential placement would deprive the student of family support and affection. The court ruled in favor of the residential placement after finding that it would provide an appropriate education and that the day placement would not.

Consistency of Programming Is Necessary

Residential placement was ordered by the district court and upheld by the court of appeals in a Third Circuit decision after it was determined that the student's unique needs required a great degree of consistency in programming. The student in *Kruelle* v. *Biggs* was a profoundly retarded, cerebral-palsied 12-year-old who could not walk, dress himself, or eat unaided. He was not toilet trained, did not speak, and had a history of emotional difficulties. His educational history began in Pennsylvania where he attended special education classes. Due to his emotional difficulties, he was eventually placed in a residential program of training and respite care. When the family moved to Delaware, he was placed in a respite care home and enrolled in a public day school for handicapped children. After two weeks his parents withdrew him from the day school and sought a residential placement. They were unsuccessful in administrative appeals and filed court action.

The district court, in ruling that a residential placement was required, found that the student's educational record indicated that his unique combination of handicaps required that he receive a greater degree of consistency of programming than many other profoundly retarded children. The court found that he would realize his learning potential only if he received more professional help than the day school's program could provide and that full-time care was necessary for him to learn. In upholding the district court, the appeals court indicated that a residential placement was necessary in this case to conform to the EHCA's mandate that specially designed instruction to meet the unique needs of the handicapped child be provided.

The First Circuit Court of Appeals upheld the district court's order for a residential placement in 1983 in *Abrahamson* v. *Hershman.* The district court had found that educational benefits could not be realized in a day program but could be realized in a residential setting. The student was a severely retarded 16-year-old youth. The district court found that the student could not dress, eat or otherwise care for himself. The student, who had a mental age between 1 and 4, had very few communication skills and did not recognize danger to himself. He had attended day programs for several years and then entered a residential school. After four years in the residential school, the local school system proposed an Individualized Education Program (IEP) that called for placement in a public school day program. The student's parents rejected the proposed placement; however, it was upheld in administrative appeals.

The district court found that the student needed consistent instruction and reinforcement on a round-the-clock basis. This, according to the court, could be provided only through either a residential placement or a day program with an accompanying residential component. The appeals court held that the district court's decision was not erroneous. In reaching its decision, the appeals court applied the *Rowley* standard and held that the school district was only required to place the student in a program that provided the opportunity for some educational progress. The court interpreted *Rowley* to mean that a handicapped student who would make educational progress in a day program was not entitled to a residential school placement merely because the latter would better enable the student to reach his or her full potential. Since the student in this case would not make educational progress in a day program alone, residential placement was found to be appropriate.

Emotional Support Is Needed

A state appellate court ordered a residential placement in *San Francisco U.S.D.* v. *California* when it determined that a student's home environment was not conducive to his making satisfactory progress. The student had a history of academic and behavioral problems. His family history was chaotic and marked with conflict, and in school he had problems with peer relations and school attendance. An evaluation team found him to be severely emotionally disturbed and functioning academically one or two years below grade level in spite of his having above-average intellectual potential. An IEP proposed that he be placed in a learning disabilities class with special support services for approximately half the school day. His guardian, however, felt that he needed a residential placement and rejected the proposed IEP. The hearing officer concluded that the student needed a residential placement because his home did not provide him with the emotional support necessary to compensate for his learning difficulties. This decision was approved by the Superintendent of Public Instruction but was set aside by the trial court.

The appeals court concluded that substantial evidence supported the hearing officer's finding that the student's emotional problems adversely affected his educational achievement. The court found that his emotional problems were so linked with his learning problems that an IEP providing for residential placement was justified since it appeared that the student needed to be removed from his home environment to make satisfactory progress. The trial court's decision was overturned.

To Develop Self-sufficiency and Independence

The district court, in another District of Columbia case, weighed the needs of the student against the preference for education in the least restrictive environment in *Capello* v. *District of Columbia Board of Education*. The student, an 18-year-old autistic, mentally retarded youth, had been attending a day facility for children with special needs for several years. His mother requested that his placement be changed to a residential facility and, when the school system refused to do so, requested a hearing. The hearing officer found that the day placement no longer met the student's needs. The hearing officer, however, also found that the school district's responsibility for the student, according to its own rules, would end in June of that year, but would begin again 14 months later in September 1980 by EHCA mandate. The hearing officer gave the school district 40 days to develop a plan with other state agencies to meet the student's needs. When no such plan was developed, a preliminary injunction and order for residential placement was sought.

The district court denied the preliminary injunction, but ordered the school district to develop a plan to meet the student's needs through his twenty-first birthday, taking into consideration the hearing officer's finding that the current placement was appropriate. In denying the preliminary injunction, the court stated that a court-mandated placement of a student in a residential setting was a drastic step that should only be taken when it was clearly necessary for the student's education or well-being.

The school district later submitted the court-ordered plan, again recommending a day school placement. In the meantime the student's parents had enrolled him in a residential facility and filed court action requesting an order that the school district pay for the residential placement. Evidence submitted at the trial indicated that the student had regressed toward the end of the day placement but had shown marked improvement since being placed in the residential facility. A pediatric neurologist also recommended the residential placement.

The court found that the evidence supported a residential placement for the student. The court indicated that an appropriate education for the student should provide an opportunity for him to progress in developing self-control, self-awareness, self-sufficiency, and basic academic skills. The court determined that the residential facility provided such an opportunity, whereas the day facility did not.

For Students Who Are Dangerous

An Illinois appellate court found residential placement to be appropriate for an emotionally disturbed student whose behavior had become violent. The student in *Walker* v. *Cronin* had been placed in a self-contained class for severely emotionally disturbed students for half a day with some mainstreaming and assistance from a social worker. His grades and behavior began to deteriorate so that his mother requested a residential placement. The school system, however, recommended that his present placement continue. His mother requested a hearing, but before the hearing was held, the student's behavior became so violent that his mother placed him in a private residential facility. When the hearing was held, the hearing officer determined that a residential placement was appropriate. That determination was overruled by the state Office of Education.

The trial court determined that a residential placement was appropriate because the student's needs were so profound, complex, and unique that the public schools could not appropriately meet them. The appeals court found that ample support existed for the trial court's findings and affirmed.

In *Hines* v. *Pitt County Board of Education,* the court held that the particular residential placement made must be one that is appropriate for the student. The student in *Hines* was a 10-year-old emotionally handicapped student whose problems were evident as early as the age of 5. He had experienced learning and behavior problems throughout his schooling, but these problems became so acute that in the third grade an evaluation team recommended that he be placed in a special school for emotionally disturbed students. His problems also persisted at this school, and his parents had a psychiatric evaluation performed on him. He was diagnosed as having a schizoid personality, and placement in a residential treatment center was recommended. Instead, however, the student was returned to his former school, and an additional staff member was hired to help meet his needs. He was later taken out of school and given homebound instruction when his disruptive and aggressive behavior continued. Residential placement was again recommended, but the particular facility recommended served students between the ages of 11 and 17. The student's parents objected to this recommendation and, after failing to gain relief through administrative appeals, filed court action.

The court heard testimony that the student needed social interaction with other children of approximately the same developmental level. Since the student was below average in his overall development, an appropriate peer group would consist of children between the ages of 8 and 10. There was also an indication that the student would withdraw in a setting with older children. The court found three other facilities that it deemed appropriate and ordered the school district to place the student in one of them. The court noted that the state could not refuse to provide the funds to send the student to one of these schools under the pretense that it could not afford the costs.

When Public School Programs Are Not Available

The district court in *Matthews* v. *Campbell* ordered a residential placement when it determined that the student had made little progress in a public school setting. The student was a profoundly retarded child. In previous action the school department had been ordered to take steps to provide him with an appropriate education. In this regard school officials had placed the student in a public school program and had retained an advisory panel of experts to assist in preparing an IEP. The student's parents contended that this was not appropriate and that a residential placement was required.

Evidence submitted at the trial indicated that the student had made little or no progress in crucial daily living and self-care skills during the previous semester. The student was assessed to be totally dependent on others in almost every respect. However, evidence also indicated that residential facilities presented some problems as well, such as high staff turnover, limited exposure to nonhandicapped children, and the emotional trauma associated with removal from the home and family.

In spite of the statutory preference for educating students in the least restrictive environment, the court ordered residential placement. The court based its order on a conclusion that the public school placement was not appropriate and that the public schools could not develop an appropriate program.

In *Cox* v. *Brown* the court ordered the Department of Defense to provide and fund residential placements for two severely learning disabled students when it determined that the government's overseas school system's special education programs were insufficient to meet the students' specific special education needs. The court ordered the residential placements when it determined that the students would suffer the irreparable harm of lacking an appropriate education that was sensitive to their particular disabilities. During the trial the court heard testimony that the students would not benefit educationally or survive emotionally in the program proposed by the overseas school system.

In *Norris* v. *Massachusetts Department of Education* the district court ordered a private day school placement when it determined that the student was not making sufficient progress in the public schools. The student had received special education services for severe learning disabilities for several years within the public schools. His learning problems had caused him to perform poorly in academics, become easily frustrated, and feel inadequate. The school department proposed an IEP for the student's sixth grade year that called for him to be placed in a program of at least 60 percent special education. His parents rejected that plan, but it was found to be appropriate on appeal. The following year the school department proposed an IEP that called for substantially less special education, stating that a more intensive program was not available at the junior high school. The student's parents again appealed and were successful this time. The hearing officer found that the student's educational and emotional needs required his placement in a private school.

The district court noted that the student had failed to show significant growth in the public school program and had failed to close the gap between his level of achievement and that of his age group peers. The court found that the evidence indicated that the student's special education needs required an environment that provided careful monitoring, intensive instruction, small groups of only learning disabled students, minimum distractions, and individual attention. Since the public schools had not provided, and appeared to be unable to provide, that environment, private school placement was ordered.

The district court ordered residential placement in *Colin K.* v. *Schmidt* after determining that the severity of the student's handicaps required a highly individualized, highly structured, and closely monitored program for them to learn and progress. The students had moved to Rhode Island from Washington, D.C., where they had attended a private day school for learning disabled children. After they moved, their father requested funding for a similar residential school since an appropriate day school did not exist within commuting distance. The students were evaluated by local officials who determined that they could be educated in a self-contained special education class within the public schools. The students' father rejected that proposal. The local hearing officer decided that the proposed program was not appropriate as it was not intensive enough. This decision was affirmed on appeal. A new IEP was developed that proposed essentially the same program with the addition of psychological counseling. The local hearing officer determined that this IEP was appropriate and that the residential school was not appropriate as it was not the least restrictive environment. That decision was reversed on appeal, and court action followed.

Testimony at the trial indicated that both students suffered from severe to profound learning disabilities with associated emotional disturbance. Staff from the day school in Washington testified that the proposed public school was insufficient to meet the student's needs and that mainstreaming could be detrimental to them. Witnesses for the public schools testified that the students were severely learning disabled but that they could be educated within the public schools.

The court found that the proposed IEP calling for public school placement was inappropriate and that the residential placement provided at least an appropriate placement. Since the record was insufficient, the court was unable to decide whether a more intense nonresidential placement would be appropriate. In ordering the residential placement over the public school placement, the court determined that both students had severe learning disabilities and significant emotional problems and that the severity of these handicaps warranted a highly individualized, highly structured, and closely monitored program. That program, in the court's opinion, could not be provided by the public schools. The First Circuit Court of Appeals affirmed.

PLACEMENTS FOR OTHER THAN EDUCATIONAL REASONS

In another District of Columbia case, *North* v. *District of Columbia Board of Education,* the district court ordered the school board to provide a residential placement when it determined that the student's educational, emotional, social, and medical needs were so intimately intertwined that it was impossible to treat them separately. The student was a 16-year-old multiply handicapped youth who had been diagnosed as being epileptic, emotionally disturbed, and learning disabled. It was determined that the student required a residential placement that would provide special education, medical supervision, and psychological support. The student was placed in a school that provided all of these; however, one year later the school notified his parents that it could no longer deal with his emotional and other problems. His parents requested that the school department provide an alternate placement; however, that was not done. When his parents also refused to take him, the student was placed in a residential psychiatric treatment center that also provided educational and medical services. The school department claimed that it was not responsible for providing for the student's living arrangements since his problems were emotional, social, and otherwise noneducational.

The court disagreed, however, finding that it was not realistically possible to determine whether the student's social, emotional, and medical problems or his educational problems were dominant, and thus be able to assign responsibility to the appropriate human service agency. The court held that it was clear that under federal law the school board had the responsibility to provide the student with a residential placement since all these needs were so intimately intertwined.

The district court in *Erdman* v. *State of Connecticut* found, as did the *North* court, that it could not separate the student's emotional needs from his educational needs and ordered the school district to pay the full costs of a residential placement. In this case a high school student, who had received special education services since third grade because of behavioral and academic difficulties, had been suspended for breaking another student's nose. Following the suspension an evaluation team, based on a psychiatric assessment, recommended placement in a therapeutic community for other than educational reasons and determined that the school system was to pay the educational costs only. The student's parents appealed, claiming that although the residential program was appropriate, it was necessary for educational reasons. The hearing officer upheld the school system's decision.

The court found that the student was emotionally handicapped and that his emotional needs interfered with his ability to learn; thus, it was impossible to separate his emotional needs from his academic needs. It determined that the student could learn only in a structured environment and that the local schools could not provide such an environment. The court noted that both the EHCA and Section 504 regulations provided that if residential placement was necessary to provide special education and related services, it was to be at no cost to the student's parents. Since the student required a residential placement to receive an appropriate education, the local school system was required to pay the full costs of the program.

The district court in *McKenzie* v. *Jefferson* held that the school district was not responsible for the residential component costs of a program for a student who was in a private psychiatric hospital and school. The student had suffered a severe psychotic breakdown while the family was temporarily living out of the country and was placed in a psychiatric facility in the United States. One year later, after her parents had returned home, they placed her in a private psychiatric hospital and school on a residential basis. They subsequently requested that the local school system provide for her special education and related services there. The school system proposed that they pay for the student's educational tuition costs only, but not her residential costs. Her parents contended that this was not appropriate and appealed. The hearing officer ruled that a residential program was appropriate and directed the school system to pay for it. The school system appealed that determination to the district court.

The court found that the primary reasons for the student's placement at the psychiatric hospital were medical, not educational. The court determined that the particular services needed required hospitalization and, thus, were medical services and as such did not fall within the realm of related services. The EHCA includes those medical services required for evaluation and diagnostic purposes only within the definition of related services. Treatment, especially long-term medical treatment, is not included according to the court. The court held that in this case the hospital had little to do with special education, but rather, was for medical treatment.

The district court in *Ahern* v. *Keene* found that a multihandicapped student did not require a residential placement in spite of having emotional problems because those emotional problems did not interfere with her achievement. The student's parents placed her in a private residential facility out of concern for her emotional stability and social development after she began to exhibit behavioral problems in reaction to a stressful home environment. The court found that the evidence indicated that the student was achieving academically up to expectations for her capacity and that she was making progress in social development. Since the school district could provide an appropriate education, a residential placement was not necessary.

MUST BE AT NO COST TO PARENTS

The costs of the residential placement were litigated in *Michael P.* v. *Maloney*. A class action suit had been filed on behalf of handicapped students requiring residential placement alleging that they had been denied a free appropriate education by a state policy that required their parents to contribute to the cost of their residential special education.

The suit was settled by a consent decree that provided that the costs of residential placements made by a local education agency would be at no cost to the students' parents, including nonmedical care and room and board. It was also stipulated that this agreement could not cause a change in placement for a handicapped child unless the change in placement was recommended by an evaluation team. The district court approved the consent decree.

The district court ruled in *Parks* v. *Pavkovic* that the school system was responsible for all costs of a residential placement. A 17-year-old student who suffered from autism, mental retardation, emotional disorders, speech and language impairments, and behavioral difficulties had been placed in a residential facility. He was transferred to a new facility by the state Department of Mental Health and Developmental Disabilities when it appeared that his former school might close. The school department and state agencies, however, refused to pay all the residential costs at the new facility. After a large bill accumulated, the student's parents were notified that he would be discharged if the bill was not paid. The parents requested a due process hearing at which the hearing officer ruled that the school department would have to pay all further costs, but did not order them to pay the outstanding bill. The student's parents appealed, but when no decision was reached after a long delay, they filed court action.

The court found that the refusal of the school district and state agencies to pay all residential costs was based on state law. Since that state law was inconsistent with federal law, it could not stand. The court ruled that the federal mandate was unambiguous in its requirement that special education and related services were to be provided at no cost to the handicapped student's parents.

The *Parks* case came before the district court in Illinois again one year later. A class action suit was filed challenging the section of the Illinois Mental Health and Developmental Disabilities Code that provided that responsible relatives of recipients of the department's services were to be assessed a portion of the costs of services rendered according to their income. Under this provision, the parents of handicapped children were often assessed a portion of the costs of the special education services provided by the Department of Mental Health and Developmental Disabilities. The plaintiffs claimed that this provision violated the EHCA.

The district court issued an enjoinment to prevent the enforcement of the challenged provision and ordered the department to reimburse parents of handicapped children for past assessments. The court found the challenged provision to be in conflict with federal law and invalidated it under the supremacy of federal law clause of the U.S. Constitution.

The district court in *Christopher T.* v. *San Francisco Unified School District* ruled that handicapped students were entitled under the EHCA to have their residential placements paid for by the school district. The court's order invalidated the practice of requiring the parents of handicapped students to turn over guardianship of the students to the Department of Social Services for them to receive a residential placement. This suit involved two students with emotional difficulties. The first student was diagnosed as having childhood schizophrenia and mild mental retardation. He had attended a residential school in another state, but when the family moved to California his parents were informed that a residential placement could take place only if the Department of Social Services assumed guardianship. The second student had a history of emotional difficulties, but when his behavior deteriorated, his parents sought psychiatric counseling and, later, residential placement. They were also informed that a residential placement could take place only if the Department of Social Services assumed guardianship. In both cases the parents relinquished guardianship but, later, upon learning that funding was available under the EHCA, applied to the school district for such funding. These efforts were unsuccessful. Both students had been evaluated by psychiatric experts on several occasions, and residential placement was consistently recommended as the best method of meeting their needs.

The district court found that both students required residential placements to benefit from special education. The school district was ordered to assume all costs of such placements.

ADDITION OF OTHER SERVICES IN A LESS RESTRICTIVE ENVIRONMENT

In *Stacey G. v. Pasadena Independent School District* the court determined that a residential placement was not necessary because the student could be educated in a less restrictive environment if additional related services were provided. The student was a severely handicapped child who had been enrolled in special education programs for the mentally retarded and emotionally disturbed since the age of 4. There had been some disagreement as to whether she was mentally retarded with autistic tendencies or autistic with secondary mental retardation. After four years in the public schools, her parents unilaterally placed her in a private residential facility and attempted to have the school district pay all costs. The school district refused, feeling that it could provide educational services. The hearing officer denied the parents' request for residential placement but ordered the school district to provide year-round educational programming and counseling services for the parents. The parents appealed to the district court.

Testimony at the trial indicated that the student's abnormal behaviors had decreased and that improvements had been noted in social, academic, and self-help skill areas while she had been enrolled in the public schools. The court concluded that an appropriate education could be provided in the public schools on a year-round basis with additional training and counseling for the student's parents.

The court noted that the EHCA mandated that under appropriate circumstances, local school districts must provide handicapped children with residential placements but that the EHCA also mandated that handicapped children were to be educated in the least restrictive environment. The court held that if the circumstances required a residential placement, the mainstreaming requirement became secondary and could not preclude such a placement. The court also noted that since educational funding was limited, the personal and unique needs of an individual handicapped child had to be balanced against the realities of limited funding and the requirement to educate all handicapped children.

The Supreme Court of Kansas upheld a trial court's order for a residential placement for a legally blind student when it found that the residential school for the visually handicapped had the facilities and trained staff to deal with all the student's needs. In addition to being legally blind with a prognosis for total blindness, the student in *Bailey* v. *Unified School District* also had learning disabilities and emotional problems. He had attended the local school system for ten years where he received special education and counseling services. During those years he had been maintained in regular classes by having a qualified teacher sit with him in those classes to provide assistance. The student was evaluated before entering high school, and it was concluded that the local high school would not be the best placement for him because of the open setting, the increased mobility that would be required, and the diversity of the subjects he would be required to take. Instead, a residential school for the visually impaired was recommended. His parents objected, however, preferring continued placement at the local high school.

The school district's recommendation was upheld in administrative appeals and by the trial court. The Supreme Court of Kansas affirmed, finding the recommended placement to be clearly appropriate since it would provide the student with all the necessary services, including academic training and counseling to help him accept his blindness. The court also noted that it would cost $187,000 per year to maintain the student at the local high school.

EFFECTS OF *ROWLEY*

A court applied the *Rowley* standard to a residential placement question for the first time in *Lang* v. *Braintree School Committee*. Here a mentally retarded, mentally ill, and epileptic student had attended a private day school for a number of years. When her family moved to a new community, the local school district developed an IEP for her that called for placement in a public school program. Her parents objected to this plan, but it was upheld in administrative hearings. Testimony during the hearings indicated that the program offered by the public schools was educationally sound.

The district court, finding *Rowley* controlling, determined that where a school district was providing the student with an education that was of some benefit and was utilizing an approach that was at least minimally acceptable, the court could not interfere. The court also held that in this case there was every reason to believe that the student's placement in a public school setting with appropriate special education and related services would be more beneficial to her than would the private school placement. Since the school district would provide an educational program that would benefit the student in a less restrictive environment, the court held that the proposed IEP was satisfactory.

The question of residential placement for learning disabled students was one of the issues involved in *Riley* v. *Ambach*. This action was brought on behalf of 18 handicapped children by their parents seeking an enjoinment of the enforcement of certain regulations and policies of the Commissioner of Education concerning the education of learning disabled children in New York. One of the challenged actions was the removal of all residential schools for the learning disabled from the commissioner's list of approved schools. This action, in effect, eliminated residential schools as an option for the education of learning disabled children.

The district court granted the enjoinment, finding that residential treatment was the least restrictive environment for some children and that not all local school districts had programs that were adequate to serve all learning disabled children. The court stated that residential school placement must be an option open to local officials charged with the responsibility of appropriately placing handicapped children. To deny that option, according to the court, to one category of handicapped children would amount to discrimination. Also, blanket denial of that option violated the EHCA provision that placement decisions were to be made on an individual basis. The appeals court, however, reversed because it found that the plaintiffs had failed to exhaust all their administrative remedies prior to filing court action.

One of the original plaintiffs subsequently exhausted his administrative remedies and returned to the district court seeking a residential placement. The plaintiff was a severely learning disabled student with dyslexia. He had spent several years in local special education programs, but later attended private residential schools out of state. Since those schools were not on the commissioner's list of approved schools, his mother paid all costs. After attending those schools for three years, the local schools' evaluation team recommended that he return to the public schools since their resource room program could provide him with an adequate education. His mother rejected that proposal and appealed, requesting that the school system fund a residential placement. The hearing officer concluded that a residential facility was the appropriate placement; however, the commissioner reversed. The student remained in the residential school and the following year the evaluation team made a similar recommendation. The student's mother again appealed. The hearing officer found the facts to be substantially the same but felt bound by the commissioner's previous decision. The commissioner affirmed.

The court, using the *Rowley* standard, framed the issue as being not whether the school district could provide the best possible education or even a program that would maximize the student's potential commensurate with that of nonhandicapped students but, rather, whether the local schools could provide a program that was reasonably calculated to benefit the student educationally. The evidence indicated that the local school district's program would do that, and thus, the court ruled that it conformed to the EHCA as interpreted by *Rowley*.

In an early 1983 case, the Fourth Circuit Court of Appeals held that once a public school program has been determined to be appropriate, there is no duty to consider a private placement. The student in *Hessler* v. *State Board of Education of Maryland* was a 17-year-old youth who had attended a private school for eight years. Her parents requested that the local school district provide special education services since the student was having academic difficulties. The school district conducted an evaluation and determined that it could provide the student with an appropriate education in a public school self-contained classroom. The student's mother rejected that recommendation and filed a due process appeal. She then enrolled the student in a private nonspecial education school. In the appeal, the mother sought payment and reimbursement for the private school costs claiming that the proposed public school placement was inappropriate. The hearing officer held that the proposed placement was appropriate and denied payment of the private school costs. The state Board of Education and the district court upheld the hearing officer's findings and this appeal followed.

In the appeal the student's parents claimed that the proposed public school placement was inappropriate because the private school was more appropriate and that the school district had a statutory duty to consider placing the student in a private school. The appeals court rejected both claims. The court held that although state and federal laws indicate that private school placements may be required in some circumstances, they are limited to instances where appropriate public school programs are not available. Since it had been determined in this case that a public program was appropriate, there was not duty to consider a private placement. The court also ruled that just because a given program may be more appropriate than another program, it did not make the less appropriate program inappropriate, and that there was no duty, according to *Rowley,* to provide the student with the best education money could buy.

The district court in *Clevenger* v. *Oak Ridge School Board* found that a state residential school would provide an appropriate placement under the *Rowley* standard for an emotionally disturbed 18-year-old student who had attended the local public schools except for periods when he was placed in a psychiatric hospital by the Department of Corrections or his mother. The school district proposed an IEP calling for placement in a state school that provided educational and psychiatric services on a residential basis. His mother objected, preferring an out-of-state facility, and requested a due process hearing.

The hearing officer found the recommended placement to be appropriate. The district court affirmed, applying the *Rowley* standard. The court found that the state school provided an educational component as well as psychiatric therapy, social interaction, and family planning and counseling. However, the appeals court reversed and remanded finding that the program approved by the district court was inappropriate because the student required long-term placement and this program specialized in short-term treatment, the student required a secure locked facility which the approved facility was not, and the approved facility did not want the student due to his oppositional behavior. The district court was instructed on remand to approve the parent's chosen facility.

RETURN TO PUBLIC SCHOOLS

The district court in *Zvi D.* v. *Ambach* ruled that a private school did not have to be found to be inappropriate for a student to be transferred from it to a public school program. The student, who had minimal brain dysfunction, attended the public schools until grade 3 and was then placed in a private school. When the student reached junior high school, the local evaluation team recommended that he return to a special class in the public schools. His mother objected and requested a hearing; however, before the hearing was held, the school department made an agreement with her that it would fund the private school for the current year with the stipulation that the student's status would be reviewed at the end of the school year with consideration for a public school placement. The student was reevaluated at the end of the year, and public school placement was again recommended. The student's mother challenged this, claiming that he could not be transferred unless the private school was found to be inappropriate. The school department's recommendation was found to be appropriate by the hearing officer; however, the student was allowed to remain at the private school at public expense because a physician had not been present at the evaluation conference as required by state law. One year later, the transfer to the public school was again recommended, and once again, the student's mother objected. The recommendation was upheld in administrative appeals.

The district court, in upholding the school district's recommendation, found the public schools to be less restrictive while still appropriate. Since the student had made marked improvement in the areas covered by his IEP, the court felt that he should be able to be educated in the less restrictive environment. The court also noted that the public schools offered educational and vocational opportunities that were not available in the private school. The court totally rejected the mother's claim that the student could not be transferred unless the private school was found to be inappropriate.

The district court weighed the benefits of a return to the public schools against the risks the change presented in *Grkman* v. *Scanlon*. A hearing impaired student had attended a private school for the deaf since the age of $1\frac{1}{2}$ years because the local school system had no facilities for preschool-aged deaf children. When she reached school age, the private school placement approval was withdrawn as the local system operated a facility for deaf students of school age. The student's parents objected, but the school district's decision was upheld in administrative appeals.

The court ruled that the preponderance of the evidence indicated that continued placement in the private school was appropriate. The court noted that the student was making progress and felt that it was important that momentum be maintained. The court stated that the risks of change outweighed the possible benefits and that it was a suitable time to do nothing.

The Fourth Circuit Court of Appeals in *Matthews* v. *Davis* affirmed the district court's decision that a severely handicapped student no longer required a residential placement by refusing to substitute its judgment for that of school officials. The student, who suffered from mental retardation and myoclonic seizures, had attended a residential institution until his family moved to another state when he was 11. The new school system proposed that he attend an elementary school program for severely and profoundly retarded youngsters. The student's parents, preferring a residential placement, appealed that decision. After failing to prevail in administrative hearings, they brought court action.

The district court initially found that the public school placement was not appropriate but later approved a program that combined continued attendance in the public schools with a residential apartment program staffed by public school personnel. Three years later the school department requested that the residential component of the program be terminated. The court, relying on *Rowley,* found that a residential component was no longer a necessary prerequisite to the provision of an appropriate education for the student.

On appeal by the student's parents, the circuit court affirmed stating that the courts should not substitute their judgment for that of school authorities on matters of educational policy. The court noted that the primary responsibility for formulating an educational program for a handicapped child was left by the EHCA to the states and local school districts. The court further stated that if the school system could provide an appropriate education in a day program, further enhancement was not required.

OBLIGATION TO MAINTAIN A PLACEMENT

The state has an obligation to maintain a student's residential placement until an appropriate alternative placement is found according to the court of appeals in *Vander Malle* v. *Ambach.* Here an emotionally disturbed student had been placed in a psychiatric hospital. At the time the placement was made the hospital was on the state's list of approved residential schools; however, it was later removed when the state determined that it was a hospital rather than a school and was thus inappropriate. The district court issued a preliminary injunction ordering the state to maintain the student's placement at the hospital until an alternate appropriate placement could be made. The state appealed this decision.

The Second Circuit Court of Appeals upheld the district court's decision, ruling that once a placement had been made by an evaluation team, the state had an obligation to continue that placement until either an appropriate alternative was found or the student was determined to be no longer handicapped. The court also ruled that if the local evaluation team failed to carry out its obligation in this regard, the state could not disclaim its legal responsiblities.

Late in 1982 the First Circuit Court of Appeals upheld a district court decision ordering that a residential placement be maintained. The student in *Doe* v. *Anrig* was a Down's syndrome child who had never lived with his parents, but had been raised and educated in residential programs at his parent's expense. When he was 10 years old his parents requested that he be evaluated by the public schools. The school district proposed an IEP that called for nonresidential public school placement. The parents rejected this plan but eventually agreed to a residential placement on a cost-sharing basis whereby the parents paid the noneducational residential costs and the school district paid the educational expenses. Two years later he was evaluated again, and a new IEP calling for nonresidential public school placement was proposed. The student's parents rejected this plan and sought administrative review. In administrative appeals it was held that the proposed IEP was appropriate, but that a transitional program should be developed to facilitate the student's move from a residential to a nonresidential placement. Court action followed.

The district court held that the parents had proven by a preponderance of the evidence that a residential program was appropriate. That evidence indicated that the student had spent his entire life in a residential program, that the teachers in the proposed program had no experience with children who had never lived in a nonresidential setting, and that it was likely that the student would regress if moved into a new home and school environment. The appeals court affirmed the district court's decision. On appeal the school district argued that the student's parents' unwillingness to have him live at home was a familial concern that was not relevant to whether or not the proposed IEP was appropriate. The appeals court disagreed, finding that forcing the student into an unreceptive or even hostile environment would have a negative effect on his educational development.

REFERENCES

Abrahamson v. *Hershman,* 701 F.2d 223 (1983).

Adams Central School District v. *Deist,* 334 N.W.2d 775, 338 N.W.2d 591 (1983).

Ahern v. *Keene,* 593 F.Supp. 902 (1984).

Bailey v. *Unified School District,* 664 F.2d 1379 (1983).

Capello v. *District of Columbia Board of Education,* 551 EHLR 190, 551 EHLR 500 (1980).

Christopher T. v. *San Francisco Unified School District,* 553 F.Supp. 1107 (1982).

Clevenger v. *Oak Ridge School Board,* 744 F.2d 514 (1984).

Colin K. v. *Schmidt,* 715 F.2d 1 (1983).

Cox v. *Brown,* 498 F.Supp. 823 (1980).

DeWalt v. *Burkholder,* 551 EHLR 550 (1980).

Diamond v. *McKenzie,* 602 F.Supp. 632 (1984).

Doe v. *Anrig,* 692 F.2d 800 (1982).

Erdman v. *State of Connecticut,* 552 EHLR 218 (1980).

Gladys J. v. *Pearland Independent School District,* 520 F.Supp. 869 (1981).

Grkman v. *Scanlon,* 528 F.Supp. 1032 (1981).

Hessler v. *State Board of Education of Maryland,* 700 F.2d 134 (1983).

Hines v. *Pitt County Board of Education,* 497 F.Supp. 403 (1980).

Kruelle v. *Biggs,* 489 F.Supp. 169 (1980), aff'd Sub. Nom. *Kruelle* v. *New Castle,* 642 F.2d 687 (1981).

Ladson v. *Board of Education of the District of Columbia,* 551 EHLR 188 (1979).

Lang v. *Braintree School Committee,* 545 F.Supp. 1221 (1982).

Matthews v. *Campbell,* 551 EHLR 264 (1979).

Matthews v. *Davis,* 742 F.2d 825 (1984).

McKenzie v. *Jefferson,* 554 EHLR 338 (1983).

Michael P. v. *Maloney,* 551 EHLR 155 (1979).

Norris v. *Massachusetts Department of Education,* 529 F.Supp. 759 (1981).

North v. *District of Columbia Board of Education,* 471 F.Supp. 136 (1979).

Parks v. *Pavkovic*, 536 F.Supp. 296 (1982), 557 F.Supp. 1280 (1983).

Riley v. *Ambach*, 508 F.Supp. 1222 (1980), 554 EHLR 180 (1982).

Rowley, Board of Education v., See Chapter Two.

San Francisco Unified School District v. *State of California*, 131 Cal. App. 3d 54, 182 Cal. Rptr. 525 (1982).

Stacey G. v. *Pasadena Independent School District*, 547 F.Supp. 61 (1982).

Walker v. *Cronin*, 438 N.E.2d 582 (1982).

Zvi D. v. *Ambach*, 520 F.Supp. 196 (1981), 694 F.2d 904 (1982).

Figure 3-1

LEADING CASES

North v. *District of Columbia,* 471 F.Supp. 136 (1979)

Since the student's social, emotional, medical, and educational needs are so intimately intertwined, it is impossible to separate them and assign responsibility for both to an appropriate agency; the school district is responsible for providing a residential placement.

Gladys J. v. *Pearland I.S.D.,* 520 F.Supp. 869 (1981)

The student requires a residential placement to provide her with a constant structured environment, a 24-hour behavior modification program, and an intensive language program.

Parks v. *Pavkovic,* 536 F.Supp. 296 (1982)

Placement of a handicapped child in a residential facility must be cost-free to the child's parents. Any state laws that are not consistent with the federal mandate in this regard cannot stand.

Hessler v. *Maryland,* 700 F.2d 134 (1983)

Once it has been determined that a public school placement is appropriate, the school district is not required to consider a private placement. Just because a given program may be more appropriate than another program, it does not make the less appropriate program inappropriate.

Abrahamson v. *Hershman,* 701 F.2d 223 (1983)

A handicapped child who would progress in a day program is not entitled to a residential program simply because the residential program would better enable the child to reach his full potential.

Figure 3-2

DETERMINING THE NEED FOR A MORE RESTRICTIVE PLACEMENT

A private day school may be necessary when

> The student has not progressed in the public schools and the school district is unable to provide a more appropriate program.
>
> The student requires specialized techniques or resources that are not available within a public school program.
>
> The student requires a specialized environment that is not available within the public schools.
>
> The student has a low-incidence-type handicap and should be educated with students who have a similar disability.

A residential program may be necessary when

> A 24-hour program of instruction and care is required.
>
> The student requires extreme consistency of approach between the school and home environment.
>
> An appropriate program cannot be provided in a day placement even with additional supportive aids and services.
>
> The student requires total immersion in the program for progress to be made.

Figure 3-3

RIGHTS TO A PRIVATE PLACEMENT

1. Every handicapped child is entitled to receive a free, appropriate, public education designed to meet his or her unique special educational needs.

2. Every school district must ensure that a continuum of alternative placements is available to meet the needs of all handicapped children.

3. When a private day or residential school placement is necessary to provide the student with an appropriate education, consideration should be given to provide mainstreaming to the maximum extent appropriate.

4. The private facility chosen should be as close to the child's home as possible.

5. The private facility placement must be at no cost to the child's parents, and in the case of a residential placement, the entire program, including nonmedical care and room and board, must be free of cost to the parents.

Figure 3-5

HOW TO EVALUATE THE APPROPRIATENESS OF A PRIVATE FACILITY

1. Are all staff members properly trained and certified?

2. Is the facility licensed by the department of education or other appropriate agency?

3. Are the techniques and methods used generally accepted by the profession?

4. Are the staff-to-student ratios proper for the student's disability?

5. Are appropriate support services available?

6. Is the facility financially sound?

7. Is the physical plant safe and appropriate?

8. Does the facility have a good reputation among professionals?

9. Does the facility have a reputation for cooperating with public school officials?

10. Does the facility provide periodic progress reports on its students?

11. Does the facility have an appropriate amount of equipment and materials? Are they in good condition?

12. What is the rate of staff turnover?

13. Does the facility make every possible effort to communicate with the student's parents and involve them in the educational program?

Figure 3-6

LETTER AUTHORIZING PRIVATE SCHOOL PLACEMENT

Date: _____

Private School: _____

Address: _____

_____ Phone: _____

Contact Person: _____

Dear _____ :

    In accordance with the IEP developed for _(student)_ , the _(school district)_ authorizes placement in your school for the time period _____ to _____ .

    All terms and conditions outlined in the IEP must be adhered to, and all services specified in the IEP must be provided. If for any reason you are unable to implement fully the enclosed IEP, please contact this office immediately.

    We agree to pay you the sum of _____ per annum as established by the Rate Setting Commission in four equal quarterly installments. Payment is contingent on our receiving quarterly progress reports. Bills may be sent directly to me at the address listed on this letterhead.

    If at any time you are unable to continue to provide the services outlined in the IEP, we require thirty days' notice of such inability.

    We reserve the right to make four annual site visits to your school to monitor the services you are providing. Such visits will be made by the Special Education Administrator or designee.

(Special Education
Administrator's Signature)

Figure 3-7

ALTERNATIVE FUNDING FOR RESIDENTIAL PLACEMENTS

If a residential placement is made for other than educational reasons, the following state agencies may be contacted to cost-share the placement:

Department of Mental Health if the residential placement is necessary for emotional or psychological reasons.

Department of Social Services if the residential placement is necessary because of the familial situation or if the student has been removed from the home by the courts.

Department of Youth Services if the student has been judged by the courts to be delinquent and remanded to a residential facility.

Figure 3-8

COST-SHARE AGREEMENT

Date: _____

_____(school district)_____

_____

_____

and

_____(agency)_____

_____

_____

hereby agree to cost-share the placement of _____(student)_____ at the _____ School for the time period _____ to _____ . The (school district) agrees to pay _____ % and the (agency) agrees to pay _____ % of the per annum costs of _____ as established by the Rate Setting Commission.

_____   _____
School District Representative   Agency Representative

Figure 3-9

ADMINISTRATOR'S CHECKLIST

Questions to ask in determining whether or not a private day or residential placement is necessary:

1. Does the student require a 24-hour program to attain the objectives of his IEP? _

2. Does the student require a continuously structured environment? _____ Why?

   _____

3. Does the student require a consistency of approach that cannot be obtained between the school and the home? _____ Why? _____

4. Does the student require techniques, resources, or a specialized environment that is not available within the public schools? _____ Describe _____ Why is such a program not available within the public schools? _____

5. Can the school district provide an appropriate program within the public schools with supportive and other related services? _____ What additional services would be needed? _____

6. Would the student be better off in a mainstreamed environment with additional supportive services? _____ Explain _____

7. Can the staff of the public school be trained to provide appropriate educational and/or therapeutic services within the mainstream? _____ What type of training would be necessary? _____

8. Is the private day or residential program necessary for educational reasons? _____ Explain _____

Chapter 4

WHEN IS IT NECESSARY TO PROVIDE SERVICES BEYOND THE TRADITIONAL SCHOOL YEAR?

> *This court concludes that the Handicapped Act requires that full consideration be given to the individual educational needs of each child in the development of a program for that child. To the extent that a state has a policy which prohibits, or even inhibits, such full consideration, the court is of the opinion that such policy constitutes a violation of the Handicapped Act.*
>
> **District Judge Ward**
> *Georgia A.R.C. v. McDaniel*
> **511 F.Supp. 1263 at 1277 (1981)**

The Education for All Handicapped Children Act (EHCA) and its implementing regulations do not specifically address the provision of special education programs that extend beyond the traditional school year. Many parents and advocates for the handicapped have contended that in some instances such services are needed to provide a particular student with an appropriate education. This contention usually arises in the case of a severely handicapped child who requires constant reinforcement and who would regress significantly if services were interrupted for several weeks. Since the law and the regulations are silent on the issue, we must turn to the courts to determine if, and when, extended school year programs are mandated.

ESY MUST BE AN AVAILABLE OPTION

The district court in *Georgia Association of Retarded Citizens* v. *McDaniel* found that the state of Georgia's practices that effectively limited consideration of educational programs to 180 days were in violation of federal statutes. Court action was initiated when the parents of a profoundly mentally retarded child requested, and were refused, a 12-month educational program for their son. After they failed to gain relief in administrative appeals, a class action suit was filed alleging that the state and the local school system had policies or practices of refusing to consider the educational needs of mentally retarded students for programs in excess of 180 days.

The court found that Georgia's state plan did not require local school systems to provide for educational services beyond the traditional school year, but did not prohibit the provision of such services. The court did find, however, that the local school district had uniformly found mentally retarded children to require only 180 days of schooling, apparently because this was all that was required or funded by the state. The court also found that the state Board of Education had never ordered a local district to consider the provision of educational services beyond 180 days. The court concluded that both the state and local educational agencies, therefore, had policies that prohibited the consideration of programs beyond the traditional school year for mentally retarded children.

The court held that the EHCA requires full consideration of the individual educational needs of each child in the development of a program for that child. The court reasoned that if a state had a policy that prohibited or inhibited such full consideration, that policy would violate the EHCA. Georgia's policy of limiting the provision of schooling to 180 days was held to contravene its obligation to make a case-by-case determination of a child's needs, and thus, it violated the statute. The defendants were ordered to provide extended school year programs to any child who might need them to be provided with an appropriate education. The Court of Appeals for the Eleventh Circuit affirmed, finding that the refusal to provide education beyond the traditional school year violated both prongs of the *Rowley* standard in that it failed to follow the EHCA's mandate to make individual determinations and failed to allow the development of Individualized Educational Programs (IEPs) that were reasonably calculated to bring about educational benefits to the plaintiff class.

In a 1983 case, *Yaris* v. *Special School District of St. Louis County*, the district court applied the *Rowley* standard in finding that any policy that refused to consider extended school year programs violated the EHCA. A class action suit was filed seeking declaratory and injunctive relief from the school district's policy of not providing educational programs beyond the traditional school year. The state educational agency did not consider on an individual basis whether handicapped children required educational programming in excess of 180 days and did not require local and special school districts to do so.

Testimony at the trial indicated that a practice existed whereby the special school district refused to consider or provide for a handicapped child's educational needs beyond 180 days. Summer school was, however, provided by many local districts for nonhandicapped children, partly through state and federal funds. The court concluded, based on testimony at the trial, that many handicapped children do regress after an extended break and that the extent of such regression could only be determined on an individual basis.

The court held that educators must examine the individual needs of a handicapped child to determine if there are enough support services present to permit the child to benefit educationally. The court found the state's policy of refusing to consider the provision of programs in excess of 180 days to be incompatible with the EHCA and the standards enunciated by the U.S. Supreme Court in *Rowley*. The state, according to the court, was thus refusing to provide the plaintiff class with a free appropriate public education by failing to consider their educational needs in excess of 180 days. To the extent that this policy also precluded the consideration of individual needs and to the extent that summer programs were offered to the nonhandicapped, the court ruled that Section 504 had also been violated.

The Court of Appeals for the Fifth Circuit invalidated a state's policy of refusing to provide instruction beyond the traditional 180-day school year in *Crawford* v. *Pittman*. The plaintiffs in this case, six severely handicapped children and their parents, filed suit claiming that the state of Mississippi's refusal to develop IEPs that provided educational programs beyond the traditional 180-day school year violated the EHCA. The defendants admitted that they provided no more than 180 days of instruction and that employees were instructed to not include instructional programs of longer duration in a child's IEP. The plaintiffs contended that certain handicapped children regress during periods of no instruction, causing them to lose much of what they have gained. In spite of the extensive body of case law mandating the consideration of extended school year programs, the district court found in favor of the defendants.

The appeals court reversed the district court's finding, however, stating that the EHCA required school districts to treat each student as an individual with unique qualities and needs that could only be served with an IEP developed with wisdom, care, and educational expertise. The court found that the EHCA did not tolerate policies or practices that would impose a rigid pattern on the education of handicapped children, but rather, favored the development of IEPs based on an individual evaluation. The court held that categorical limitations on the length of special education programs were not consistent with the EHCA's mandate that IEPs are to be developed to meet the unique needs of each handicapped child. Mississippi's policy of refusing to provide programs that extend beyond the traditional school year was found to be inconsistent with the EHCA and could not stand.

MUST BE PROVIDED AT NO COST TO PARENTS

One of the first cases to deal with the provision of services during the summer months came before the Family Court in New York City in late 1977. The parents of handicapped children who required residential placement for 12 months a year brought suit in *In re Scott K.* seeking to have the school district pay these costs for the full year. The students had been attending an approved residential facility, but the school district paid for only that portion of the total program costs that covered the normal school year.

The court ruled that the federal requirement that residential programs were to be provided at no cost to the parents applied to residential placements covering a full 12 months if the child's needs required it. The court felt that the legislature did not intend for parents to contribute toward the summer costs of residential placements.

A state appeals court, in *Mahoney* v. *Administrative School District,* also held that the summer component of a residential placement must be paid for by the school district. The student in this case attended a private facility that offered a year-round educational program and related services for trainable mentally retarded children. The student's parents initiated due process proceedings, seeking a determination that year-round residential placement was necessary and that the school district was required to pay for it. The hearing officer found the placement to be appropriate and ordered the school department to assume full costs; however, the Deputy Superintendent of Education reversed that portion of the decision directing the school department to pay summer tuition.

The court, basing its decision on both federal and state laws, held that the provision of a free appropriate public education sometimes necessitated placement in a private residential facility. Certain children also required programs in excess of 180 days. Since these programs must be provided without cost to the handicapped child's parents, it followed that the tuition expenses must be borne by the school district. The court thus reversed the decision of the Deputy Superintendent of Education.

REQUIRED TO PREVENT SUBSTANTIAL REGRESSION

In 1979 a federal district court ruled that a state's policy of not providing educational services beyond the traditional school year deprived certain handicapped students of an appropriate education. Three class action suits were combined for trial in *Armstrong* v. *Kline* that contested the Pennsylvania Department of Education's policy and practice of refusing to provide or fund an educational program for any child in excess of 180 days. The suits alleged that five students, who were classified as being severely and profoundly impaired and severely emotionally disturbed, required year-round programs to have their educational needs met. A summer break in programming, it was claimed, caused such a degree of regression that an inordinate amount of time was required for recoupment. That recoupment time lessened the amount of time that was then available for the attainment of other objectives. The students' overall rate of progress was thus limited.

The court found that interruptions in programming often caused regression in certain severely handicapped children and that, although in some cases that regression was minimal, in others it was substantial. The court also found that the time required to regain lost skills also varied as did the effects of the combined regression and recoupment time required. The court concluded that if children such as the plaintiffs in this case were not given a program in excess of 180 days, they might not attain their educational goals, particularly the goal of self-sufficiency. The court also concluded from the legislative history of the EHCA that the goal of self-sufficiency was an appropriate educational goal for handicapped children. The court thus found that the 180-day rule deprived the students and their class of an appropriate education.

The Court of Appeals for the Third Circuit upheld the district court's decision, but used a different reasoning. The appeals court concluded that the 180-day rule precluded the proper determination of the content of a free appropriate public education and, thus, violated the EHCA. The appeals court disagreed that the EHCA intended a specific educational goal but, rather, provided that the state had the responsibility of setting individual goals and establishing the means to attain them. The U.S. Supreme Court declined to review the case.

In *Stacey G.* v. *Pasadena Independent School District,* the court ordered year-round schooling when it found that regression was likely to occur if the student's program was not maintained continuously. The student, who was severely handicapped, had been enrolled in special education programs for several years. Since the public schools did not have summer programs, her parents had enrolled her in private residential facilities for two years. Her parents had requested that the school department pay for the summer schooling, but it refused. After the second summer, her parents unilaterally placed her in the private residential facility on a full-year basis and attempted to have the school district pick up the costs. That request was also denied, and the case eventually went to court.

Testimony at the trial indicated that the student would suffer serious regression if there was a long interruption in her programming, such as the usual summer vacation. The court concluded that a residential program was not required, but did order a public school program on a year-round basis. The court, finding the *Armstrong* opinion persuasive, held that under appropriate circumstances local school districts may be required to provide handicapped children with summer school programs. The court held that such a program was warranted here since regression was likely to occur if the student's program was not maintained continuously.

ADDITIONAL FACTORS TO CONSIDER

In another 1983 case, *Lee* v. *Thompson,* the district court found the Hawaii Department of Education to be in contempt of court for not fully complying with previous court orders to provide extended school year programs. The district court had previously ruled that the Department of Education was to consider the following factors in determining whether a handicapped child required services for a full year: nature of the handicapping condition, areas of learning crucial to attaining the goal of self-sufficiency and independence, extent of regression caused by an interruption in education, and rate of recoupment. One year later the Department of Education was found to be in contempt of court as they had been using only the first two criteria to determine a child's eligibility for an extended school year program. The plaintiffs filed the present motion for contempt, claiming that the department was using only the last two criteria. The department contended that this was satisfactory because it was consistent with the ruling in *Armstrong*.

The court disagreed, holding that although the initial order went well beyond *Armstrong*, it comported with the Supreme Court's decision in *Rowley* and the EHCA's regulations concerning an appropriate education. The court stated that an extended school year program could be regarded as an additional means of providing a handicapped student with a program of specialized instruction under the EHCA.

NOT REQUIRED IF REGRESSION IS MINIMAL

In *Anderson* v. *Thompson* the district court declined to order the school department to provide a summer school program after it determined that the student's regression over the summer vacation was no greater than that of a nonhandicapped child. The student had been attending a private special education facility, but was to begin a transition to a public school program under a court-ordered IEP. The court found that the student had speech and language disabilities, learning disabilities, and emotional disturbance. Her parents also requested a summer school program in addition to the special education services that were to be provided under the student's IEP.

The court held that although summer school programs may be required in some cases to assure an appropriate education, one was not required in this case. The court found that the student had been progressing from year to year without summer school and that her rate of regression was no greater than that of a nonhandicapped student. Since she would not suffer an irreparable loss of progress during the summer break, the court ruled that a summer program was not warranted.

In *Bales* v. *Clarke* the court ruled that year-round schooling was not required unless it could be shown that an irreparable loss of progress during the summer months would take place. The student in this case had been injured in an automobile accident and was subsequently placed in a residential facility for crippled children. Her father requested that the school department provide her with a summer language therapy program. Although that request was denied, her parents hired a speech therapist to provide those services during the following summer. One year later they enrolled her in a private school for severely handicapped children, and their attorney notified the school department that they would seek to have the school department pay all costs. The school department refused to do so. The student's parents, dissatisfied with her entire educational placement, filed suit in the district court seeking, among other things, funding for summer programs.

The court, stating that a student did not have the right to an ideal education, found the school district's proposed IEP, which did not include a summer component, to be appropriate. The court held that a summer program was not required if an irreparable loss of progress over the summer months was not shown. The court did not find such a showing in *Bales*.

DETERMINATION SHOULD BE MADE THROUGH A MULTIFACETED EVALUATION

The court in *Rettig* v. *Kent City School District* also declined to order a summer school program, but indicated that it would do so if such a program were called for in an IEP based on a multifactored evaluation. The student in this case was autistic and mentally retarded and functioned at a preacademic level. The court found that an appropriate education for the student would be one that gave him a reasonable chance to acquire the skills he needed to function outside of an institution. The court did not feel, however, that the school district was required to provide any and all services that might be beneficial to the student.

According to the court, a summer program would be required if it would prevent significant regression of skills or knowledge retained by the student that would seriously affect his progress toward self-sufficiency. The court, based on the evidence before it, was unwilling to order a summer program. The court did, however, state that if a summer program was called for in an IEP based on a multifactored evaluation, it would expect that such a program would be provided. That decision was affirmed by the appeals court.

SUMMER ENRICHMENT AND RECREATION PROGRAMS

Summer recreation and enrichment programs may also be required in some circumstances according to a 1982 ruling by the Sixth Circuit Court of Appeals in *Birmingham and Lamphere School District* v. *Superintendent of Public Instruction*. An autistic student had been enrolled in a public school program for children with severe behavior and language disorders. For several years that program included a summer school session that was jointly funded by the federal, state, and county governments. After federal aid was reduced, the summer program was eliminated due to a lack of funds. The student's mother appealed the decision to discontinue the summer component. The hearing officer determined that the student needed a six-week summer program of instruction and enrichment activities. This decision was based, in part, on testimony by all witnesses that the student's unique needs required some program during the summer. The trial court upheld the hearing officer's decision.

The appeals court found, based on the testimony of several witnesses, that the student needed a program that involved outdoor activities for him to receive an appropriate education. The court held that the proposed summer enrichment activities fell within the broad definitions of special education and related services in the EHCA. Special education specifically included instruction in physical education, and related services specifically included such supportive services as recreation according to the court. The appeals court thus upheld the district court's decision, and the school district was required to provide the summer enrichment program.

REFERENCES

Anderson v. *Thompson,* 495 F.Supp. 1256 (1980).

Armstrong v. *Kline,* 476 F.Supp. 583 (1979), aff'd Sub.Nom. *Battle* v. *Pennsylvania,* 629 F.2d 269 (1980).

Bales v. *Clarke,* 523 F.Supp. 1366 (1981).

Birmingham and Lamphere School District v. *Superintendent of Public Instruction,* 554 EHLR 318 (1982).

Crawford v. *Pittman,* 708 F.2d 1028 (1983).

Georgia Association for Retarded Citizens v. *McDaniel,* 511 F.Supp. 1263 (1982), aff'd 716 F.2d 1565 (1983), vac'd and rem'd 104 S.Ct. 3581 (1984), on rem'd 740 F.2d 902 (1984).

In re Scott K., 400 N.Y.S.2d 289 (1977).

Lee v. *Thompson,* 554 EHLR 429 (1983).

Mahoney v. *Administrative School District No. 1,* 601 P.2d 826 (1979).

Rettig v. *Kent City School District,* 539 F.Supp. 768 (1981), aff'd in part vac'd and rem'd in part 720 F.2d 463 (1983).

Rowley, Board of Education v., See Chapter Two.

Yaris v. *Special School District of St. Louis County,* 558 F.Supp. 545 (1983), aff'd 728 F.2d 1055 (1984).

Figure 4-1

LEADING CASES

Armstrong v. *Kline,* 476 F.Supp. 583 (1979)
The state's policy of not providing educational services beyond the traditional school year deprived certain handicapped students of an appropriate education. If the student's regression combined with the time required to recoup lost skills substantially interferes with the attainment of the IEP's objectives, a summer program may be required.

Anderson v. *Thompson,* 495 F.Supp. 1256 (1980)
A school district is not required to provide a summer school program if the student's regression over the vacation period is no greater than that of a nonhandicapped child.

Bales v. *Clarke,* 523 F.Supp. 1366 (1981)
Year-round schooling is not required unless it can be shown that an irreparable loss of progress will take place during the summer.

Georgia A.R.C. v. *McDaniel,* 716 F.2d 1565 (1983)
State practices that effectively limit consideration of educational programs to 180 days violate the federal statutes.

Yaris v. *Special School District,* 558 F.Supp. 545 (1983)
Any policy that refuses to consider extended school year programs violates the EHCA under the Supreme Court's *Rowley* standard.

Lee v. *Thompson,* 554 EHLR 429 (1983)
In determining the need for an extended school year program, a school district must consider the nature of the handicapping condition, the severity of the handicap, areas of learning, extent of regression, and the rate of recoupment.

Figure 4-2

RIGHTS TO AN EXTENDED SCHOOL YEAR

1. The EHCA and its regulations guarantee each handicapped child "a free appropriate education and related services to meet their unique needs." (34 C.F.R. § 300.1)

2. The EHCA, as interpreted by the U.S. Supreme Court (*Board of Education* v. *Rowley,* 102 S.Ct. 3034 (1982)), guarantees the handicapped child services that are "individually designed to provide educational benefit to the handicapped child." (at 3048)

3. Although a handicapped child is not entitled to the best possible education, the student is entitled to an education that will enable him or her to reach the goals and objectives of his or her IEP.

4. If the amount of regression a handicapped student suffers over the course of a vacation period combined with the recoupment time required to relearn lost skills substantially interferes with the attainment of reasonable educational expectations for that child, the student is entitled to a program that extends beyond the traditional school year.

5. A state or local education agency may not have laws, regulations, policies, or procedures that either prevent or interfere with the consideration of extended school year programs.

Figure 4-3

DETERMINING THE NEED FOR AN EXTENDED SCHOOL YEAR

A handicapped student may need an extended school year program when

The cumulative effect of regression over a vacation period combined with the recoupment period required to regain lost skills seriously interferes with the student's attainment of yearly goals and objectives as stated on the IEP.

The regression/recoupment process is impairing the student's ability to become independent and self-sufficient.

The combined regression/recoupment process is significantly greater than is that of a nonhandicapped student.

Other students with a similar handicapping condition typically require year-round programming.

Figure 4-4

QUESTIONS ADMINISTRATORS OFTEN ASK ABOUT EXTENDED SCHOOL YEAR

1. *What is an extended school year?*

The term "extended school year" refers to the duration of any educational program that goes beyond the normal school year. Generally, it refers to full-year programming or programs with a summer component.

2. *Who is entitled to an extended school year?*

Any handicapped child who suffers such regression during a break in programming combined with an inordinate recoupment period that it substantially interferes with the attainment of educational objectives. Generally only severely handicapped students meet this criteria.

3. *Don't all students suffer regression during a summer vacation?*

Most students do regress during the summer vacation, which is why every school year begins with a few weeks of "review." However, most students recoup lost skills rather quickly. Some handicapped students, however, suffer from severe regression and do not recoup those skills very quickly. For these students, the cumulative effect of the regression/recoupment process is very little or no educational gain over a period of time. Without a summer component, the student's educational program does not provide any educational benefit. In such an instance the child does not receive the appropriate education guaranteed by the EHCA.

4. *What if a state has a policy that prohibits the provision of educational services beyond the normal school year for any child?*

Such a policy would violate the EHCA, and under the principle of supremacy of federal legislation it could not stand.

5. *What handicapped children are not entitled to an extended school year?*

Those whose regression/recoupment is not substantially greater than that of nonhandicapped children. This constitutes the vast majority of handicapped children.

Figure 4-5

SAMPLE IEP STATEMENTS CONCERNING EXTENDED SCHOOL YEAR PLACEMENTS

When an ESY Placement Is Required

The evaluation team has determined that the student will suffer such regression as a result of a break in programming over the summer recess that, combined with the time required to recoup those lost skills, the student's progress toward the goals of the IEP will be severely compromised. Therefore, the team proposes that the student's educational program be extended throughout the summer months.

When an ESY Placement Is Not Required

The evaluation team has been asked to consider an extended school year program for the student. A review of assessments and past progress reports indicate that the student's regression/recoupment rate is not so severe that it substantially interferes with the student's progress toward the goals of the IEP. Therefore, an extended school year program is not recommended.

Figure 4-6

OPTIONS TO CONSIDER AS ALTERNATIVES TO ESY PROGRAMS

Summer Camp. There are many day camp programs offered by charitable organizations specifically for handicapped children. These are often low cost or cost-free.

Recreation Programs. Many cities and towns offer recreation programs that are appropriate for handicapped children. These are generally sponsored by the Parks and Recreation Department and are usually cost-free. Recreation programs are also often sponsored by nonprofit groups that would be low cost.

Local Colleges. The special education department of a local college may offer a summer recreational or instructional program for handicapped children.

Figure 4-7

ADMINISTRATOR'S CHECKLIST

Questions to ask in determining whether or not a handicapped child needs an extended school year program:

1. How much regression will the student suffer over the summer vacation? _____ Specifically, what skills will be lost? _____

2. How long did it take originally for the student to acquire those skills? _____ How long will it take the student to relearn those skills? _____

3. What is the cumulative effect of this regression/recoupment process? _____ Specifically, what will the effect be on the attainment of the student's educational goals? _____

4. If the student is not provided with an extended school year program, will the total educational program be of little or no benefit? _____ Will it substantially compromise the total educational experience for the student? _____

5. What is the nature of the student's handicap? _____ Do other students with a similar handicap normally require an extended school year program? _____

6. Will the absence of a summer program prevent or seriously impair the student's ability to become self-sufficient and independent? _____

7. What other options are available besides a school district—sponsored extended school year program? _____
   Would any of these programs satisfy the student's need for continuous programming? _____

Chapter 5

WHAT MUST BE DONE TO CHANGE A HANDICAPPED STUDENT'S PLACEMENT?

> *When parents become convinced that their child is not receiving an appropriate education, the potential for reimbursement from the school system would encourage them to be assiduous in protecting their child's rights, yet the potential of having to repay the school system for a change to a private school would militate against impulsive or unfounded actions: a balance is struck.*
>
> **Circuit Judge Bownes**
> *Doe v. Brookline School Committee*
> **722 F.2d 910 at 920 (1983)**

The Education for All Handicapped Children Act (EHCA) regulations provide that

> Written notice . . . must be given to the parents of a handicapped child a reasonable time before the public agency:
> (1) Proposes to initiate or change the identification, evaluation, or educational placement of the child or the provision of a free appropriate public education to the child, or
> (2) Refuses to initiate or change the identification, evaluation, or educational placement of the child or the provision of a free appropriate public education to the child. (34 C.F.R. § 300.504 (a))

The parents also have the right to contest any decision made by school officials concerning the educational placement of their child (34 C.F.R. § 300.506).

The phrase "change in placement" has generated a fair amount of controversy in the past few years. School systems, as a result of declining enrollments and fiscal difficulties, have attempted to make physical and programmatic changes in their total educational offering. Special education programs have been affected by several of these changes. Just how far a school district could go before these changes and revisions constituted a change in placement has not always been clear. Again, the regulations provide little guidance as to what precisely constitutes a change in placement. The courts have, however, provided some answers.

RELOCATION OF SPECIAL EDUCATION PROGRAMS

In an early District of Columbia case, the district court ruled that the relocation of a special education class did not constitute a change in placement. The plaintiffs in *Brown* v. *District of Columbia Board of Education* were students in a local deaf-blind class. The class had been located in a public school that also housed programs for nonhandicapped students. At this school the students had been in a self-contained classroom with mainstreaming for lunch, recess, and assemblies. As a result of a monitoring report that indicated that these students needed supportive services that were not available in their then current school, the class was relocated to another facility that housed only programs for the handicapped. The students' parents were not provided with notice or other due process safeguards prior to the move. The parents filed court action seeking injunctive relief.

The court, in refusing to issue the injunction, held that the EHCA appeared to contemplate the use of due process procedures only for changes that affected the form of educational instruction being provided to handicapped children. The court thus ruled that the transfer of the class from one school to another was not a change in placement. The court also felt that the need for additional supportive services outweighed the goal of educational integration in this case. The court did, however, state that if the change in location of the class required a change in a student's Individualized Educational Program (IEP), parental participation would be required.

The Second Circuit Court of Appeals in a similar factual situation also held that the transfer of handicapped children from one school to another, with their programming remaining substantially the same, did not constitute a change in placement. In *Concerned Parents and Citizens* v. *New York City*, a public school was closed for budgetary reasons. Approximately 185 out of 310 students at the school were handicapped and in special education classes. All the school's students were transferred to other schools in the district, with the teachers and their classes being kept as intact as possible. The parents of several of the students filed court action alleging that the transfer of handicapped students violated the EHCA and Section 504. The district court ruled that the transfer constituted a change in placement under the EHCA requiring notice and a prior hearing. The school district appealed this ruling.

The appeals court held that the term "educational placement" referred only to the general type of educational program in which a handicapped student is placed. A change in placement, according to the court, did not refer to the various adjustments in that program that the school system may determine are necessary. The transfer of students from one school to another, with little change in the general program, did not constitute a change in placement sufficient to require prior notice and a hearing. The U.S. Supreme Court let the decision stand by declining to review the case.

TRANSFER FROM AN INAPPROPRIATE PROGRAM

In 1981 the district court in *Dima* v. *Macchiarola* ruled that the transfer of students from a private school that was found to be lacking to another more appropriate private school did not constitute a change in placement. The school department had notified the parents and guardians of students scheduled to attend a private school for handicapped children that the school department had not signed a contract with the private school for the coming year. The students were offered alternative educational sites. The school department had decided not to sign the contract with the private school after an audit disclosed that the school had mismanaged public funds and had serious educational deficiencies. The parents and guardians of the students affected filed court action claiming that the transfer of the students to other schools violated the EHCA's due process provisions.

The court ruled that the school department had the right to refuse to continue a contract with a private school that, in their discretion, they believed to be inappropriate. The court felt that the school department should be permitted to make an independent determination about the suitability of private schools to meet the needs of the school system without affording the parents and students due process. Accordingly, the court held that a transfer, such as the transfer in the present case, which resulted in the removal of all handicapped students from the school, as opposed to an individual transfer, did not require the due process of the EHCA.

The Supreme Court of Kings County, New York, also ruled that the transfer of students from a private school to other similar placements was not a change in placement. In *Cohen* v. *Board of Education* the school district decided not to renew its contract with a private school after a four-year period of continuous contracting, effectively causing the school to close. The contract was not renewed allegedly because of financial mismanagement. The school department had offered alternate placements to a majority of the affected students and was seeking placements for the others. Officials of the private school and the parents of one of the students brought suit in an attempt to prohibit the transfers.

In denying relief to the plaintiffs, the court stated that a change in schools was not by itself a change in educational placement under the EHCA. The court indicated that in some cases a transfer from one school to another would constitute a change in placement but that in the present case there was not sufficient proof of irreparable injury to the students to warrant a stay preventing the closing of the school. Such irreparable injury could be shown by the educational uniqueness of the former school or by a showing that the new school would not similarly aid the student, according to the court.

MINOR PROGRAMMATIC CHANGES

The Third Circuit Court of Appeals in *DeLeon* v. *Susquehanna Community School District* held that the important element in determining whether a change in placement has taken place is whether the change is likely to affect the student's learning in some significant way. In this case the school district had made minor changes in the student's transportation plan and the student's parents filed suit claiming that a due process hearing was required before the change could take place. The district court disagreed and the appeals court affirmed, holding that the minor changes would not have an impact on the student's learning and did not constitute a change in placement.

The Court of Appeals for the District of Columbia held in *Lunceford* v. *District of Columbia Board of Education* that a student's discharge from a private hospital was not a change in placement under the EHCA. A multihandicapped student with profound mental retardation and crippling conditions had lived in an institution for the mentally retarded for several years. Pursuant to a hearing officer's order he had been placed in a private hospital serving children with chronic ill- nesses and handicapping conditions. The hospital staff later determined that he could be discharged but recommended that he continue in their education program on an outpatient basis. The student's surrogate parent objected and contended that such a move was a change in placement and could be accomplished only according to the EHCA's change in placement procedures. The trial court held in favor of the surrogate parent.

The appeals court reversed, holding that according to settled case law, a student must show at a minimum that a fundamental change in or an elimination of a basic element of the education program took place for the move to constitute a change in placement. The court found that this standard had not been met since the only differences between the hospital and institution programs were minor.

TERMINATION OF A PROGRAM FOR FISCAL REASONS

The U.S. Court of Appeals for the Sixth Circuit held that a change in place- ment took place in *Tilton* v. *Jefferson County Board of Education* but that the EHCA's procedural protections did not apply since the change was necessitated by the closing of a treatment center. The plaintiffs were emotionally disturbed students who had been receiving treatment and education at a day treatment facility oper- ated by the state's Department of Human Resources. The treatment facility, which had provided the only 12-month day treatment program for seriously emotionally disturbed children available in the county, closed for budgetary reasons. The students unsuccessfully sought a preliminary injunction to prevent the closing from the district court.

The appeals court found that the programs of the alternate placements offered to the students were not comparable to those of the treatment facility. In particular, the alternative placements offered to the students were limited to 180 days, whereas the treatment facility provided a year-round program. The court noted that a change in placement usually cannot take place without the procedural protections of the EHCA, including the requirement that a child remain in the then current placement pending final resolution of any proceedings. School officials, however, by electing to receive EHCA funds, did not abdicate their traditional control of fiscal decisions, according to the court. To apply the EHCA's procedural protections to a situation where a change in placement is caused solely by economic decisions, the court reasoned, would result in a transfer of power. Plaintiffs in such a situation could forestall such a closing for years by pursuing complaints through the procedural framework. The court ruled that if a program must be discontinued for purely economic reasons, the procedural requirements of the EHCA do not apply. The court noted that the students could bring complaints concerning their new programs through the EHCA's due process mechanism if they were dissatisfied with them.

ELIMINATION OF A MAJOR PROGRAM COMPONENT

In *Gebhardt* v. *Ambach* the district court ruled that the discontinuance of a summer school program constituted a change in placement. Court action was initiated on behalf of students who attended a state school for the blind when it was learned that a scheduled summer program at the school was to be eliminated due to renovations and construction at the facility. The students' IEPs called for year-round residential placement. The plaintiffs claimed that the school officials' summary elimination of the summer component of the students' placement violated the EHCA since no opportunity was provided for the students and their parents to challenge the decision.

The court referred to the Second Circuit Court of Appeals definition in the *Concerned Citizens* case of a change in placement being a change in the general type of educational program that is provided by the school. The district court found that in the present case, students who were entitled to year-round programming had been notified that such programming was to be shortened, with no provision having been made for an alternate placement. The court held that a change which shortened a program by two months was of such critical magnitude that it constituted a change in placement. The court ordered the school to reinstate and maintain the summer program unless the procedural requirements of the EHCA were complied with.

GRADUATION IS A CHANGE IN PLACEMENT

The Supreme Judicial Court of Massachusetts held that the graduation of a handicapped student also constituted a change in placement under the EHCA. The student in *Stock* v. *Massachusetts Hospital School* was mentally and physically disabled and had attended a state-operated hospital school for disabled children since the age of 14. He was awarded a high school diploma in June 1981, which ended his eligibility for special education services under state law. Neither the student nor his parents had been given formal written notice that graduation would terminate special education services nor were they informed of their procedural rights under the law. They also had not been invited to participate in the development of the student's final IEP prior to graduation. The IEP also made no mention of the impending graduation. After graduation, the student failed to adapt either to a sheltered workshop or to independent living. A suit was filed on his behalf seeking to have his diploma rescinded and his eligibility for special education restored.

The state's high court held that graduation, because it terminates a student's special education services, is a change in placement. The court stated that the termination of special education is a serious issue worthy of parental involvement and procedural protections. The failure to provide the student's parents with formal written notice of the graduation decision, the failure to provide notice of their rights to involvement in that decision, and the failure to notify them of their due process rights all violated state and federal law, according to the court. The court further indicated that the awarding of a diploma to an 18-year-old student, thus ending special education services, was substantively inappropriate where evidence indicated that the student would be unable to earn a diploma under normal requirements even by the age of 22.

DISCIPLINARY ACTION

Several courts have held that the disciplinary expulsion of a handicapped student is tantamount to a change in placement. Students who are dangerous, however, can be removed from their special education programs and transferred to another, more appropriate program without prior due process. Although this issue will be discussed in much greater detail in Chapter Seven, it may be helpful at this point to present one case that provides an example of an emergency situation in which school officials can change a student's placement without going through the time-consuming due process procedures outlined in the EHCA.

The student in *Jackson* v. *Franklin County School Board* had been suspended for three days for disruptive sexual conduct. During his suspension, the youth court placed him in a state hospital for treatment. The following year he attempted to return to school; however, school officials determined that they could not meet his needs for counseling, vocational training, and academics. A private facility was recommended instead. The student rejected all options offered by the school department and initiated due process appeals. He contended that until the dispute was settled, he was entitled to return to his previous public school program. The school system contended that because the student's behavior was disruptive and since he suffered from a psychosexual disorder that made him a possible danger to others, placement in a public school setting was not advisable.

The court held that the school system's refusal to allow the student to return to the public school setting was based on the reasonable conclusion that he would disrupt the educational process for others. The court further stated that the public interest was best served by the school district being able to provide a safe and effective environment for learning. This consideration, in the court's opinion, far outweighed any harm suffered by the student from being excluded.

STATUS QUO PROVISION—PLACEMENT PENDING APPEALS

The EHCA's provision that the status quo is to be maintained during any due process proceedings has been the subject of much additional litigation. The law specifically states that

> During the pendency of any proceedings conducted pursuant to this section, unless the State or local educational agency and the parents or guardian otherwise agree, the child shall remain in the then current educational placement of such child, or, if applying for initial admission to a public school, shall, with the consent of the parents or guardian, be placed in the public school program until all such proceedings have been completed. (20 U.S.C. § 1415(e)(3))

The implementing regulations are almost identical to the law itself. Simply stated, this provision does not permit a child's placement to be changed during a complaint proceeding unless the parents and school district agree otherwise. Problems have developed, however, when the then current placement was inappropriate, or eliminated, and the parents and school district were unable to agree on an alternate placement. As we will see, the courts have often been asked to intervene.

When Current Programs Are Clearly Inappropriate

Monahan v. *State of Nebraska* involved two students whose then current placements were clearly inappropriate, but their parents and the school district were unable to agree on alternate placements. The first student was a multihandicapped child who had attended a private school for the mentally retarded with his tuition being paid by the local school district. When he became confined to a wheelchair, he was unable to continue at the private school since it was not able to accommodate wheelchair-bound students. The student's father made arrangements to enroll the student in a program in a neighboring school district and requested his local district's approval. The local district agreed to allow the placement, but refused to pay the costs, contending that it had a similar program within its own district. The father enrolled the student in the neighboring school district, paying the costs himself, and filed court action. The question arose as to where the student should be placed pending final resolution of the litigation.

The court, referring to the EHCA's status quo provision, noted that it was powerless to place a child in any provisional program except for his then current placement. In this case, however, the child was unable to remain at his former placement because of his physical condition. Since the parties agreed that the student could remain in the neighboring school district's program pending resolution of the lawsuit, the court treated that as the student's then current placement. However, to maintain the status quo, the court held that the father should continue to pay the costs of the placement as he had been doing.

The second student in the *Monahan* case was also multihandicapped, but attended a program at a local junior high school. When she was not progressing, school officials proposed a change to a state school for the deaf. Her father objected and requested a due process hearing. After being unsuccessful in administrative appeals, he filed court action. The parties agreed that pending resolution of the litigation, the student should attend a program at another local junior high school, receiving basically the same education she received at her former school. However, after two weeks the father removed the student from the local school and enrolled her in a private school. The question again arose as to what was the status quo.

The court held that the EHCA's status quo provision did not require that a student must be placed in the school she had been attending all along, but that she could be placed in another school offering the same type of education. The status quo provision could be satisfied by placement in any local program that was similar to the one the student had been attending.

The Eighth Circuit Court of Appeals affirmed that portion of the decision concerning the placement of the children pending the outcome of appeals. The case was remanded on other grounds, however.

When Current Program Loses State Approval

The Second Circuit Court of Appeals in *Vander Malle* v. *Ambach* held that a student was to be maintained in a placement that had lost its approval until an appropriate alternative could be found. The student had been placed in a psychiatric hospital by an evaluation team. At the time the placement was made, the hospital was on the state's approved residential schools list. One year later, however, the hospital was removed from that list when the state determined that it was not a school and was thus inappropriate. The student's parents sought to have his placement at the hospital maintained until an appropriate placement that would be permanent could be found. The district court issued an injunction requiring that the hospital placement be maintained and the state appealed.

The appeals court, in upholding the district court decision, held that once a placement has been made by an evaluation team exercising its responsibilities under law, the state has an obligation to continue that placement until an appropriate alternative can be found or until the student is determined to no longer be handicapped. The court further held that if the local evaluation team failed to carry out its obligation to make an alternate placement, the state could not disclaim its statutory responsibilities.

School District Must Continue to Fund a Program Until a Proper Change in Placement Occurs

In 1983 the District Court for the District of Columbia upheld a hearing officers' determination that a residential school was the then current educational placement of a handicapped student. The plaintiff in *Jacobson* v. *District of Columbia Board of Education* was a 17-year-old learning disabled student who had attended a private special education school for several years. Since he had completed that school's most advanced program, he could no longer attend it. An IEP was developed by the private school without the participation of public school representatives that called for residential placement. Public school officials, however, proposed that the student attend a local high school learning disabilities program. Eventually the school district agreed to fund the residential placement. One year later, however, the school district advised the student's parents that it saw no need for continued residential placement and would no longer be financially responsible for such a placement. The school district again recommended that the student attend the public schools. The student's parents appealed the school department's recommendation. The hearing officer was unable to make a determination as to what was the appropriate placement due to insufficient information, but determined that the residential school was the student's current educational placement and directed the school district to continue funding it.

The district court found that when the school department assumed responsibility for the residential placement, it gave no indication that it intended to do so for one year only. The student's parents were thus free to assume that the public schools would continue to fund that program until a proper change in placement, including the exhaustion of any appeals, took place. The residential school was thus held to be the student's current placement.

When a Placement Is no Longer Available

Sometimes the student's then current placement is no longer available and therefore cannot be maintained. In such an instance the District of Columbia Court of Appeals has held that the school district is obligated to locate and fund a similar program. In *McKenzie* v. *Smith* the student had attended private schools since entering school. His then current private school determined that it could no longer meet his needs. A dispute arose between the student's parents and public school officials as to what would be an appropriate placement. Since he could no longer remain in his current program while the dispute was pending, his parents enrolled him in another private facility and sought funding for that program. The court held that since his then current placement was no longer available, the school district was required to locate and fund a similar program during the pendency of the appeals process.

Courts May Determine an Interim Placement

The question arose in *Doe* v. *Brookline School Committee* as to which party should pay private school costs pending final resolution of a due process complaint under the EHCA. The student in this case had been unilaterally placed in a private school by his parents while due process action was still pending. The private school was eventually determined to be the appropriate placement, and the school department was ordered to assume all costs of that placement. Later the school district attempted to develop an IEP providing for the student's return to a public school program. The IEP was rejected and another round of due process appeals began. Eventually the court was asked to determine which party was responsible for the private school costs while due process action was pending. The issue is critical since these proceedings could take several years, especially if they reach the court level.

The First Circuit Court of Appeals held that the courts may use their judicial powers of equity to make a determination as to which party should bear the costs of a private school placement during the appeals process. However, the court further held that the party seeking to modify the status quo bears the burden of proof. In making this determination, the court found that Congress did not intend to freeze a possible inappropriate placement for the three to five years of review proceedings. In a situation such as the one that existed in the present case, parents could obtain the relief sought, maintenance of a publicly funded private placement, simply by filing appeals if the status quo provision was interpreted to require the party paying costs at the time of appeals to continue to do so throughout the process. Similarly, school districts could avoid their obligation to provide private placements by filing a series of appeals.

Parents May Rely on a Final Hearing Decision

As has been discussed in previous sections, the due process appeals procedures can be very drawn out. Throughout the process contravening decisions can be handed down at different levels. The question arises as to which decision should be followed while a final judicial resolution is pending. The First Circuit held in *Town of Burlington* v. *Department of Education of Massachusetts* that where the parents of a handicapped child rely on a final administrative hearing decision in placing their child in a private school at public expense, the school district may not later recover those funds for the time period covered by that order even if it is later reversed by the courts.

The issue was similar in *Board of Education of the City of New York* v. *Ambach.* In this case an emotionally disturbed student had been placed in an alternative school by his parents pursuant to a court order that was issued in response to New York's failure to implement fully the EHCA in a timely manner. That court order authorized parents of handicapped children who had not been offered an appropriate placement to enroll their child in a private school at public expense. After the student in the present case had been enrolled in the alternative school the evaluation team recommended that he be placed in a class for the emotionally handicapped in the public schools. The student's mother sought a due process review of that decision. The hearing officer determined that the evaluation team had not been properly constituted, did not follow proper procedure, and failed to substantiate the appropriateness of its recommendation. The hearing officer ordered that the school department continue to fund the alternative school for the then current school year. At the end of that school year, the school district again proposed a transfer to a public school placement and the student's mother again objected. This time, however, that recommendation was upheld by the hearing officer. The State Commissioner of Education upheld that decision but held that the Board of Education was responsible for the private school tuition until its proposal was finally confirmed by the commissioner.

The district court held that the alternative school was the student's then current placement as defined by the EHCA until all review proceedings had been completed. In upholding the commissioner's decision, the court stated that the board was not relieved of its duty to finance that placement until all such proceedings had been completed. The board is responsible only until the date of the commissioner's decision, however, and not until the end of the school year.

REIMBURSEMENT TO PARENTS FOR UNILATERAL PLACEMENT CHANGES

The issue of reimbursing parents of handicapped children for tuition and other costs incurred in unilaterally placing their handicapped child in a private school if that placement was later determined by the courts to be the appropriate placement for the child has proven to be the most controversial legal dispute under the EHCA. This dispute also provides us with an example of how legal thinking can change over time and how an issue that was assumed to be settled can suddenly become unsettled. Since courts in various circuits had provided contrary opinions, the U.S. Supreme Court finally had to settle the dispute.

The EHCA's procedural safeguard provisions give the courts the authority to "grant such relief as the court determines is appropriate" (20 U.S.C. § 1415(e)(2)(c)). Neither the law nor the regulations give any indication of what type of relief may be appropriate or in what instances relief may be warranted. The EHCA's status quo provision, discussed earlier, has been the subject of much litigation concerning monetary relief. The parents of handicapped students, feeling that their child's program was inappropriate, have often unilaterally placed the child in another program and subsequently sought reimbursement for the costs incurred. School officials, on the other hand, have contended that the EHCA's status quo provision also places a duty on the parents to keep the child in the then current placement until any disagreements are resolved.

Initially the courts were fairly unanimous in holding that reimbursement was not generally available under the EHCA unless exceptional circumstances were present that warranted the unilateral move. However, late in 1983 the First Circuit Court of Appeals parted company with the other courts and challenged that rationale by declaring that reimbursement was, in fact, generally available if the parents prevailed in having their choice of a program determined to be the appropriate placement. A second similar ruling by that same court prompted the U.S. Supreme Court to rule on the issue in 1985.

Background

One of the first cases litigating the reimbursement question came before the Fourth Circuit Court of Appeals, which held that the EHCA's status quo provision placed a duty on parents to maintain their child's educational placement throughout due process proceedings. The student in *Stemple* v. *Board of Education of Prince George's County* had a history of physical and emotional difficulties and had attended self-contained special classes for a number of years. The school department began to mainstream her for part of the school day; however, after several months her parents, dissatisfied with her progress, withdrew her from the public schools and placed her in a private day school. Her parents then requested that the county pay for her private schooling. That request was denied, and the denial was upheld in administrative appeals. The district court also upheld the denial.

The appeals court, in affirming the district court's decision, stated that the language of the EHCA's status quo provision created a duty on the part of parents who avail themselves of the due process review provisions of the act to keep their child in the current educational placement until the review proceedings are completed, unless they agree with school district authorities to some other arrangements. The court recognized that the state could not enforce that duty, but held that any action on the part of parents in violation of that duty would negate any right on their part to later recover private school tuition costs incurred through such a violation. The U.S. Supreme Court let that decision stand by declining to review this case.

The district court in *Tatro* v. *Texas* awarded tuition reimbursement to the parents of a physically handicapped student when it determined that the child's health would have been in danger if the parents had not made the placement. The student required catheterization approximately every four hours. The school system claimed that it was not responsible for providing the catheterization and the student's parents filed suit seeking an order requiring the school to provide it. In the meantime, the parents enrolled the student in a private school where she would be catheterized as needed. The parents eventually prevailed in their suit and sought reimbursement.

The district court held that the student's parents were entitled to recovery of the costs incurred by them to furnish the student with private educational services, qualified by their duty to mitigate those costs. The court reasoned that reimbursement for substitute educational services was consistent with the congressional purpose of the EHCA that handicapped children were to be provided with a free, appropriate public education.

The Court of Appeals for the Fifth Circuit affirmed. The case eventually went to the U.S. Supreme Court; however, reimbursement was not one of the issues considered by the high court.

Reimbursement Allowed Under Exceptional Circumstances

The Seventh Circuit Court of Appeals held that reimbursement for educational services unilaterally acquired by the parents of a handicapped child was appropriate only under exceptional circumstances in *Anderson* v. *Thompson*. The school district, after evaluating the student, recommended that she be placed in a public school program of special education. The student's parents declined that placement and enrolled her in a private school. Two years later she was reevaluated and again, a public school placement was recommended. The parents again declined and appealed the recommendation. The parents eventually prevailed and sought reimbursement of the private school costs. The district court declined to award compensatory damages.

The appeals court, in affirming the district court's decision, held that compensatory damages were appropriate in only two circumstances. The first circumstance is when, as in the *Tatro* case the child's physical health would have been endangered if the parents had not made alternate arrangements to those offered by the school system. The second circumstance is when the school district fails to comply with the EHCA's due process provisions in an egregious fashion. The court further held that a damage remedy was not available if the school system had made an incorrect placement decision, absent these exceptional circumstances.

In *Department of Education, State of Hawaii* v. *Katherine D.*, the Ninth Circuit Court of Appeals found a third exceptional circumstance that it felt warranted reimbursement. That exception exists when the school district fails to offer a public school placement when one is clearly appropriate, leaving the child's parents with little choice but to seek a private placement. The student in the present case was a young handicapped child who had to wear a tracheotomy tube to breathe and to expel mucus from her lungs. At various times during the day she needed to have her tube attended to by trained personnel. She was otherwise capable of attending public school classes. A dispute arose over whether or not the EHCA required the school department to provide the personnel to attend to the student's health needs. Pending resolution of the dispute, her parents enrolled her in a private facility after the school department offered only a minimal homebound instruction program as an alternative. The district court eventually ruled that the student was entitled to attend the public schools and have the necessary health services provided. The court also awarded her parents reimbursement of all costs associated with the private school placement they had chosen unilaterally.

In upholding the district court, the appeals court found that this situation did not precisely fit the exceptions outlined in *Anderson*. However, it found that the Department of Education's behavior was exceptional in that it failed to offer a public school classroom placement when the student's ability to function in such a placement was clearly demonstrated. The private school offered her parents the only feasible way to assure her an appropriate education in a regular educational environment.

In an early 1984 case, the Court of Appeals for the Fifth Circuit rejected an attempt to expand the *Anderson* exceptional circumstances to include the possibility of regression as a reimbursable reason for making a unilateral change in placement. The student in *Scokin* v. *State of Texas* was an emotionally disturbed youth who had attended a public school program for emotionally disturbed children. In the middle of her second year in that program, her parents requested that she be placed in a residential school because she had shown some regression. That request was denied, and appeals were filed. Before the appeals process was completed, her parents unilaterally placed her in the residential facility. The state Board of Education upheld the school district, and court action was filed. The district court found that in spite of the student's regression, she had benefited from the public school program, and it was therefore appropriate. Reimbursement for the residential school costs was also denied.

On appeal, the student's parents claimed that their situation consituted yet another exceptional circumstance that should result in reimbursement: the student would have continued to regress if she remained in the public school program. The appeals court held that the student's period of regression did not amount to a type of exceptional circumstance that would justify reimbursement. The court noted that while regression is unfortunate, in an emotionally disturbed student, it is neither surprising nor exceptional.

A Controversy Develops

In the majority of reimbursement cases cited in the preceding section, the parents of the handicapped student have claimed that they were entitled to reimbursement because the school district failed to provide an appropriate program as required by the EHCA and that the only way they could gain the needed services was to unilaterally enroll their child in a private school. School districts, on the other hand, have argued that the EHCA also places a duty on the parents to maintain the status quo until the dispute is finally settled. As we have seen, the courts had unanimously agreed with the school districts' arguments.

Late in 1983, however, the First Circuit Court of Appeals issued an opinion in *Doe* v. *Brookline School Committee* in which it strongly disagreed with the prevailing *Anderson* rationale. Although the *Brookline* decision represents the first time a court stated that reimbursement could be awarded under the EHCA without the presence of exceptional circumstances, it was not without precedent in the First Circuit. Earlier in 1983 the Massachusetts District Court issued an opinion in *Doe* v. *Anrig,* a case it had decided on remand from the First Circuit Court of Appeals. The appeals court had denied reimbursement under the EHCA but remanded the case for a determination under state law. The district court awarded reimbursement under the state special education statute and criticized the appeals court for its denial of reimbursement under the federal law stating that it did not feel that Congress intended for a successful parent to be left with what should have been the school district's expense in the first place. The lower court urged the appeals court to reconsider its position.

The appeals court had that opportunity in the *Brookline* case. The student in this instance had severe specific learning disabilities. His parents rejected a proposed IEP, subsequently unilaterally placed him in a private school for learning disabled children, and filed an appeal. The state Bureau of Special Education Appeals ruled that the proposed IEP was inadequate and that the private school was the appropriate placement. The school department was ordered to pay all costs associated with that placement. After the student had attended the private school for two years, the school department developed an IEP that called for him to return to a public school program. The student's parents again rejected the IEP; however, this time it was upheld in administrative hearings. The student's parents filed court action seeking to have the court determine an appropriate IEP and to order the school department to fund the private school placement until final resolution of the dispute. The school department refused to pay the student's private school tuition the following year but was later ordered to do so by the district court. The school district complied with the order but appealed the decision.

The appeals court framed two issues concerning the EHCA's status quo provision: Who should pay the private school costs pending final resolution of the complaint? and Was reimbursement of costs available to the prevailing party? In its decision the court deviated from the previous decisions that had held that whoever was paying the costs of the private placement at the time the complaint was filed would continue to do so and that reimbursement was generally not available to the prevailing party absent exceptional circumstances.

The court was troubled by the fact that in situations such as the present one, parents could obtain the relief sought—maintenance of a publicly funded private placement—simply by filing appeals if the status quo provision was interpreted to require the school district to continue paying private school costs throughout the appeals process, especially if reimbursement was barred to the prevailing party. Similarly, school districts could avoid their obligation to provide private placements if reimbursement was barred to parents who made a unilateral private placement and were later upheld. The court stated that it did not feel that Congress intended to freeze a possible inappropriate placement and program for the three to five years of review proceedings. The court found that the EHCA did not create a duty to maintain the status quo but, rather, created a preference for it. The courts could, however, use their traditional judicial powers of equity to make a determination as to which party would maintain the placement pending resolution since the EHCA granted courts the authority to fashion appropriate equitable relief. The party seeking to modify the status quo had to bear the burden of proof according to the appeals court.

In regard to reimbursement, the court disagreed with the Seventh Circuit's decision in *Anderson* that reimbursement was available only in exceptional circumstances. In parting from the prevailing judicial interpretations regarding reimbursement awards under the EHCA, the court stated

> We believe that the best approach to this issue is to require each party to bear the costs of its own errors of judgment in determining what a "free appropriate education" for a child requires in the pertinent circumstances. When parents become convinced that their child is not receiving an appropriate education, the potential for reimbursement from the school system would encourage them to be assiduous in protecting their child's rights, yet the potential of having to repay the school system for a change to a private school would militate against impulsive or unfounded actions: a balance is struck. Similarly, the right to reimbursement would create the appropriate incentive for the local school committee. . . . If school systems are forced to pay interim tuition eventually . . . greater incentive exists for making the initial placement the correct placement. (pp. 920–21)

The court felt that permitting reimbursement would promote the purpose of the EHCA. If the parents were incorrect in their decision that a proposed IEP provided an inappropriate education, they would pay for giving their child a private education. If, however, the school system's proposed IEP was held to be inappropriate, reimbursement would put all parties in the position the EHCA sought to achieve. The court ruled that reimbursement was available to the prevailing party under the EHCA. In ruling as it did, the First Circuit Court reversed its own previous ruling that reimbursement was not generally available.

In light of the remedial nature of the EHCA and its many provisions for parental input into the decision-making process, the *Brookline* decision had greater merit than did the *Anderson* rationale. A standard that allows parents to recover the costs involved in successfully exercising their duty to seek an appropriate education for their handicapped child is more consistent with the act's general purpose than is a standard that would reward a school district for failing to provide the required appropriate education in the first place.

The Supreme Court Settles the Controversy

In 1985 the U.S. Supreme Court settled the reimbursement dispute by holding in *Burlington School Committee* v. *Department of Education* that reimbursement was generally available under the EHCA. The student in this case was a learning disabled boy who received special education services in the public schools through grade 3. At the end of his third grade year, his father rejected a proposed IEP and had an independent evaluation completed at the local hospital. The hospital evaluators recommended that the student be placed in a private school for learning disabled children. Believing that the school department's proposed placement was inappropriate, the student's father unilaterally placed him in the recommended private facility.

After a hearing on the matter, the Massachusetts Bureau of Special Education Appeals found that the proposed public school placement was inappropriate and that the private school was the least restrictive environment. The hearing officer ordered the school department to fund the private school placement and to reimburse the parents for expenses they had already incurred.

The school department appealed the hearing officer's decision to the courts. School officials agreed to pay the current costs of the private school but not the past costs after they had been threatened by the State Department of Education with a cut-off of funds if they did not fund the private placement. This threat came even though the case was still on appeal. Eventually the courts found the proposed public school placement to be appropriate and ruled that the school district was not responsible for the private school costs. The school district and the student's father each then sued for reimbursement of the costs each had expended on the private school. The district court held that the student's father was required to reimburse the school district. The court was also critical of the Department of Education's interference in ordering the school district to fund the private school under the threat of withholding of funds.

The student's father appealed that decision. The First Circuit Court of Appeals held that the EHCA did not bar reimbursement when the parents of a handicapped student unilaterally changed the student's placement if their action was eventually held to be appropriate. Reimbursement is not, however, available if the school district had proposed and had the capacity to implement an appropriate IEP according to the court. The court further held that where the parents of a handicapped child rely on the final state administrative decision that orders a school district to fund a private school placement, the school district may not later obtain reimbursement for the time period covered by that decision, which is usually one year.

On appeal the U.S. Supreme Court squarely addressed the issue of whether or not the EHCA allowed reimbursement of expenses to the parents of a handicapped child who unilaterally placed that child in a private school if their choice was later determined to be appropriate. The majority held that the EHCA did, in fact, authorize reimbursement in such instances. In affirming the First Circuit's decision, the Court disagreed with the reasoning of a majority of the circuits on the issue.

Justice Rehnquist, writing for the majority, stated that if reimbursement were not available in such an instance "the child's right to a *free* appropriate public education, the parents' right to participate fully in developing a proper IEP, and all of the procedural safeguards would be less than complete" (P. 2003). By empowering the courts to grant appropriate relief, Congress intended to include retroactive reimbursement as an available remedy according to the high court. Justice Rehnquist further stated that "Reimbursement merely requires the Town to belatedly pay expenses that it should have paid all along and would have borne in the first instance had it developed a proper IEP" (2003).

The Court's ruling indicates that a parental violation of the EHCA's status quo provision does not constitute a waiver of reimbursement. The Court noted that the EHCA was intended to give handicapped children an appropriate education and a free one and that it should not be interpreted to defeat one or the other of those objectives. The Court cautioned, however, that parents who unilaterally change their child's placement to a private facility do so at their own financial risk since they won't be reimbursed if the courts ultimately determine that the school system had proposed and had the capacity to implement an appropriate IEP.

The *Burlington* decision has been hailed as the Supreme Court's most important EHCA decision thus far. Many feel that it has strengthened the EHCA's mandate that school districts must provide handicapped children with a free appropriate public education as it provides school systems with the incentive to develop an appropriate program from the beginning and provides the parents with equitable relief if the school district fails to do so.

Post-Burlington Decisions

The *Burlington* decision settled the controversy among the various circuits over whether or not reimbursement was generally available under the EHCA to parents who prevailed in having a private facility judged to be the appropriate placement for their handicapped child. After the issuance of that opinion, all courts throughout the country were required to rule accordingly in reimbursement cases.

McKenzie v. *Smith* provides an example of how the courts have responded to *Burlington*'s pronouncements. In this case a learning disabled student who also had emotional problems had received special education services in private day schools since the time he first entered school. A dispute arose when the staff of the school he had been attending and his parents determined that he needed a residential placement, but public school officials disagreed and proposed a public high school learning disabilities class placement. The student's parents rejected that proposal and enrolled him in a residential facility.

Eventually, the residential placement was determined by the district court to be the apporopriate placement for the student. The Court of Appeals for the District of Columbia upheld a reimbursement award, declaring that the parents were entitled to be reimbursed under *Burlington* since their choice of a residential placement was determined to be appropriate.

REFERENCES

Anderson v. *Thompson*, 658 F.2d 1205 (1981).
Board of Education, City of New York v. *Ambach*, 612 F.Supp. 230 (1985).
Brown v. *District of Columbia Board of Education*, 551 EHLR 101 (1978).

Burlington School Committee v. *Department of Education,* 105 S.Ct. 1996 (1985).

Cohen v. *Board of Education of the City of New York,* 454 N.Y.S.2d 630 (1982).

Concerned Parents and Citizens v. *New York City Board of Education,* 629 F.2d 751 (1980).

DeLeon v. *Susquehanna Community School District,* 747 F.2d 149 (1984).

Department of Education, State of Hawaii v. *Katherine D.,* 727 F.2d 809 (1983).

Dima v. *Macchiarola,* 513 F.Supp. 565 (1981).

Doe v. *Anrig,* 561 F.Supp. 121 (1983).

Doe v. *Brookline School Committee,* 722 F.2d 910 (1983).

Gebhardt v. *Ambach,* 554 EHLR 130 (1982).

Jackson v. *Franklin County School Board,* 765 F.2d 535 (1985).

Jacobson v. *District of Columbia Board of Education,* 564 F.Supp. 166 (1983).

Lunceford v. *District of Columbia Board of Education,* 745 F.2d 1577 (1984).

McKenzie v. *Smith,* 771 F.2d 1527 (1985).

Monahan v. *State of Nebraska,* 491 F.Supp. 1074 (1980).

Scokin v. *State of Texas,* 723 F.2d 432 (1984).

Stemple v. *Board of Education of Prince George's County,* 623 F.2d 893 (1980).

Stock v. *Massachusetts Hospital School,* 467 N.E.2d 448 (1984).

Tatro v. *State of Texas,* 625 F.2d 557 (1980), on rem'd 516 F.Supp. 968 (1981), aff'd 703 F.2d 823 (1983).

Tilton v. *Jefferson County Board of Education,* 705 F.2d 800 (1983).

Town of Burlington v. *Department of Education of Massachusetts,* 736 F.2d 773 (1984).

Vander Malle v. *Ambach,* 673 F.2d 49 (1982).

Figure 5-1

LEADING CASES

Concerned Parents v. *New York City*, 629 F.2d 751 (1980)

The transfer of handicapped children from one school to another, with programming remaining substantially the same, does not constitute a change in placement under the EHCA.

Gebhardt v. *Ambach*, 554 EHLR 130 (1982)

The elimination of a major component of an educational program constitutes a change in placement.

Stock v. *Massachusetts Hospital School*, 467 N.E.2d 448 (1984)

Graduation of a handicapped student, and the subsequent termination of special education services, constitutes a change in placement that requires prior due process.

Anderson v. *Thompson*, 658 F.2d 1205 (1981)

Reimbursement of private school tuition costs generally is not available to parents who unilaterally place their child in such a school even if they eventually prevail in having their choice upheld as the appropriate placement, unless exceptional circumstances existed to warrant such a move.

Doe v. *Brookline*, 722 F.2d 910 (1983)

Reimbursement is available to parents who unilaterally place their child in a private school if their choice is eventually determined to be the appropriate placement.

Burlington v. *Department of Education*, 105 S.Ct. 1996 (1985)

The EHCA authorizes reimbursement of private school expenses to the prevailing party in a special education placement dispute.

Figure 5-2

PROCEDURAL STEPS REQUIRED PRIOR TO CHANGING A HANDICAPPED
STUDENT'S PLACEMENT

1. Prior to changing a handicapped student's placement the school district must provide the student's parents with written notice of the proposed change in placement. That notice must include

   a. An explanation of the EHCA's due process safeguards
   b. A description of the proposed change as well as a description of any other options considered with an explanation of why they were rejected
   c. A description of all assessments used in making the determination
   d. A description of any other relevant factors used in making the determination
   The notice must also
   a. Be written in language understood by the general public
   b. Be written in the parents' native language or other mode of communication
   c. Be provided orally if the parent cannot communicate in written language
   Such written notice must be provided a reasonable time prior to the proposed change in placement.

2. If the handicapped student's parents object to the proposed change in placement, they are entitled to a hearing conducted pursuant to state regulations. The hearing decision may be appealed to the state education agency or to the courts.

3. Until the dispute is finally resolved, the student's placement may not be changed unless the school district and the parents agree to a change, or unless the court orders a change. However, the school district may use its normal procedures to deal with a disruptive or dangerous student.

Note: State due process regulations may provide for additional procedural safeguards.

Figure 5-3

WHAT CONSTITUTES A CHANGE IN PLACEMENT?

1. A change in placement occurs whenever a school district makes programmatic changes that substantially affect the delivery of services to a handicapped child.
   Examples

   a. Graduation with its subsequent termination of services
   b. A transfer from one program to another program that is not substantially the same
   c. The elimination of a major component of a program
   d. Total cessation of special education services
   e. Expulsion or a long-term suspension of the student
   f. A major change in the length of the school day or yearly duration of the program
   g. A change in the amount or type of services provided

2. Minor changes that do not substantially affect the implementation of the student's IEP do not qualify as a change in placement.

   Examples
   a. The relocation of a special education class to another building where the delivery of services will remain basically the same
   b. Minor changes in transportation
   c. Changes in staffing or scheduling that do not affect the delivery of services
   d. The temporary disciplinary suspension of a student
   e. A transfer from one program found to be lacking to a more appropriate program
   f. The movement of a student from a program at one level to a similar program at another level due to grade promotion or chronological age considerations

Figure 5-4

SAMPLE IEP STATEMENTS

When it is anticipated that a handicapped student will graduate, statements similar to those that follow should be included on the final IEP prior to the graduation date:

The evaluation team anticipates that the student will graduate next June at the annual graduation exercises.

To graduate, the student must earn an additional five credits. Those credits will be earned by successful completion of the following courses as provided for in this IEP:

English for Business (1)
U.S. History (1)
Practical Math (1)
Woodworking (1)
Physical Education ($\frac{1}{2}$)
Driver Education ($\frac{1}{2}$)

Notice: All the due process rights outlined in the accompanying cover letter apply to the recommendation to graduate the student, including the right to contest that decision through an impartial due process hearing.

Figure 5-5

QUESTIONS ADMINISTRATORS OFTEN ASK ABOUT A CHANGE IN PLACEMENT

1. *If a student is promoted from an elementary school to a junior high school and his or her special education program is consequently altered, does it constitute a change in placement?*

No, as long as the amounts and types of services remain the same. Basically, a change in placement will not have occurred if the junior high program provides substantially the same educational benefit as the elementary program. Minor changes that reflect an adjustment to a new school are allowed.

2. *Would the elimination of speech therapy services, with no other changes in the total program, constitute a change in placement?*

Yes, the elimination of a major component of the student's total program of special education and related services would be considered to be a change in placement since it would have a measurable impact on the student's learning.

3. *Under what circumstances can parents be reimbursed for expenses incurred in enrolling their child in a private school?*

If the private school is determined to be an appropriate placement and if the parents successfully prove that the school district failed to offer an appropriate placement, they are entitled to be reimbursed for all reasonable expenses associated with the private placement. However, the parents will not be reimbursed if the school district can show that it had proposed and had the capacity to implement an appropriate program.

4. *What if the parents had enrolled the student in a residential school but it was determined that a private day school was sufficient?*

The school district would be required to reimburse the parents only for the educational component costs of the residential placement. They would not be required to reimburse the parents for room and board expenses.

Figure 5-6

NOTICE TO PARENTS CONCERNING A POSSIBLE CHANGE IN PLACEMENT

Date: _____

Parents: _____

Address: _____

_____

Dear _____ :

     Since recent progress reports indicate that your child _____ is [or is not] making progress in his [or her] current placement the evaluation team will be considering whether a move to a less restrictive [or more restrictive] placement may be warranted at this time. The team will meet on _____ at _____ at the _____ School to consider this question.

     You are invited to attend this meeting and participate in the decision-making process. You may bring any other person (at your own expense) with you to this meeting. If you are unable to attend this meeting, please call this office so that another time may be arranged.

     If the evaluation team determines that a change in placement is warranted and you disagree, you may reject the proposed IEP and request a due process hearing before an impartial hearing officer. If you do dispute the proposed change, your child will remain in his [or her] current educational placement until the dispute is finally settled, unless you and the school district agree to an alternate interim placement or unless your child poses a danger to himself [or herself] or others in his [or her] current placement.

     If you have any questions or concerns, please call this office.

(Special Education Administrator's Signature)

Figure 5-7

LETTER TO PARENTS INFORMING THEM OF A PROPOSED
CHANGE IN PLACEMENT

Date: _____

Parents: _____

Address: _____

_____

Dear _____ :

 At a meeting of the evaluation team on _____ it was determined that your child, _____ 's placement should be changed as
follows: _____ .

 The enclosed Individualized Education Plan outlines the program and services to
be provided in the new placement. The evaluation team has determined that this change is
warranted for the following reasons: _____ .

 In making this determination, the evaluation team considered and rejected the
other options listed below. The reasons why each option was rejected are also listed.

_____

_____

 If you agree with the proposed change in placement, please indicate your acceptance of the enclosed IEP and return it to this office as soon as possible. If you disagree,
you should indicate so by rejecting the proposed IEP. If you do reject the IEP, a due
process hearing will be scheduled to settle the dispute. If you disagree with the findings of
the hearing officer, you may appeal to a higher-level hearing panel and eventually to the
courts.

 If you disagree with the IEP but prefer not to reject it and go to a hearing, you may
contact this office to try to work out an alternative IEP that would be acceptable to you.
You also have the right to postpone a decision while you seek an independent evaluation.
If you wish to have an independent evaluation at school department expense, you must
notify this office in writing and wait for authorization.

 The proposed change in placement will not take place until you accept the IEP. If
you reject the IEP your child will remain in the current placement until the dispute is finally
settled unless you and the school district agree to an alternate interim placement or unless
your child poses a danger to himself [or herself] or others in his [or her] current placement.

 If you have any questions or concerns, please call this office.

(Special Education Administrator's Signature)

128

Figure 5-8

ADMINISTRATOR'S CHECKLIST

Questions to ask prior to making a change in placement:

1. Have the student's parents been provided with written notice of any proposed changes in the student's program? _____

2. Was the notice written in their native language? _____

3. Was the notice written in such a manner that it could be easily understood? ___

4. Did the notice contain a clear description of all due process safeguards available to the parents? _____

5. Did the notice contain clear descriptions of the proposed change, the reasons for the proposed change, and all factors that were considered in making the determination? _____

6. Did the notice contain a clear description of any other options that were considered and the reasons why they were rejected? _____

7. Was the notice provided to the parents a reasonable amount of time prior to the proposed change taking place? _____

8. Did the notice clearly inform the parents of what steps they should take if they disagree with the proposed action? _____

9. Did the notice also comply with all state due process requirements? _____

Questions to ask in determining whether a proposed change in a student's program requires prior due process:

1. After the change has been made, will the program provide substantially the same level and type of services? _____

2. Will the change alter the student's IEP or in any way affect its implementation? _____ Explain _____

3. How will the change affect the student's learning? _____

Chapter 6

WHAT ARE RELATED SERVICES AND WHEN MUST THEY BE PROVIDED?

> *In the absence of a handicap that requires special education, the need for what otherwise might qualify as a related services does not create an obligation under the Act. . . . Only those services necessary to aid a handicapped child to benefit from special education must be provided, regardless how easily a school nurse or layperson could furnish them.*
>
> **Chief Justice Burger**
> *Irving I.S.D.* v. *Tatro*
> **104 S.Ct. 3371 at 3379 (1984)**

The Education for All Handicapped Children Act (EHCA) requires that local school districts must provide handicapped students with a free, appropriate public education, consisting of any needed special education and related services. Related services are defined by the regulations as

> Transportation and such developmental, corrective, and other supportive services as are required to assist a handicapped child to benefit from special education, and includes speech pathology and audiology, psychological services, physical and occupational therapy, recreation, early identification and assessment of disabilities in children, counseling services, and medical services for diagnostic or evaluation purposes. The term also includes school health services, social work services in schools, and parent counseling and training. (34 C.F.R. § 300.13(a))

A comment to this regulation indicates that this list of related services is not exhaustive and could include other services that may be required to assist a handicapped child to benefit from special education.

The EHCA requires that related services need only be provided to a handicapped child who is receiving special education. A comment following the definition of special education in the regulations states

> The definition of "special education" is a particularly important one under these regulations, since a child is not handicapped unless he or she needs special education. . . . The definition of "related services" . . . also depends on this definition, since a related service must be necessary for a child to benefit from special education. Therefore, if a child does not need special education, there can be no "related services," and the child (because not "handicapped") is not covered under the Act. (34 C.F.R. § 300.14)

Litigation has arisen concerning whether or not certain services needed by a handicapped child constituted related services that must be provided by the school district. Although each of the categories of related services listed in the regulations are clearly defined later in the regulations, the precise parameters of each category are sometimes disputed. Also, since the list is not exhaustive, litigation is sometimes brought over whether or not a certain service could be considered a related service under the EHCA. Although there has not been a great amount of litigation in this area, enough decisions have been handed down to provide additional guidance. Issues that have thus far been litigated include the provision of psychotherapy and counseling, health-related services, specialized environments, recreation programs, transportation, and diagnostic assessments.

PSYCHOTHERAPY AND COUNSELING

One of the major disputes that has arisen over the EHCA's related services mandate is whether or not school systems are required to provide and pay for psychotherapy. Counseling services, psychological services, and social work services in the schools are clearly required related services. Psychotherapy, however, does not always fit neatly into one of those categories. In some instances psychotherapy may be considered a medical service, which is not a required related service unless it is for diagnostic purposes. How psychotherapy is classified largely depends on state regulations or licensing requirements. Some states, for example, only allow psychotherapy to be provided by a psychiatrist, while other states allow psychologists to provide psychotherapy. Consequently, whether psychotherapy is or is not a required related service may vary from state to state.

It may be helpful at this point to examine the definitions of counseling services, psychological services, and social work services contained in the regulations.

(2) "Counseling services" means services provided by qualified social workers, psychologists, guidance counselors, or other qualified personnel.

* * *

(8) "Psychological services" include:
(i) Administering psychological and educational tests, and other assessment procedures;
(ii) Interpreting assessment results:
(iii) Obtaining, integrating, and interpreting information about child behavior and conditions related to learning;
(iv) Consulting with other staff members in planning school programs to meet the special needs of children as indicated by psychological tests, interviews, and behavioral evaluations; and
(v) Planning and managing a program of psychological services, including psychological counseling for children and parents.

* * *

(11) "Social work services in schools" include:
(i) Preparing a social or developmental history on a handicapped child;
(ii) Group and individual counseling with the child and family;
(iii) Working with those problems in a child's living situation (home, school, and community) that affect the child's adjustment in school; and
(iv) Mobilizing school and community resources to enable the child to receive maximum benefit from his or her educational program. (34 C.F.R. § 300.13(b))

Defined as Psychological Services

The Supreme Court of Montana in 1979 determined that psychotherapy fell within the classification of psychological services and was thus a required related service, by turning to the dictionary definition of psychotherapy. The student in *In re "A" Family* had been classified as mildly mentally retarded for several years and had been placed in special education classes with some mainstreaming. His parents felt that he was not progressing and that he had periods of emotional regression that made him a danger to himself and others. They had him evaluated at a children's hospital where he was diagnosed as being functionally retarded as a result of severe emotional disturbance. His parents presented the evaluation report to local school officials and requested that the student be placed in a residential school program with intensive psychotherapy. That request was denied by the school system's evaluation team, who determined that the student was mildly mentally retarded, not severely emotionally disturbed. A hearing officer found that the student was severely emotionally disturbed and in need of an intensive psychotherapy program in a residential school. That finding was upheld by a state-level hearing officer and the trial court.

The Montana Supreme Court sustained the finding that the student was severely emotionally disturbed and in need of a residential school. To determine whether psychotherapy was a required related service, the court turned to the dictionary and found that although the word "psychotherapy" was not specifically mentioned in the EHCA or regulations, it fell within the meaning of "psychological services" because Webster's *Seventh New Collegiate Dictionary* defined psychotherapy as treatment of mental or emotional disorders or of related bodily ills by psychological means. Since psychological services are required related services, psychotherapy was also held to be required.

Required If Needed to Benefit from Educational Programs

A federal district court in Illinois held that psychotherapy was a required related service because it could be necessary for some children to benefit from their educational programs. The plaintiffs in *Gary B.* v. *Cronin* attended residential schools because the public schools did not have appropriate special education programs for them. They filed court action seeking declaratory and injunctive relief regarding a rule adopted by the Governor's Purchased Care Review Board that excluded counseling and therapeutic services from being provided as part of special education and related services as mandated by the EHCA.

The court found that the rule on its face appeared to be inconsistent with the definitions of related services in the EHCA and its regulations. The defendants had claimed that psychotherapy was related to mental health not educational needs, but the court held that psychotherapy may be related to mental health, but it may also be required before a child can derive any benefit from education. The court ruled that if psychotherapy was part of the recommended residential placements for the students, it must be provided at public expense.

In *T.G. and P.G.* v. *Board of Education of Piscataway,* the district court ordered the local school district to pay for a handicapped student's psychotherapy. The 11-year-old student had been diagnosed by the local evaluation team as being emotionally disturbed. It was recommended that he be provided with a totally therapeutic environment in a special education day school for the emotionally disturbed. The chosen day school provided psychotherapy in conjunction with an educational program. The psychotherapy was provided by a staff member with a Masters in Social Work degree under the supervision of a psychiatrist. The costs of the psychotherapy were assessed to the student's parents who unsuccessfully sought to have the school system assume that responsibility. The school system refused on the grounds that psychotherapy was not part of the Individualized Educational Program (IEP), that the New Jersey Department of Education had issued a policy statement indicating that psychotherapy was not a related service, and that nothing in the EHCA required it to pay for these services.

The district court disagreed, however, holding that although there is no explicit mention of psychotherapy in either the EHCA or its regulations, the definitions of related services indicated that Congress intended to include it among the services to be provided. The court further found that the therapy was an essential service that allowed the student to benefit from his educational program but was not supplied to maximize his performance. The court also indicated that psychotherapy could appropriately be described as a counseling or psychological service which are specifically included as related services in the EHCA.

Exempted Medical Service or Required Related Service

The district court in *Papacoda* v. *State of Connecticut* found that psychotherapy did not fall within the realm of exempted medical services and was a required related service. The student was an emotionally disturbed youth who had a history of academic and discipline problems. Throughout her education she had received treatment at various mental health facilities. At the beginning of her senior year she entered an in-patient psychiatric program at a local hospital. When she was discharged from that hospital, she entered a private residential school on the advice of hospital staff. The residential school offered a structured and therapeutic environment. The local school system approved the placement; however, the state Department of Education held that the placement was primarily for noneducational reasons and that the school system was not responsible for medical treatment or psychotherapy expenses.

The court found that the student must be placed in a facility with a therapy program because the treatment was necessary to render her educable. The very purpose of the residential placement, according to the court, was to provide an educational program in a therapeutic environment. The court found that the purpose of the EHCA was to provide education for handicapped students regardless of the source or severity of their problems, and thus, placement in a facility whose purpose was to educate students with a particular handicap must be recognized as having an educational purpose. The court ruled that psychological services that were required to assist a handicapped student in benefiting from a special education program were not exempted medical services, but rather, were required related services.

In a similar factual situation in *McKenzie* v. *Jefferson,* the federal district court for the District of Columbia held that the school department was not responsible for paying for the residential component costs of a placement in a psychiatric hospital and school. The court in this situation found that the placement was made primarily for medical reasons and had little to do with the provision of special education. The services required by the student were classified as medical services because they required hospitalization. Since the services were determined to be medical services, the court held that they were not related services.

The courts in *North* v. *District of Columbia* and *Erdman* v. *State of Connecticut,* discussed in the chapter on residential placements, found that the educational, emotional, social, and medical needs of the students were so intertwined that they could not be separated. As a result residential placements were required because all these needs had to be dealt with in an integrated fashion. The courts held that the school systems were required to pay all costs associated with the residential placements. Again, therapeutic services were required as part of the total effort to educate the students and could thus be considered required related services.

The district court in *Darlene L.* v. *Illinois State Board of Education* held that a student with severe behavior disorders was not entitled to have her placement at a psychiatric hospital publicly paid for. An evaluation team had recommended that the student be placed in a private psychiatric hospital but the state Board of Education refused to approve that placement as it considered psychiatric services to be medical services. The student brought suit to compel the department of education to approve and pay for her placement at the hospital. The court found that psychiatrists were licensed physicians and determined that their services were exempted medical services, not required related services. The state Board of Education's decision was upheld.

COUNSELING AND TRAINING FOR PARENTS

One of the required related services specifically mentioned in the EHCA's regulations is parent training and counseling, which is further defined as "Assisting parents in understanding the special needs of their child and providing parents with information about child development" (34 C.F.R. § 300.13(b)(6)). As was seen in the chapter on residential placements, many children require consistency of approach between the school and the home or follow-through in the home of what has been taught in school. These children have often been given residential placements because such consistency and follow-through was not available in the home environment. In many cases a less restrictive environment would be appropriate if the parents could be taught to employ the techniques used in the school environment.

Such was the case in *Stacey G. v. Pasadena Independent School District* where the court ordered the school district to provide parent training and counseling instead of residential placement. The student was a severely handicapped child who had been enrolled in special education programs since the age of 4. Her parents later unilaterally placed her in a private residential school at their own expense, but subsequently requested that the local school district maintain that placement. The school district, feeling that it could provide an appropriate program, refused. A hearing officer denied the request for a residential placement, but ordered the school department to provide a full-year program in conjunction with counseling for the student's parents.

The court found that an appropriate placement for the student would be one that provided a highly structured environment and was designed to meet the student's unique needs. Such a program, the court held, could be provided through a day placement within the district on a year-round basis. To ensure that the highly structured environment was maintained after school hours, the court ordered the school to provide the student's parents with training in behavioral techniques for the management of the student's abnormal behaviors and counseling to help relieve the emotional stress of the burdensome demands placed on them by their daughter's disability.

CONTROLLED ENVIRONMENT

Although no mention of it is made in the EHCA or the regulations, school systems may be required to make alterations to the physical plant to allow a handicapped student to participate fully in and benefit from the educational program. The district court in *Espino* v. *Besteiro* ordered the school district to provide an air-conditioned classroom for a child who needed a temperature-controlled environment. The student was a multihandicapped child who, because of injuries sustained in an accident, was unable to regulate his body temperature. He was a quadraplegic, had damage to his sympathetic nervous system, and may have suffered brain damage in the hypothalamus area. Due to his inability to regulate his body temperature, he needed a temperature-controlled environment at all times.

The student received his kindergarten education in a school for the handicapped that was fully air conditioned. It was felt, however, that the school for the handicapped was too restrictive, so an IEP was proposed that would place him in a regular first grade in an air-conditioned classroom. When the student reported to the first grade, however, it was discovered that school officials had constructed a small air-conditioned Plexiglas cubicle within the classroom for him instead of providing the air-conditioned classroom. He was confined to that cubicle between 25 and 75 percent of the school day, depending on the outside temperature. School officials defended the use of the cubicle, stating that it was more economical and would avoid several potential problems. The student's parents objected to the cubicle; however, the school district was upheld in administrative appeals.

Testimony at the trial indicated that the student was achieving satisfactorily, but was restricted in his ability to socialize and participate in group activities. The court found the cubicle to be a violation of the least restrictive environment mandate of the EHCA because it caused the student to miss out on a great deal of class participation and group interaction which were important to his education. Placement in the cubicle thus deprived the student of a full educational opportunity. The school district was ordered to provide the air-conditioned classroom.

CATHETERIZATION

The EHCA's regulations on related services provide that school health services, which are defined as "services provided by a qualified school nurse or other qualified person" (34 C.F.R. § 300.13 (b)(10)), are required to be provided. Medical services, however, are expressly exempted, unless they are for evaluation purposes. Controversy often develops over whether a certain health-related service falls within the required school health services or the exempted medical services. One such controversial issue is whether local school systems are required to provide catheterization.

The Fifth Circuit Court of Appeals in *Tatro* v. *State of Texas* held that catheterization was a required service under the EHCA. The student was a 4-year-old child who suffered from spina bifida. As a result of this condition, she was unable to empty her bladder voluntarily and had to be catheterized every three to four hours using a procedure known as clean intermittent catheterization (CIC). The student was eligible for participation in the early childhood education program offered by the local school district. The IEP developed for her, however, failed to provide for catheterization. Her parents objected, contending that this failure violated the EHCA and Section 504.

After failing to gain relief in administrative appeals, the student's parents filed court action. The district court ruled that CIC was not a related service required by the EHCA. The court held that to be related, the service had to arise out of the effort to educate. The court also held that failure to provide CIC did not violate Section 504. The student's parents appealed.

The appeals court reversed and remanded, finding that without the provision of CIC, the student could not benefit from the special education program she was entitled to because she could not be physically present in the classroom. CIC was thus held to be a supportive service required to assist the student in benefiting from her special education. The court also found that to exclude the student by not providing CIC would violate Section 504. The court also helped to clarify where a school system could draw the line between required health services and exempted medical services by indicating that any health-related activities that must be performed by a licensed physician were excluded. Services, such as CIC, that could be performed by a school nurse or other trained health personnel were required. Also, the court indicated that a life support service would not be a related service if it did not have to be provided during school hours. On remand the district court ruled that the student was entitled to have her IEP modified to include the provision of CIC. The appeals court affirmed.

Eventually the case went to the U.S. Supreme Court, where the decision that catheterization was a required related service was affirmed. In its opinion the Court stated that services like CIC that permit a child to remain at school during the day are no less related to the effort to educate than are services that allow the child to reach, enter, or exit the school. The Court noted that school nurses have long been a part of the public schools and that it was reasonable to assume that Congress did not intend to exclude their services as medical services.

The Court also provided further clarification of when related services must be provided to a handicapped student by holding that in the absence of a handicap that requires special education the need for related services does not create an obligation under the EHCA and that only those services that are necessary to aid a handicapped child in benefiting from special education must be provided. This holds true regardless of how easily a school nurse or trained layperson could provide the services.

In *Tokarcik* v. *Forest Hills School District* the Court of Appeals for the Third Circuit also held that CIC fell within the definition of required related services. The student in this case also was unable to empty her bladder voluntarily because of spina bifida and required CIC approximately every four hours. The local school system refused to provide CIC so that family members had to go to the school each day to provide it. As a result of the school district's refusal to provide CIC, the parties were unable to agree on an IEP. The parents were unsuccessful in administrative appeals and filed court action. The district court, finding *Tatro* persuasive, ordered the school system to provide CIC.

On appeal, the circuit court found that CIC required no more than a few minutes a day, could be performed by a school nurse or health aide, and would cost little or nothing. In holding that CIC was a required related service, the court noted that the student could be predominantly educated in a regular classroom but that such a placement had to be physically accessible to her. That could be accomplished through the provision of transportation and reasonable health services. The U.S. Supreme Court declined to review the case.

OTHER HEALTH NEEDS

As mentioned in the preceding section, the EHCA requires that school health services must be provided as a related service, but medical services need not be. It is sometimes difficult to draw the line between a health service and a medical service. In the catheterization cases, the courts determined that CIC was a health service rather than a medical service because it could be provided by a school nurse.

The district court in *Department of Education, State of Hawaii* v. *Katherine D.* used a similar reasoning in finding that the school department was required to provide health services to a handicapped child who wore a tracheotomy tube. The student suffered from cystic fibrosis and tracheomalacia and required the tube to breathe and expel mucus from her lungs. Occasionally the tube became dislodged and had to be reinserted. Mucus also had to be suctioned from her lungs, and she needed to have medication administered. These procedures could be performed by a school nurse or trained layperson.

The student had attended a private child care facility and kindergarten where her mother was employed and received speech therapy at home. While at this school, her mother attended to her health needs. Her parents had requested that she attend the public schools and receive speech therapy there, however, they would allow this only if a trained person were available to attend to her health needs. The Department of Education offered a homebound placement that was rejected by her parents. A hearing officer ruled that the department failed to provide an appropriate education in that home instruction was not the least restrictive environment. An IEP was later offered calling for a public school placement; however, that plan never materialized because of administrative difficulties in training school personnel to attend to the student's health needs.

The district court found that the home instruction program clearly did not satisfy the concept of least restrictive environment. The court further found that the health services needed by the student fell within the definition of related services as they could be provided by the school health services or trained laypersons. The court held that the Department of Education was required either to provide those services or to pay the student's expenses at a private school that would provide them.

Whether or not a school district is required to pay for health services that may be performed by a nonphysician but in actuality are provided by a physician was the issue in *Max M.* v. *Thompson*. The student in this case received psychotherapy from a psychiatrist, but state law allowed nonpsychiatric professionals to provide this service. The court noted that under the EHCA health services that *must* be performed by a physician were not required related services but health services that may be provided by a nonphysician were required. The court held that this did not mean that services that may be performed by a nonphysician, but in actuality were provided by a physician were excluded. However, in such an instance, the court held, a school district could be required to fund such services only to the extent of the costs of their being performed by a nonphysician.

RECREATION PROGRAMS

The EHCA's regulations provide that recreation is one of the required related services that must be provided to handicapped children, if needed to allow them to benefit from their educational programs. Recreation is further defined as including

(i) Assessment of leisure function;
(ii) Therapeutic recreation services;
(iii) Recreation programs in school and community agencies; and
(iv) Leisure education. (34 C.F.R. § 300.13 (b)(9))

The EHCA's regulations also provide that handicapped students are to be provided with "non-academic and extracurricular services and activities in such a manner as is necessary to afford handicapped children an equal opportunity for participation in those services and activities" (34 C.F.R. § 300.306(a)). Under these regulations handicapped students should be provided with access to a school system's extracurricular programs, if appropriate, or should have extracurricular programs developed in which they may participate.

The district court in *Rettig* v. *Kent City School District* held that under the EHCA's regulations a school system was required to provide after-school activities for a handicapped student on an equal basis with nonhandicapped students. The student in this case was a 16-year-old autistic and mentally retarded youth who functioned on a preacademic level. The student's parents had challenged the adequacy of his IEP on several points. The court found that the IEP was basically appropriate but that the school system had failed to provide any after-school activities for the student as it did for nonhandicapped students. The court ordered the school system to provide the student with one hour of extracurricular activities per week. That decision has, however, been overturned by the appeals court. The appeals court held that the EHCA regulation requiring that a handicapped student be provided with an "equal opportunity" to participate in extracurricular activities conflicted with the U.S. Supreme Court's *Rowley* decision that the EHCA only creates a basic floor of opportunity for handicapped children. The Supreme Court allowed the appeals court decision to stand by declining to review its decision.

As it now stands, school districts cannot deny a handicapped student the right to participate in the regular extracurricular program if that student is able to meet all the normal criteria for participation. Such denial would amount to discrimination under Section 504. School systems are not required to develop extracurricular programs specifically for handicapped students unless it can be shown that such a program is necessary to assist an individual student in meeting the objectives of his or her IEP.

The Court of Appeals for the Sixth Circuit affirmed the district court's finding that a handicapped student needed a six-week summer enrichment and instructional program in *Birmingham and Lamphere School District* v. *Superintendent of Public Instruction*. The student was a 14-year-old autistic youth. For several years he had attended a public school program for children with severe behavior and language disorders that had included a summer school session. That summer school program, which had been partially federally funded, was eliminated after federal aid was reduced. The student's mother contested the elimination. The hearing officer determined that the student required a summer program of instruction and enrichment, based in part on testimony by all witnesses that such a program was needed by the student. The district court found that sufficient evidence existed for the hearing officer to rule as he did and upheld.

The appeals court, in affirming the district court, found that the student needed a program which involved outdoor activities for him to receive an appropriate education. The court held that the proposed summer enrichment activities fell within the broad definitions of special education and related services in the EHCA since special education specifically included instruction in physical education and related services specifically included such supportive services as recreation.

TRANSPORTATION

The EHCA also requires school districts to provide handicapped students with transportation as a related service. A student cannot benefit from a special education program if he or she is unable to get to that program. The district court in *Hurry* v. *Jones* affirmed the transportation mandate by awarding damages to the parents of a handicapped student after the school district failed to provide appropriate transportation. The student was physically handicapped and had received special education and related services for several years. After he had gained some weight he was denied assistance in getting from his house to the school bus. He was unable to get to the school bus without this assistance. His father transported him to school for the next two years; however, due to a change in personal circumstances, his father was not able to continue transporting him. The student did not attend school for approximately 18 months due to a lack of transportation. Several attempts to get the school department to resolve the transportation problem, including requests for due process hearings, failed. The student's parents then filed court action. A satisfactory solution was worked out; however, the student's parents still sought damages.

The court found that transportation was the full responsibility of the school department as it was a related service under the EHCA. The court also found that the school department had failed to solve the transportation problem for an inexcusably long time, even though the statutes and regulations clearly defined their responsibility to do so. The court awarded the student's parents compensation for the costs they incurred in transporting him to school. The First Circuit Court of Appeals affirmed the judgment of the district court.

The *Hurry* decision also indicates that transportation involves more than simply providing bus service. The transportation provided must be appropriate and must enable the student to get safely to the special education program with a minimum of inconvenience. In some instances the transportation mandate may require that the handicapped student be transported from the house to the bus and from the bus to the classroom. In the *Pinkerton* v. *Moye* case, the district court ordered the school department to provide some alternative transportation arrangements for a child whose transportation to school took more than 30 minutes even though she lived only 6 miles from school. It took more than 30 minutes because of transfers. The court found transportation to be a related service and ordered the school department to pay for a more appropriate arrangement.

The term "transportation" in the related services mandate does not include publicly supported trips home for a residential school student for therapeutic visits according to a Florida appeals court in *Cohen* v. *School Board of Dade County*. The student attended an out-of-state facility for students with severe psychiatric and emotional problems. One of the goals of the student's IEP was for him to improve his relationship with family members. The student's parents requested reimbursement from the school board for several therapeutic visits between the student and family members. The requested expenses included airfare, hotels, and meals. The school board agreed to fund only three round trips per year made by the student between his home and school. The student and his parents claimed that funding for all therapeutic trips was required under the related services mandate. The school board contended that it was only required to provide usual transportation services. A hearing officer agreed with the school board.

The court also agreed with the school board and held that the student was entitled to transportation to the residential facility to receive an education there, but was not entitled to additional trips home at public expense for therapeutic purposes. The court noted that although improved family relations was desirable, the primary goal was to educate the student and that the EHCA did not require school districts to satisfy all the particular needs of each handicapped child.

A school district may make minor adjustments to a student's transportation plan without first providing due process according to a Third Circuit Court of Appeals decision in *DeLeon* v. *Susquehanna Community School District*. The school district had assigned the student to a new transportation run which added approximately ten minutes to his return trip home. The student's parents claimed that the change in mode of transportation was a change in placement requiring due process under the EHCA; however, the district court denied a preliminary injunction. The appeals court affirmed, holding that the important element in determining whether a change in placement had taken place was whether the change was likely to affect the student's learning in some significant way. The court found that a minor change would not affect even a severely handicapped student's learning. However, the court did indicate that under some circumstances transportation could have an effect on a student's learning.

DIAGNOSTIC SERVICES

The diagnosis and evaluation of handicapped students is a vital component of the entire special education process. Proper diagnosis is mandatory to the identification of handicaps in the first place and also necessary to develop a proper IEP. The definition of related services makes it clear that the assessment and identification of handicapped children is a required related service. It is also clear that medical evaluations can be part of that process. Since diagnostic services are required related services, they must be provided at no cost to the student's parents.

Two interesting issues often arise in regard to medical evaluations of a handicapped student conducted as part of the entire special education evaluation process. The first issue is whether or not the student's parents can be required to use their private medical insurance coverage to pay for such evaluations. The second issue concerns whether or not the school district can be required to pay for subsequent medical evaluations ordered by the physician conducting the initial medical evaluation.

Each of these issues was squarely dealt with by the district court in *Seals* v. *Loftis*. The student in this case suffered from a seizure disorder, visual difficulty, and learning disabilities. After his behavior had changed and his school performance had deteriorated the school's evaluation team met to consider his situation. As part of its assessment the team recommended a pediatric evaluation. The pediatrician referred the student for a neurological evaluation, and the neurologist subsequently referred him to a psychologist. The evaluation team had not requested the latter two evaluations but did make use of them. A dispute arose over who was financially responsible for the neurological and psychological exams. A hearing officer ruled that the parents had to use their insurance coverage to pay for all the evaluations and that the school department had to pay all costs not covered by the insurance. Both parties appealed.

The district court first found that the services rendered by the neurologist and psychologist easily fit within the EHCA's definition of related services. Since the student's medical and educational needs were intertwined and these services were necessary to help him benefit from his special education the school department was responsible for payment. The court further found that the EHCA regulations indicate that an insurance carrier is not relieved from any obligation to pay for services provided to a handicapped child. However, the EHCA also states that all services provided under the act must be free of cost to the child's parents. The court concluded that a handicapped child's parents couldn't be required to use their medical insurance if the utilization of that insurance would incur a financial cost to them. In the present case the parents' lifetime benefits for psychological services would be reduced by the amount of the current bill under the terms of their insurance plan, so the court held that they could not be required to use their insurance to pay for the psychological evaluation. However, since no such limitation existed for neurological services, they were required to use their insurance for that evaluation.

REFERENCES

Birmingham and Lamphere School District v. *Superintendent of Public Instruction,* 554 EHLR 318 (1982).

Cohen v. *School Board of Dade County,* 450 S.2d 1238 (1984).

Darlene L. v. *Illinois Board of Education,* 568 F.Supp. 1340 (1983).

DeLeon v. *Susquehanna Community School District,* 747 F.2d 149 (1984).

Department of Education, State of Hawaii v. *Katherine D.,* 531 F.Supp. 517 (1982).

Erdman v. *State of Connecticut,* 552 EHLR 218 (1980).

Espino v. *Besteiro,* 520 F.Supp. 905 (1981).

Gary B. v. *Cronin,* 542 F.Supp. 102 (1980).

Hurry v. *Jones,* 560 F.Supp. 500 (1983), aff'd in part 734 F.2d 879 (1984).

In re "A" Family, 602 P.2d 157 (1983).

Irving I.S.D. v. *Tatro,* 104 S.Ct. 3371 (1984).

Max M. v. *Thompson,* 566 F.Supp. 1330 (1983), rehearing 592 F.Supp. 1437 (1984).

North v. *District of Columbia Board of Education,* 471 F.Supp. 136 (1979).

Papacoda v. *State of Connecticut,* 528 F.Supp. 68 (1981).

Pinkerton v. *Moye,* 509 F.Supp. 107 (1981).

Rettig v. *Kent City School District,* 539 F.Supp. 768 (1981), aff'd in part vac'd and rem'd in part 720 F.2d 463 (1983), rev'd 788 F.2d 328 (1986), cert. den'd 106 S.Ct. 3297 (1986).

Seals v. *Loftis,* 614 F.Supp. 302 (1985).

Stacey G. v. *Pasadena Independent School District,* 547 F.Supp. 61 (1982).

Tatro v. *State of Texas,* 481 F.Supp. 1224 (1979), rev'd 625 F.2d 557 (1980), on rem'd 516 F.Supp. 968 (1981), aff'd 703 F.2d 823 (1983), aff'd sub. nom. 104 S.Ct. 3371 (1984).

T.G. and P.G. v. *Board of Education of Piscataway,* 576 F.Supp. 420 (1983).

Tokarcik v. *Forest Hills School District,* 665 F.2d 443 (1981).

Figure 6-1

LEADING CASES

Irving I.S.D. v. *Tatro,* 104 S.Ct. 3371 (1984)

Catheterization is a required related service under the EHCA as it enables the student to remain in school and thus benefit from special education. Only services necessary to help a handicapped child benefit from special education must be provided. Only handicapped students receiving special education are entitled to related services. Life support that does not have to be performed during school hours is not required.

Hurry v. *Jones,* 734 F.2d 879 (1984)

Transportation, including transporting the student between the house or school and the vehicle, is a required related service. The transportation plan developed must be appropriate.

T.G. and P.G. v. *Board of Education,* 576 F.Supp. 420 (1983)

Psychotherapy must be provided as a related service if it is an essential service that allows a handicapped student to benefit from his educational program.

Darlene L. v. *Illinois,* 568 F.Supp. 1340 (1983)

Psychiatrists are licensed physicians whose services are appropriately designated as medical treatment. Psychiatric services are not related services.

Seals v. *Loftis,* 614 F.Supp. 302 (1985)

A handicapped student's parents may be required to use their private medical insurance coverage to pay for diagnostic medical examinations as long as such use does not incur a financial cost to them. The school district must pay for any charges not covered by the insurance policy.

Figure 6-2

RIGHTS TO RECEIVE RELATED SERVICES

1. The EHCA and its implementing regulations require school districts to provide related, or supportive, services to a handicapped child if these services are needed by the child to benefit from his educational program. Many of these related services are necessary for the child to even gain access to the special education program while others allow the child to progress in or gain benefit from the program.

2. Only handicapped children receiving special education services are entitled under the EHCA to receive related services.

3. Only those services that are necessary for the child to benefit from the special education program are required.

4. Health services that must be performed by a licensed physician are exempt.

5. Life support services that do not have to be performed during school hours are not required.

6. Any required related services provided must be appropriate to the child's needs.

7. All related services must be provided without cost to the student's parents.

Figure 6-3

DETERMINING THE NEED TO PROVIDE RELATED SERVICES

Determining the need for related services is similar to determining the need for special education services. Such determination should be made by the school district's evaluation team based on information obtained through a multidisciplinary evaluation.
A handicapped student may need related services when

> Such services are necessary for the student to gain access to the special education program.
>
> Such services are necessary for the student to remain in the special education program.
>
> The student would not make meaningful progress toward the goals and objectives of the IEP without such services.
>
> The student's various needs are so intertwined that an integrated program of special education and related services is necessary.
>
> The effort to educate depends on the resolution of other needs.

Figure 6-4

MEDICAL AND HEALTH SERVICES
(Differentiation)

Medical services are those health-related services that by law can only be provided by a licensed physician. Medical services are not required related services except for medical services that are provided for diagnostic purposes as part of a special education evaluation.

Health services are those health-related services that can be performed by a school nurse, trained health aide, or other trained layperson. Those services that are typically provided as part of a school district's school nursing services fall into this category. Other health or medical procedures are also included as long as they do not, by law, have to be provided by a licensed physician.

Figure 6-5

LIST OF REQUIRED RELATED SERVICES

1. Transportation
2. Speech pathology
3. Audiology
4. Psychological services
5. Physical therapy
6. Occupational therapy
7. Recreation
8. Medical services for diagnostic purposes
9. Counseling services
10. Early identification of handicapping conditions
11. Diagnostic, assessment, and evaluation services
12. School health services
13. Social work services
14. Parent counseling and training
15. Such other developmental, corrective, or supportive services as may be needed

Figure 6-6

QUESTIONS ADMINISTRATORS OFTEN ASK ABOUT RELATED SERVICES

1. *Psychological and counseling services are required related services, but what about psychotherapy? Isn't that a medical service?*

It depends on state laws governing the practice of medicine. Some states allow psychologists, social workers, and counselors to provide psychotherapy. In these states it would be classified as a required related service. In other states the law requires that only psychiatrists, who are usually licensed physicians, can provide psychotherapy services. In those states it would be classified as an exempt medical service.

2. *Exactly what transportation services are required?*

School districts must provide handicapped students with transportation to their special education programs if those programs are located such a distance from the student's home that walking to them is not feasible or if the student's handicap makes it impossible or not feasible for the student to walk. This includes transportation to and from residential schools. It also includes assisting students to and from the transportation vehicle. The transportation plan must be as convenient as possible and must be appropriate to the student's special needs. Transportation is required when its provision is necessary for the student to gain access to the special education program.

3. *Why are schools required to provide health services? Shouldn't this be the parents' responsibility?*

Again, the word access is the key. One of the major goals of the EHCA was to provide handicapped students with access to publicly supported special education programs. Many students could not be physically present in the program without supportive health services. Health services can be as important as transportation, wheelchair ramps, and elevators in terms of making school programs accessible to handicapped children.

4. *Does the fact that a person is a licensed physician prevent that person from providing nondiagnostic related services?*

No, as long as the service provided is one that may be performed by a nonphysician. The fact that the service provider is also a licensed physician does not exempt that person or reclassify the service as an exempted medical service. However, the school district is only required to pay the normal and customary costs of that service. If the physician's fees are higher, they do not have to fund the higher amount in full.

Figure 6-7

REQUEST FOR SPECIALIST ASSESSMENT

Date:_____

Student:_____D.O.B._____

School:_____ Grade:_____

Parents:_____

Address:_____

The evaluation team has determined that the specialist assessment indicated below is necessary to diagnose properly and place the above-named student.

Type of Assessment:

Recommended Evaluator or Facility:

Specific Questions to Be Addressed by the Specialist:

1.

2.

3.

4.

5.

Special Education Administrator's Approval_____

Date:_____

Parental Consent
I consent to the specialist assessment outlined above. I also authorize the school department to communicate with the specialist regarding the requested assessment.

_____ Date:_____
(Parent's Signature)

Parent's medical insurance coverage_____
(The above request is to be sent to the Special Education Administrator from the Evaluation Team.)

Figure 6-8

LETTER AUTHORIZING SPECIALIST ASSESSMENT

Date:_____

Specialist:_____

Address:_____

_____

Dear_____:

      The school district evaluation team has determined that a specialist assessment is needed on_____.
You are authorized to conduct that assessment as outlined on the attached "Request for Specialist Assessment" form.

      The school district will pay the cost of any authorized assessment not covered by the parents' private medical insurance. Payment is contingent upon receipt of your report by this office.

      If you have any questions regarding the requested specialist assessment you may contact the evaluation team chairperson,

_____ , at _____ .

(Special Education
Administrator's Signature)

Note: This above letter may be sent to pediatricians, neurologists, audiologists, psychologists, and so on.

Figure 6-9

MEDICAL EVALUATION SUMMARY

Date: _____

Student: _____ D.O.B. _____

School: _____ Grade: _____

Parents: _____

Address: _____

1. *Medical History.* Please list any chronic illnesses, hospitalizations, injuries, anomalies, and other pertinent information.

2. *Physical Examination.* Please list any abnormalities or areas of concern noted during the physical exam.

3. *Medications.* Please list any medications currently being administered to the child.

4. *Physical Constraints.* Please indicate any physical or medical constraints on the child's learning.

Examining Physician: _____

Figure 6-10

LETTER AUTHORIZING PSYCHOTHERAPY

Psychotherapist: _____

Address: _____

_____

Dear _____ :

      The school district's evaluation team has determined that _____ is in need of psychotherapy to benefit from the special education program. You are hereby authorized to provide those services as outlined in the enclosed IEP.

      The school department will pay for all costs of the psychotherapy not covered by the parents' private medical insurance. Bills may be sent directly to me at the above address.

      We request that you provide us with quarterly progress reports on the student's social/emotional development.

                                               (Special Education
                                             Administrator's Signature)

Figure 6-11

TRANSPORTATION PLAN

The evaluation team has determined that_____
will require special transportation as outlined below.

Home address:_____

School address:_____

Phone number where parent can be reached during the day:_____

Contact person at school:_____

Morning pickup time:_____ Arrival at school:_____

Afternoon pickup time:_____ Arrival at home:_____

Type of vehicle to be used:

Special equipment needed:

Other special requirements:

Is an aide on the vehicle required?

Will the student need assistance getting on and off the vehicle?

What type of assistance will be required?

Will the student need assistance between the vehicle and the buildings?

What type of assistance?

Figure 6-12

ADMINISTRATOR'S CHECKLIST

Questions to ask before determining the need for related services:

1. Is the student in a special education program?_____

2. Does the service have to be provided during the school day or could it be provided outside of school?_____

3. How will the provision of this service effect the student's learning and the achievement of the IEP's objectives?_____

   _____

4. Will the student benefit from the special education program without this service? _____ Explain:_____

5. What factors from the multidisciplinary special education evaluation indicate the need for a related service?_____

   _____

6. Is the service necessary or is it just beneficial?_____

7. Is this service necessary for the student to gain meaningful access to the educational program?_____
   Explain:_____

8. Is this service necessary for some of the goals of the IEP to be attained?_____
   Explain:_____

9. Is this service a necessary component of the student's total special education program?_____
   Explain:_____

Chapter 7

WHAT ARE THE SPECIAL REQUIREMENTS FOR DISCIPLINING HANDICAPPED STUDENTS?

> *An examination of the Act reveals nothing that would deprive school officials of their ever-present right to maintain discipline.*
>
> **Senior Circuit Judge Simpson**
> *Victoria L.* **v.** *District School Board*
> **552 EHLR 265 at 266 (1980)**

The disciplining of handicapped students in the public schools has been one of the more controversial issues under the Education for All Handicapped Children Act (EHCA). The act itself makes little mention of disciplinary procedures; however, many of its provisions have implications in regard to certain disciplinary actions. The EHCA requires that all handicapped children receive a free appropriate education in the least restrictive environment. The term "all handicapped children" includes children who may have behavior disorders. Excluding such children from the public schools, for whatever reason, would be a violation of their rights under the EHCA.

Suspensions and expulsions have long been used by school officials as disciplinary tools. A suspension is generally considered to be a short-term exclusion from school and an expulsion is generally considered to be a long-term exclusion. The U.S. Supreme Court in *Goss* v. *Lopez* has held that students may be suspended and expelled from the public schools as long as they are afforded certain due process safeguards. Suspensions and expulsions, however, are somewhat more complicated when the student involved is handicapped, especially since all educational services come to a halt during such a forced absence. Under the EHCA, a handicapped student has certain rights that place additional requirements on school officials when disciplining such a student.

EXPULSION IS A CHANGE IN PLACEMENT

In *Stuart* v. *Nappi*, a case decided shortly after the EHCA was implemented, the district court held that an expulsion constituted a change in placement and was inconsistent with the procedures for a change in placement enumerated in the EHCA. The student was in her junior year at the local high school and had serious academic and emotional difficulties. She had been diagnosed as having severe learning disabilities and had attended special education classes for several years. However, in her sophomore year, she stopped attending those classes and began wandering the halls. She was also involved in several incidents that resulted in disciplinary conferences. Following those conferences her behavior improved, but she still did not attend her special education classes. School officials were aware of this, but failed to take any action to correct the situation. At the beginning of her junior year, the student was involved in a schoolwide disturbance for which she was given a ten-day suspension. The superintendent later recommended that she be expelled for the remainder of the school year. The student filed a court action claiming that the EHCA prohibited the expulsion of a handicapped student.

The district court held that the EHCA prohibited disciplinary measures which resulted in a change in a handicapped student's placement, but permitted whatever measures were necessary to deal with a student who appeared to be dangerous. Since the student in this case did not appear to be dangerous to either herself or others, her expulsion was held to be inappropriate. The court reasoned that if schools were permitted to expel handicapped students, the right to an appropriate education in the least restrictive environment could be circumvented. An expulsion, according to the court, resulted in a change in placement, restricted the availability of alternate placements, and was also inconsistent with the EHCA's procedures for changing the placement of disruptive students to more restrictive settings.

The court further commented that handicapped children were not immune to discipline and that they were not entitled to participate in programs if their behavior disrupted the educational process for others. The court held that school officials could temporarily suspend disruptive students or place them in a more restrictive program by following the EHCA's change in placement procedures.

The district court in *Sherry* v. *New York State Education Department* held that a student's expulsion from a state school for blind children violated both the EHCA and Section 504. The student was legally blind and deaf and suffered from brain damage and an emotional disorder that caused her to be self-abusive. She was enrolled in a state school for blind children but shortly thereafter had to be hospitalized because of injuries resulting from her self-abusive behavior. Later, her mother was informed that the school did not have sufficient staff to supervise the student and that it would not be possible for her to return to the school until either her condition improved or the school hired more staff. A temporary program was provided by the local school system, but the student's mother requested that she be reinstated in the school for the blind. The school consequently expelled the student, stating that she would be reinstated when it appeared to be in her and the school's best interests. The student's mother filed court action seeking her daughter's reinstatement and an order requiring the school to comply with the procedural provisions of the EHCA.

The court found that the student's expulsion amounted to a change in placement which required specific procedural safeguards under the EHCA. The school's failure to provide those safeguards, including maintaining her in her then current educational placement and providing her with a hearing before an impartial hearing officer, violated the EHCA according to the court. The court further held that her expulsion also violated Section 504 in that the expulsion was caused by the failure of the school to provide the necessary supervisory personnel. The court found that a lack of staff could not justify a failure to provide an appropriate education and that the school had an obligation to provide the supervisory staff needed to allow the student to benefit from their services. The school was ordered to develop procedures that complied with the procedural protections of the EHCA.

In 1983 the Supreme Court of Nebraska held that sending home a student with instructions that he could not return amounted to an expulsion and was in violation of the EHCA in *Adams Central School District* v. *Deist.* The student, who was autistic and mentally retarded, had attended a school for the trainable mentally retarded. When his behavior became destructive and disruptive, he was sent home and his parents were informed that he could not return. When the student's parents and the school system were unable to agree on an appropriate alternative placement, his parents unilaterally placed him in a private program and filed suit to recover all costs.

The state high court ruled that the student's removal from school constituted an expulsion since his parents were informed that he could not return. The court found the expulsion to be improper since the EHCA's change in placement procedures was not followed and since no determination was made as to whether his behavior was related to his handicap. The student's parents were awarded reimbursement for costs incurred in obtaining alternate educational services. The U.S. Supreme Court let the decision stand by declining to review the case.

EHCA PROCESS REPLACES NORMAL DISCIPLINARY PROCEDURES

The district court in *P-1* v. *Shedd* approved a consent decree negotiated by the parties that provided for special disciplinary procedures for handicapped students: (1) No handicapped child was to be removed more than six times in a school year or twice in a week unless the removal was allowed by the Individualized Educational Program (IEP). (2) No child referred for an evaluation or identified as handicapped was to be suspended for more than 15 days or expelled without convening the evaluation team to determine the appropriateness of the child's placement. (3) The special education administrative process was to replace the usual disciplinary process for handicapped children. (4) The evaluation team was to be convened within one week of an emergency suspension, and (5) Any child who was suspended for 15 days or more or who was expelled was to be referred for an evaluation, and if the child was found to be handicapped, the special education administrative process would replace the usual disciplinary process. These procedures basically provided that discipline for handicapped students must be carried out in conformity with the EHCA.

Late in 1979 the Supreme Court of Iowa held that a handicapped student could be expelled, but only as a last resort and only if certain procedures were followed. In *Southwest Warren Community School District* v. *Department of Public Instruction* the superintendent of schools had recommended that a special education student be expelled for the remainder of the school year for habitual violations of school rules. Although the student was a special needs student, regular expulsion procedures were to be used. The student's mother appealed to the Department of Public Instruction who ruled that the school district lacked authority to expel a special education student. The school district appealed to the state district court and prevailed in the action.

The state supreme court found that the state legislature had given schools the right to deny admission to children whose presence could be injurious to other children or to the school. It also gave them the power to expel students who violated the rules or whose presence was detrimental to the school's best interests. However, the state special education laws required special procedures before a special education student could be expelled. Those procedures, according to the court, included reevaluation of the student by the evaluation team, a report and recommendation by that team, and after a full hearing, a determination by the school board of whether an alternative placement would meet the needs of the student and the district. The court ruled that an expulsion could be resorted to only when no other reasonable placement was available. The court further held that the school district would have been in error if it had used normal expulsion proceedings with a handicapped student.

The district court in *Blue* v. *New Haven Board of Education* held that a handicapped student could not be expelled from the public schools. The student was a 16-year-old seriously emotionally disturbed youth who had been attending a public school special education program with mainstreaming in several regular education classes. In spite of his special education program, he still experienced some difficulties. He was suspended on two occasions for disruptive behavior and received poor grades in some of his mainstream classes. These difficulties culminated in a suspension and a recommendation for expulsion after an altercation with one of his teachers. While awaiting the expulsion hearing, the student was provided with homebound instruction. The evaluation team also met during that time and recommended that, if the student was expelled, he then attend a private school or continue on homebound instruction. The evaluation team further concluded that, even if the student was not expelled, the private school placement was the most appropriate placement for the remainder of that year. The student requested a due process hearing to review that recommendation and the expulsion recommendation. Court action was also filed seeking a preliminary injunction to prevent the expulsion.

In granting the preliminary injunction, the court noted that this case was similar to the *Stuart* case. The court held that any attempt to expel the student from school or change his educational placement during the pendency of his special education complaint would violate the EHCA's status quo provision. Since the school district had already excluded him for more than ten consecutive days, and under state law such an exclusion amounted to an expulsion, the court concluded that the student was being denied his EHCA right to remain in his then current educational placement pending resolution of his complaint.

The court further held that the student was entitled to have his educational placement changed only by the evaluation team and not through the school's normal disciplinary procedures. The court also ruled that expulsion would violate the student's right to education in the least restrictive environment as it would limit the consideration of placement alternatives to programs that may be more restrictive than was necessary. The court stated that the EHCA could not be circumvented by use of normal disciplinary procedures.

MANIFESTATION OF HANDICAP DOCTRINE

The district court in *Doe* v. *Koger* ruled that a handicapped student could not be expelled if the disruptive behavior was caused by the handicap, but a school district could expel a student if there was no relationship between the behavior and the student's handicap. In this case the student attended the public schools classified as a mildly mentally handicapped student. He was suspended for disciplinary reasons, and the principal recommended that he be expelled for the remainder of the year. After an expulsion hearing, he was formally expelled but the expulsion was appealed. He was placed in an interim education program pending the outcome of the proceedings.

The district court found that the EHCA clearly intended to limit a school's right to expel a handicapped student. The court held that schools could not expel a handicapped student whose offensive behavior was caused by the handicap, but could only transfer the student to an appropriate, more restrictive environment. The court did state, however, that not all expulsions of handicapped children were prohibited by the EHCA. If the disruptive behavior was not caused by the student's handicap, the student could be expelled. This determination, however, had to be made through the EHCA's change in placement procedures.

The court also extended the expulsion prohibition to informal expulsions, such as indefinite suspensions. The court further indicated that a handicapped student could be suspended only if the school were unable to place the student in a more restrictive environment and only until such time as the student may be appropriately placed.

The Court of Appeals for the Fifth Circuit ruled that the expulsion of a handicapped student constituted a change in placement under both the EHCA and Section 504. In *S-1* v. *Turlington* a number of students were expelled from a local high school for a period of almost two full school years. The students, who were classified as mildly or educably mentally retarded, were expelled for conduct that ranged from sexual acts to willful defiance of authority. Each student was given the normal due process protections prior to the expulsions. One student requested, and was granted, a hearing to determine if his misconduct was a manifestation of his handicap. The superintendent determined that it was not since the student was not classified as emotionally disturbed. The district court ruled that the students were denied their rights to a free appropriate public education under the EHCA as a result of the expulsions.

In affirming the district court, the appeals court stated that in deciding the issue of whether an expulsion constitutes a change in placement, the statutes should be interpreted liberally in favor of providing a free appropriate public education to handicapped students. The court held that a termination of educational services caused by an expulsion was a change in placement sufficient to invoke the procedural protections of the EHCA. The court further held that the determination of whether or not the misconduct was a manifestation of the student's handicap had to be made by a specialized and knowledgeable group of persons.

The court also held that the expulsion of students was a proper disciplinary measure under both the EHCA and Section 504 if the proper procedures were used and under the proper circumstances. The court ruled, however, that the complete cessation of educational services during an expulsion period was not authorized.

The court further held that in view of the remedial nature of the EHCA and Section 504, the burden was on local and state officials to raise the question of whether or not the student's handicap caused the offensive behavior. The U.S. Supreme Court declined to review the case and allowed the decision to stand.

The Court of Appeals for the Sixth Circuit adopted the analysis of the Fifth Circuit's *Turlington* decision in ruling that the expulsion of a handicapped student constituted a change in placement. The student in *Kaelin* v. *Grubbs* was a 15-year-old ninth grader who had been identified as handicapped and placed in classes for the educable mentally handicapped since kindergarten. He was suspended and later expelled from school for defying the authority of his teacher, destroying a worksheet, refusing to complete assignments, breaking a coffee cup, and assaulting the teacher. In expelling him the school board did not consider the relationship between his handicap and his misbehavior, or consult with the school's evaluation team. His request for a due process hearing under the EHCA was denied and court action followed. The district court held that expulsion was a change in placement requiring the due process safeguards of the EHCA. The school district appealed.

The appeals court adopted the *Turlington* analysis and also held that an expulsion from school was a change in placement within the meaning of the EHCA. The court did note, however, that a handicapped student was not totally immune from a school's disciplinary process. According to the court, a handicapped student could be temporarily suspended, or even expelled in appropriate circumstances, if the proper procedures were followed. The court held that a handicapped child could not be expelled, however, if the child's misbehavior was a manifestation of his handicap. In affirming the district court, the appeals court noted

> [H]andicapped children can generally be disciplined in the same manner as non-handicapped children. Only the procedural safeguards for removing a handicapped child are affected by our conclusion that an expulsion is a change in educational placement within the meaning of the Handicapped Children's Act. (P. 602)

The Court of Appeals for the Fourth Circuit upheld a district ruling that a handicapped student could not be expelled since a relationship existed between his handicap and his misconduct in *School Board of the County of Prince William* v. *Malone*. Here a learning disabled student who had been receiving special education services in a self-contained classroom was suspended and later expelled for acting as a go-between for other students in several drug transactions. Prior to his expulsion a committee of special education professionals determined that there was no causal relationship between his handicap and misconduct even though his IEP indicated that he had difficulty behaving appropriately and had borderline intelligence.

A hearing officer, however, determined that such a relationship did exist and invalidated the expulsion. A state reviewing officer affirmed. The district court also held that the relationship did, in fact, exist because the student's learning disability caused him to have a poor self-image which in turn caused him to seek peer approval even by acting as a "stooge" for other students. His learning disability also prevented him from understanding the long-term consequences of his actions, according to the court. The appeals court held that the district court's finding was not clearly erroneous and ruled that the student's expulsion was not proper. The court noted that to allow such an expulsion would not be fair or in keeping with the purpose of the EHCA since the student would be expelled for behavior over which he had no control.

SUSPENSIONS

Several of the courts in the foregoing expulsion cases indicated that handicapped students can be suspended for short periods of time for disciplinary reasons. Suspensions are generally considered to be an appropriate means of dealing with emergency situations and a method for teaching a disruptive student appropriate behavior.

In *Board of Education of the City of Peoria* v. *Illinois State Board of Education,* the district court held that a suspension was not a change in placement and that a handicapped student could be suspended for a short period of time. An eleventh grade learning disabled student had been suspended for five days for verbally abusing a teacher. The student's parents protested and requested a due process hearing in accordance with the EHCA. The hearing officer determined that the student had violated school policy and that his act was not perpetrated by his handicap. The suspension was upheld; however, the state Superintendent of Education reversed, holding that a handicapped student could be suspended only if he was dangerous.

The district court noted that this case did not deal with an expulsion or the termination of special education services, but rather, dealt with a brief suspension for a flagrant offense. The court found that the suspension was designed to teach the student and felt that the loss of classroom work did not outweigh the educational value of the suspension. The court held that the law did not free handicapped students from classroom discipline and that a brief period of forced absence, such as a five-day suspension, could not reasonably be considered a change in placement. The suspension was, therefore, upheld.

Lengthy suspensions, however, are generally treated in the same manner as expulsions by the courts. In the *Adams Central* case an indefinite suspension was held to be an expulsion. Historically, courts have considered any suspension of more than ten days' duration to be an expulsion. Also, serial suspensions that cumulatively exceed ten days would be treated as an expulsion.

The district court in *Lamont X.* v. *Quisenberry* held that a lengthy suspension was a change in placement and was not justified under the EHCA even though the students were provided with alternate education services during the suspension period. The two students in the case were classified as being severely behaviorally handicapped. They lived in a children's home and attended special education classes in the local public schools. Each student was involved in several incidents of disruptive and violent behavior. During the first week of the 1984–85 school year, the students were removed from school due to behavior that endangered other students. Each student was given a suspension of several months. Home tutoring was offered to the students during the suspension period. The students were also prosecuted and determined to be delinquent under state law.

The district court found that the substantial programmatic modification which occurred during the suspension period fell clearly within the definition of a change in placement. Since this change was not accomplished through the EHCA's change in placement procedures it was held to be invalid. The court noted that the EHCA allowed school officials to use their normal procedures to deal with students who are a danger to themselves or others. However, the court found that the long suspensions and home instruction program were not normal procedures for the school system to use in dealing with disruptive students. A normal procedure under such an emergency situation would have been a one- or two-week suspension. The court ordered the parties to work out an agreement that would allow the students to return to class.

EMERGENCY SITUATIONS

The EHCA does not prevent school administrators from taking swift action in emergency situations. The courts recognize that school administrators not only have the right, but have the duty to maintain an orderly educational environment. This includes the right to take whatever action may be necessary to quell a disruption. The courts have held that school officials may use normal disciplinary procedures to deal with handicapped students who present a danger to themselves or others or who disrupt the educational environment.

In one case involving a student determined to be a danger, the district court allowed the school district to use its normal disciplinary procedures to bar the student from public school classes. The student in *Jackson* v. *Franklin County School Board* had originally been suspended for three days because of disruptive sexual conduct, but during his suspension period the youth court placed him in a state hospital for treatment. When he attempted to return to school the following September, school officials determined that they could not meet his needs for counseling, vocational training, and academics and recommended a private placement. The student rejected all options and initiated due process appeals. He contended that until the dispute was settled, he was entitled to return to his previous public school program. The school district contended that because his behavior was disruptive and since he suffered from a psychosexual disorder that made him a possible danger to others, placement in the public school setting was not advisable.

The district court found that the school system's refusal to allow the student to return to his public school placement was based on the reasonable conclusion that he would disrupt the educational process for others and, thus, did not violate the EHCA. The court noted that the public interest was best served by the school district being able to provide a safe and effective environment for learning which far outweighed any harm suffered by the plaintiff. The Fifth Circuit Court of Appeals agreed, stating that the public schools unquestionably retained their authority to remove any student who disrupts the educational process or poses a threat to the safe school environment.

TREATMENT OF STUDENTS UNDERGOING AN EVALUATION

One of the stipulations in the *P-1* consent decree indicates that a child referred for an evaluation is to be treated basically as a handicapped child. In *Mrs. A.J.* v. *Special School District,* however, the district court ruled that a child referred for an evaluation was not to be treated as handicapped. The student had been experiencing behavior problems in school and was consequently referred for a special needs evaluation. Before the evaluation was completed, however, she was given a 15-day suspension for fighting with another student. Prior to the suspension she was given the normal due process hearing, but none of the EHCA's special procedures were employed. The student filed suit, contending that school officials knew, or should have known, that she was handicapped at the time of the suspension, and therefore should have employed the EHCA's more formal procedural safeguards prior to suspending her.

The court disagreed, however, holding that she was not identified as handicapped at the time of the suspension so the EHCA's procedures were not required. The court found that the EHCA was designed to minimize the risk of misclassifying children as handicapped or not handicapped. To treat a child as handicapped based on suspicions that the child was handicapped, the court reasoned, would violate the law concerning the identification and classification of students as handicapped. The court ruled that since the student had not been identified as handicapped at the time of the suspension, school officials had no obligation to afford her the more formal EHCA due process safeguards.

INDIVIDUALIZED DISCIPLINE PROGRAM NOT REQUIRED

The district court held that a handicapped student was not entitled to an individualized disciplinary program in *Pratt* v. *Board of Education of Frederick County*. The student had been placed on a disciplinary probation, given a three-day and a five-day suspension, and was finally placed on an indefinite suspension and was provided with home tutoring for the remainder of the year. During this time, school officials had been considering the question of what school program would be best for the student. A day school program had been recommended; however, his mother appealed on the grounds that it was overly restrictive. The hearing officer determined that a more restrictive residential placement was required, but again, the student's mother appealed. The state-level hearing review board determined that a special education class within the public schools was appropriate and ordered the school system to develop an IEP that included objectives for the student's behavior. While the IEP was being developed a school official stipulated that none of the provisions of the IEP were to be inconsistent with any of the provisions of the school system's policy handbook. The student's mother then filed court action seeking to require the school system to develop an IEP that included an individualized disciplinary program.

The court noted that all IEPs, including the present one, must be individually tailored to meet the needs of the individual student. Subject to that requirement, the court held, the provisions of the school system's policy handbook could be made applicable to any case, including the present one. The evaluation team was ordered to reconvene to develop an IEP. Each party was granted the right to appeal to the state-level hearing review board concerning what should or should not be included in the IEP.

TRANSFER TO A MORE RESTRICTIVE ENVIRONMENT

Several courts have held that a disruptive handicapped child may be transferred to a more restrictive environment if the student's behavior interferes with the education of others or if the child is a danger to himself (or herself) or to others. The EHCA and Section 504 regulations also indicate that this may be done.

One case has arisen that deals specifically with this issue. The district court in *Victoria L.* v. *District School Board of Lee County* ruled that school officials could bring about an involuntary change in placement for disciplinary reasons. The student was a 15-year-old youth with a specific learning disability. She had been placed in a special education program for approximately two hours per day at a public middle school with mainstreaming for the rest of the day. She began to experience behavioral difficulties, and these difficulties continued even after she was transferred to the high school. Her behavior culminated in a suspension after she was determined to be a danger to other students. This determination was made when the student brought a martial arts weapon and a knife to school and threatened another student. Following the suspension, school authorities recommended that the student be transferred to an alternative learning school. When the student's parents refused to consent to the transfer, an order was given for an involuntary change in placement. The school department's decision was upheld in administrative appeals, and court action was filed seeking a preliminary injunction to prevent the transfer.

In denying the preliminary injunction, the court found that an examination of the act revealed nothing that would deprive school authorities of their ever-present right to maintain discipline. The court further found that the EHCA's regulations allowed a transfer to a more restrictive placement when the handicapped student's behavior was so disruptive that it impaired the education of other students. The court felt that the issuance of a preliminary injunction in a case such as this could undermine the authority of school officials to maintain discipline. The court declined to do so.

On appeal the Eleventh Circuit Court of Appeals affirmed the district court's ruling. The appeals court agreed that the uncontradicted evidence left no doubt that the student's behavior at the high school posed a threat to both students and school personnel. Accordingly, the court found that school officials properly exercised the traditional disciplinary authority that they retained under the EHCA.

Victoria L. indicates that an involuntary change in placement to a more restrictive environment can take place for disciplinary reasons if the student's behavior poses a danger. If the student refuses to accept the proposed change in placement and initiates due process appeals, the student can be barred from the public schools during the appeals process according to the Fifth Circuit Court of Appeals. In the *Jackson* case a behaviorally disordered student needed placement in a private school, but the student rejected all proposals and sought to return to the public schools during the appeals process. The school district, considering him to be potentially dangerous to other students, refused. The district court and eventually the appeals court upheld that refusal, holding that school authorities have the right to remove any student, whether handicapped or not, who posed a threat to the safe and effective operation of the schools.

The Fourth Circuit Court of Appeals in *Malone* indicated that if a relationship between a student's handicap and his misconduct is found to exist, it suggests consideration of some change in the child's educational placement be made. In this case the courts had invalidated the expulsion of a handicapped student after the district court determined that a relationship between the student's handicap and the behavior initiating the expulsion did, in fact, exist. The appeals court suggested that although expulsion was improper, a less harsh form of discipline or a change in placement was warranted.

REFERENCES

Adams Central School District v. *Deist,* 334 N.W.2d 775, mod. 338 N.W.2d 591 (1983)

Blue v. *New Haven Board of Education,* 552 EHLR 401 (1981).

Board of Education of Peoria v. *Illinois State Board of Education,* 531 F.Supp. 148 (1982).

Doe v. *Koger,* 480 F.Supp. 225 (1979).

Goss v. *Lopez,* 419 U.S. 565 (1975).

Jackson v. *Franklin County School Board,* 606 F.Supp. 152 (1985), aff'd 765 F.2d 535 (1985).

Kaelin v. *Grubbs,* 682 F.2d 595 (1982).

Lamont X. v. *Quisenberry,* 606 F.Supp. 809 (1984).

Mrs. A.J. v. *Special School District No. 1,* 478 F.Supp. 418 (1979).

P-1 v. *Shedd,* 551 EHLR 164 (1979).

Pratt v. *Board of Education of Frederick County,* 501 F.Supp. 232 (1980).

S-1 v. *Turlington,* 635 F.2d 342 (1981).

School Board of the County of Prince William v. *Malone,* 762 F.2d 1210 (1985).

Sherry v. *New York State Education Department,* 479 F.Supp. 1328 (1979).

Southeast Warren Community School District v. *Department of Public Instruction,* 285 N.W.2d 173 (1979).

Stuart v. *Nappi,* 443 F.Supp. 1235 (1978).

Victoria L. v. *District School Board of Lee County, Florida,* 552 EHLR 265 (1980), aff'd 741 F.2d 369 (1984).

Figure 7-1

LEADING CASES

Stuart v. *Nappi,* 443 F.Supp. 1235 (1978)

Expulsion is a change in placement under the EHCA. A handicapped student may not be expelled, but school officials may take whatever action is necessary to deal with a dangerous situation.

Mrs. A.J. v. *Special School District,* 478 F.Supp. 418 (1979)

A student referred for a special needs evaluation, but not yet determined to be handicapped, may be disciplined as a nonhandicapped student. However, the disciplinary process may not interfere with the evaluation process.

Doe v. *Koger,* 480 F.Supp. 225 (1979)

Schools may not expel a handicapped student whose disruptive behavior is caused by the handicap. This prohibition also includes informal expulsion such as an indefinite suspension. If the behavior is not a manifestation of the handicap, the student may be expelled.

S-1 v. *Turlington,* 635 F.2d 342 (1981)

The determination of whether a student's misconduct is caused by a handicap must be made by a group of knowledgeable persons. Even when a handicapped student is expelled, a complete cessation of educational services is not permitted.

Kaelin v. *Grubbs,* 682 F.2d 595 (1982)

A handicapped student may be temporarily suspended, or may be expelled in appropriate circumstances if proper procedures are followed.

Victoria L. v. *District School Board,* 741 F.2d 369 (1984)

School authorities may involuntarily transfer a disruptive handicapped student to a more restrictive program.

Figure 7-2

PROCEDURAL STEPS

When a handicapped student misbehaves, the following steps should be taken:

1. Take whatever immediate measures are necessary to restore order and maintain discipline.

2. If more drastic measures are necessary, or if the student's misconduct has been persistent, refer the student to the school's special education evaluation team.

3. The evaluation team should determine if there is any relationship between the student's handicap and the misbehavior.

4a. If the evaluation team determines that no such relationship exists, more drastic action such as an expulsion may be taken.

4b. If the evaluation team determines that a relationship does exist, the evaluation team should develop an appropriate course of action to prevent further disruption to the educational process.

5. If the student is expelled, an alternative plan for the delivery of special education services needs to be developed.

6. In steps 1–5, the student and his or her parents or guardian must be provided with the due process safeguards that are guaranteed by the EHCA's change in placement provisions. Those safeguards include written notice of the proposed action, involvement of the evaluation team, and the right to appeal any action taken.

Figure 7-3

SAMPLE IEP STATEMENTS

The following statement may be included in the IEP of a student whose handicap should not cause behavioral problems:

The evaluation team has determined that the student's handicapping condition is not one that will cause the student to misbehave or in any way prevent the student from observing the usual rules and regulations of the school. Therefore, the student is expected to conform to the school's disciplinary code as outlined in the student handbook. Any and all infractions will be dealt with in accordance with procedures set out in the student handbook.

The following statement may be included in the IEP of a student whose handicap may cause behavioral problems:

The evaluation team has determined that the student's handicapping condition may on occasion cause the student to misbehave or in some way disrupt the educational process. Therefore, an individual disciplinary policy has been established for the student that is attached to and becomes a part of this IEP. The student is expected to conform to the individual disciplinary policy, and any and all infractions will be dealt with as outlined in that policy. However, nothing in that policy is intended to prevent school authorites from taking whatever emergency or immediate steps that may be necessary to restore order, maintain discipline, or otherwise prevent a dangerous situation from existing.

Figure 7-4

SAMPLE INDIVIDUAL DISCIPLINARY POLICY

The evaluation team recognizes that the student's handicap will on occasion cause the student to manifest behavior that does not conform to the usual rules and regulations of the school. However, the team also recognizes that a standard of discipline must be maintained for the protection of all students and to minimize disruption to the educational process. Therefore, this individual disciplinary policy has been developed as part of the student's IEP.

The student has been placed in a special education program, and an IEP has been developed that is designed to reduce the effects of the student's handicap and allow the student to perform according to his or her potential. This program is also designed to help the student learn appropriate behavior through the use of behavior modification techniques.

The student may not engage in any activity that will endanger himself or herself, other students, or staff members. The student also may not engage in any behavior that will damage school property. Also, the student is not permitted to engage in activities that will interfere with the educational process for other students. To these ends, the student may not engage in any behavior that is prohibited by the student handbook. (Enclose copy of handbook.)

The following steps will be taken in the event of an infraction:

1. The teacher will employ usual classroom disciplinary procedures.

2. If step 1 fails to correct the misconduct, the teacher will seek assistance from the school guidance counselor and/or school principal.

3. If the misconduct continues, the student may be removed from the classroom and temporarily detained in a time out area.

4. If the misconduct continues, the student may be sent home for the remainder of the school day.

5. If the misconduct continues when the student returns to school, the student may be suspended for three to five days. During the suspension period the student will be expected to complete all school assignments as provided by the teacher.

6. If the student is sent home or suspended for a cumulative total of ten school days in any school year, the evaluation team will reconvene within five days to determine if a more restrictive placement may be necessary or to develop some other appropriate alternative plan of action to curb the disruption.

Figure 7-5

QUESTIONS ADMINISTRATORS OFTEN ASK ABOUT DISCIPLINE

1. *Can a handicapped student be expelled?*

Yes, a handicapped student can be expelled if the evaluation team has determined that a relationship does not exist between the misconduct and the child's handicap. If a relationship does exist, then the student may not be expelled.

2. *How can a student with behavioral or emotional handicaps be disciplined?*

Obviously, a relationship between misconduct and the child's handicap would exist in the case of a student with a behavioral or emotional disorder. School administrators may take emergency action and may suspend such a student. If the misconduct is persistent, school authorities may move the offending student to a more restrictive environment.

3. *Can a disciplinary policy be written into a handicapped student's IEP?*

Yes, however, that policy must meet the student's individual needs and should specify what is expected of the student and what action will be taken if those expectations are not met.

4. *Are there any special precautions that must be taken in suspending a handicapped student?*

Generally there are not. A suspension is generally considered to be either an emergency measure used to restore order quickly or remove a dangerous student. It can also be used to teach a student appropriate behavior. However, administrators need to remember that indefinite or serial suspensions will be treated as expulsions by the courts.

5. *Doesn't the EHCA, in effect, create a dual system of discipline?*

No, handicapped students can be held to the same standard of discipline as nonhandicapped students. The EHCA only requires additional due process safeguards to ensure that the disciplinary process is not used to circumvent the mandates of the EHCA.

6. *Can a handicapped student have special education services terminated for disciplinary reasons?*

No, even in the case of an expelled student, an alternative program of services must be developed. This could include placement in a more restrictive environment or homebound instruction.

Figure 7-6

LETTER TO PARENTS REGARDING SUSPENSION

Date:_____

Parent:_____

Address:_____

_____

Dear_____:
 This is to inform you that a disciplinary hearing will be held regarding your child,_____, on_____ at_____ at the_____ School. A decision will be made following the hearing as to what disciplinary action, if any, will be taken. One option to be considered will be a brief suspension. You are invited to attend this hearing.
 The specific reasons for the disciplinary hearing are_____

_____

The hearing will be very informal; however, your child will be given full opportunity to respond to the above complaints.
 Since your child is receiving special education services, the school's evaluation team has been notified of this action. The team chairperson has been invited to attend the hearing.
 A suspension is not considered to be a major disciplinary action and requires only minimal due process. If, however, your child receives over ten days of suspensions in a school year, more elaborate due process procedures will be utilized. These procedures will conform to all the EHCA's due process safeguards for a handicapped student. Those procedures are the same as for a student facing expulsion and are outlined in the enclosed notice.

(School Principal's Signature)

Figure 7-7

NOTICE OF RIGHTS TO A HANDICAPPED STUDENT FACING EXPULSION

1. The student has the right to have the evaluation team determine whether or not the disciplinary code infraction is related to the student's handicapping condition.

2. If the team determines that such a relationship exists the student may not be expelled.

3. The student has the right to have the evaluation team make a determination of whether or not the current special education program is appropriate to meet the student's needs.

4. If the team determines that the current program is not appropriate, the student has the right to be appropriately placed.

5. Any determinations made by the evaluation team may be appealed to an independent hearing officer. The hearing officer's decision may be appealed to a higher-level hearing panel and eventually to the courts.

6. If the evaluation team determines that no relationship exists between the student's conduct and handicap, the student may be expelled. However, any decision to expel the student is also subject to the appeals listed in entry 5.

7. Until all such due process proceedings are completed, the student has the right to remain in the current placement unless the student's presence would constitute a danger to the student or others or would cause a substantial disruption to the educational process.

(School Principal's Signature)

Figure 7-8

RECORD OF DISCIPLINARY ACTION

School Year: _____

Student: _____ School: _____

Grade: _____

Date	Disciplinary Code Infraction	Action Taken

Figure 7-9

ADMINISTRATOR'S CHECKLIST

Questions to ask in disciplining a handicapped student

1. Have all normal disciplinary sanctions been exhausted?_____

   Describe previous action taken:_____

2. Has the IEP been modified to address the child's behavioral needs?_____ Describe those modifications:_____

3. Would additional services prevent further infractions of the disciplinary code?_____ What services are needed?_____

4. Does the evaluation team feel that the child's misbehavior is a manifestation of his or her handicap?_____

   Why?_____

5. Would the child's unique needs be more appropriately addressed in a more restrictive environment?_____ What type of program is necessary?_____

6. Is the student a danger to himself or herself or to others or is there reasonable cause to predict that his or her presence in the school will cause a disruption to the educational process?_____

   Explain:_____

7. If the child needs to be excluded from school, what services will be required to assure him or her an appropriate education during the exclusion period?_____

8. Is it possible that the child's behavior is an indication that he or she may have additional handicaps that are currently undiagnosed and are not being provided for in the IEP?_____

   Explain:_____

Chapter 8

WHAT ARE THE REQUIREMENTS FOR TESTING, RECORD KEEPING, AND PROVIDING SERVICES TO PAROCHIAL SCHOOL STUDENTS?

> *Congress perceived the EHA as the most effective vehicle for protecting the constitutional right of a handicapped child to a public education.*
>
> **Mr. Justice Blackmun**
> *Smith v. Robinson*
> **104 S.Ct. 3457 at 3470 (1984)**

The previous chapters have dealt with legal issues that directly impact the provision of special education and related services to handicapped children. The issues previously discussed have been heavily litigated in the courts. There are, however, numerous other issues that for various reasons have not been widely litigated. It would be impossible to discuss each and every issue related to the Education for All Handicapped Children Act (EHCA) that may at some time cause concern for a school administrator. In this chapter less litigated issues that may have an important impact on a school district's delivery of special education services will be presented. Many of these issues may at some time in the future be more prominent in the courts.

Issues selected for inclusion in this chapter were chosen because of their potential impact on the total special education program. Although they have not often been before the courts, these issues are still controversial. All have specific legal implications for the school district's handicapped education policies.

Issues to be discussed include the implications of minimum competency testing on handicapped students, the rights of parochial school students to receive special education services, student record requirements, native language testing and evaluation, and the awarding of attorney's fees to the prevailing party in a special education dispute.

MINIMUM COMPETENCY TESTING

During the past several years, many politicians, educators, and the general public have called for greater accountability in the nation's classrooms. We are all well aware of the various studies, reports, and media reviews that have made the contention that many high school graduates have not mastered the basic skills but have been awarded diplomas.

Minimum Competency Testing and the EHCA

Minimum competency testing is not adressed by the EHCA or its regulations. However, the advent of increased administration of these tests has many implications for handicapped children. First, these tests have great diagnostic value and can be one tool to help identify children who may have learning handicaps. The EHCA requires that school districts take affirmative steps to identify all handicapped children. The minimum competency testing program can easily be coordinated with a school district's child find activities. Indeed, identifying students who need remediation is one of the main purposes of basic skills testing.

There are even more critical implications when the tests are used for promotion and graduation decisions. Handicapped children, by the very nature of their handicaps, represent a high-risk category for failure. The implications are also especially critical for the handicapped student who is educated substantially in the mainstream. The severely handicapped student who is educated in a substantially separate program is an unlikely candidate to take a standard minimum competency test; however, students with mild to moderate handicaps may be required to participate in the school district's testing program.

Awarding Diplomas to Handicapped Students

The purpose of requiring students to pass a minimum competency test to earn a high school diploma is to guarantee that a student holding the diploma has attained a certain level of skill proficiency. Those who do not pass the test may be awarded a certificate of attendance that indicates that they have completed a prescribed course of study.

Various practices exist throughout the country in regard to awarding diplomas to handicapped students. A school district must award a diploma to a handicapped student who has clearly earned it by meeting the usual requirements. Some school districts also award a diploma to handicapped students who have not met the usual requirements but who have successfully completed the requirements of their Individualized Educational Programs (IEPs). Other districts award a special diploma or a certificate of attendance in that situation. In districts where passing a minimum competency test is a diploma requirement, handicapped students may also be required to pass the test to receive a regular diploma.

Recent Litigation

It is well settled that states have the power to develop and administer minimum competency tests. States also have the authority to set graduation requirements and, thus, have every right to require that a student pass the test to receive a diploma. Exactly how the tests are developed and administered has been a judicial issue, however. The leading case involving minimum competency tests, *Debra P.* v. *Turlington,* arose in Florida where passing a minimum competency test was a prerequisite to earning a high school diploma. After a long and complicated legal dispute, the case culminated in a decision by the Eleventh Circuit Court of Appeals that Florida's testing program was constitutional as long as certain safeguards were built into it. During this litigation, the federal courts established that to be acceptable as a diploma requirement, minimum competency tests must be a valid measure of the curriculum that has actually been taught to the students taking the test. Also, before a minimum competency test can become a diploma requirement, the students who must pass it should be given sufficient notice. The test also may not be racially or ethnically discriminatory. However, a minimum competency test can be used solely as a diagnostic tool without meeting those requirements.

The issue of requiring handicapped students to pass a minimum competency test to receive the usual high school diploma has not yet been widely litigated. However, the courts that have ruled on the issue have basically held that such a requirement is not a violation of either the EHCA or Section 504. However, to be a valid diploma requirement students expected to take the test must be given sufficient notice and their IEPs should include instruction in the areas to be tested (*Board of Education* v. *Ambach, Anderson* v. *Banks, Brookhart* v. *Board of Education*).

Modified Testing

Just as modifying the physical plant to provide handicapped students with access to the school building has been an issue, modifying the minimum competency tests so that handicapped students can take them has also been an issue.

Many students with physical handicaps could not possibly take the tests without some modifications. For example, a blind student would need to take the test in braille, and a physically handicapped student may need assistance in marking the answer sheet. A refusal to allow such modifications would be a violation of Section 504 if the students were "otherwise qualified" to take the tests. Whereas modifications in the administration of the test to provide access are required, alterations in the content of the test items are not. Students who do not have the academic ability to answer certain test items are not "otherwise qualified" in the sense intended by Section 504.

Exemptions from Testing

Handicapped students can also be exempted from taking the minimum competency tests; however, if the test is a diploma requirement, such an exemption would automatically foreclose the possibility of earning the diploma unless state law provides otherwise. Many severely handicapped students would have no hope of passing a standard minimum competency test and should be exempted.

Need to Develop Policies

The foregoing indicates that it is imperative for a school district to have a clear policy regarding the minimum competency testing of handicapped students. As with all components of a handicapped student's IEP, any decisions regarding the testing should be made by the special education evaluation team and should be clearly spelled out in the IEP. While these decisions must be made on a case-by-case basis, a general policy is needed to guide the evaluation team to ensure that the decisions made are consistent across all cases. A school district could run into difficulty if some students were exempt from the testing requirement while other similarly situated students were required to take the test.

As with other components of a handicapped child's IEP, any decisions regarding minimum competency testing are subject to the EHCA's due process safeguards. If the parents of a handicapped student object to any of the evaluation team's decisions regarding the administration of the tests, they may appeal those decisions to an impartial hearing officer.

The litigation concerning the applicability of minimum competency testing requirements on handicapped students is sparse to date. However, it is reasonable to assume that this litigation will increase as more states make passing the tests a requirement for the award of a high school diploma. School administrators need to be aware of their state's policies and any administrative hearing decisions or court opinions regarding those policies.

SERVICES TO PAROCHIAL SCHOOL STUDENTS

With regard to children who are enrolled in parochial schools or other private schools, the EHCA's regulations make the following provisions:

If a handicapped child is enrolled in a parochial or other private school and receives special education or related services from a public agency, the public agency shall:

(a) Initiate and conduct meetings to develop, review, and revise an individualized education program for the child, in accordance with [the regulations]; and

(b) Insure that a representative of the parochial or other private school attends each meeting. If the representative cannot attend, the agency shall use other methods to insure participation by the private school, including individualized or conference telephone calls. (34 C.F.R. § 300.348)

and

(a) Each local educational agency shall provide special education and related services designed to meet the needs of private school handicapped children residing in the jurisdiction of the agency. (34 C.F.R. § 300.452)

When originally written, the regulations included statements indicating that public school personnel could be made available in private school facilities to the extent necessary to provide needed services. Provisions were also made for administrative control over those services and for the use of public school equipment and materials on the premises of the private school. However, those provisions were deleted from the 1986 edition of the regulations. This deletion most likely was in response to the Supreme Court's *Aguilar* decision, which is discussed in the next section. A note to section 300.348 in Appendix C of the regulations indicates that the Department of Education is considering publishing a separate document concerning the education of handicapped students in parochial or private schools.

Provision of Remedial Services on Private School Premises

A recent U.S. Supreme Court decision in *Aguilar* v. *Felton* has implications for the provision of services to handicapped children in parochial schools. *Aguilar* was not concerned with the EHCA but did involve another federally funded program, Title I of the Elementary and Secondary Education Act. Title I (now known as Chapter I) provided funds for school districts to meet the needs of educationally disadvantaged children from low-income families. For many years the New York City School Department used a portion of its Title I funds to provide remedial instruction in reading and math, English as a second language, and guidance services. Those who taught in the parochial schools were supervised by field personnel who made frequent unannounced visits. Teachers were instructed to avoid involvement with religious activities, to remove religious materials from their classrooms, and to minimize contact with parochial school personnel. All materials and equipment purchased with public funds were to be used solely in the Title I program.

Six taxpayers filed court action claiming that the city's Title I program violated the Establishment Clause of the U.S. Constitution. The district court upheld the program, but the U.S. Court of Appeals for the Second Circuit reversed, finding that the Establishment Clause had been violated. The U.S. Supreme Court agreed, holding that the supervisory system established by the school district and the administrative cooperation that was necessary to maintain the program created an excessive entanglement between the church and the state in violation of the Establishment Clause.

Provision of Services to Handicapped Students

Thus far there have not been any serious court challenges to the provision of special education services to handicapped parochial school students. The Supreme Court has provided guidelines, however, concerning what may and may not be provided. It is reasonable to assume that special education and related services may be provided to eligible parochial school students; however, in view of the *Aguilar* decision, it would be prudent to avoid providing these services on the premises of the parochial school. If services are needed, they should be provided in a public school building.

The excessive entanglement bar is cause for concern as contact between public and parochial school officials is necessary to diagnose initially and program the student. The Establishment Clause has not been held to bar all such contact, however. Contact between the public school staff and the parochial school staff should be kept to a minimum and should exist only to the extent that it is necessary to ensure that the child's special education services will result in educational benefit.

Transportation

One other issue that has not yet been resolved is whether or not the public schools are responsible for providing transportation to the public school building for handicapped parochial school students so that they can receive special education services. Transportation is a related service under the EHCA, and providing it to a parochial school student probably would not violate the Establishment Clause. However, school systems may not necessarily be required to provide transportation between the parochial and public school buildings.

This is an issue that really needs to be settled by the courts, as the EHCA and the regulations do not directly address it. It is a well-settled facet of case law that school districts may provide certain services, such as transportation, to parochial school students, without violating the Establishment Clause, under what is known as the child benefit theory. This does not mean that such services must be provided. Even in the case of a handicapped student, it is reasonable to assume that transportation would not be the responsibility of the school system. The child has the option of attending the public schools on a full-time basis. If the child's parents elect to send the child to a parochial school, the school district should not be required to provide transportation to the public school building so that the child may receive services that are not available in the parochial school.

STUDENT RECORDS

Under the Family Educational Rights and Privacy Act (FERPA), also known as the Buckley Amendment, school systems are required to provide eligible students with certain rights regarding their educational records (20 U.S.C. § 1232g). These rights are available to all students, not just handicapped students. Many of these rights are reiterated in the regulations implementing the EHCA.

Basically, FERPA, which was passed one year prior to the EHCA, provides parents and students over the age of 18 with the rights to inspect their educational records and request that they be amended if there is a disagreement over their contents. FERPA also restricts access to school records by a third party.

EHCA Regulations on Record Reviews

Specifically, the EHCA provides the following rights of access to educational records:

(a) Each participating agency shall permit parents to inspect and review any education records relating to their children which are collected, maintained, or used by the agency under [the EHCA]. The agency shall comply with a request without unnecessary delay and before any meeting regarding an individualized education program or hearing relating to the identification, evaluation, or placement of the child, and in no case more than 45 days after the request has been made.

(b) The right to inspect and review education records under this section includes:

(1) The right to a response from the participating agency to reasonable requests for explanations and interpretations of the records;

(2) The right to request that the agency provide copies of the records containing the information if failure to provide those copies would effectively prevent the parent from exercising the right to inspect and review the records; and

(3) The right to have a representative of the parent inspect and review the records.

(c) An agency may presume that the parent has authority to inspect and review records relating to his or her child unless the agency has been advised that the parent does not have the authority under applicable state law governing such matters as guardianship, separation, and divorce. (34 C.F.R. § 300.562)

In addition, the school district must maintain a log of all access to educational records by a third party. The log must include the name of the party, date of the access, and the purpose of the access. Also, the school district, on request, must provide the parents with a list of the types of records maintained and their location. A fee may be charged for any copies of records as long as the fee does not effectively prevent access (34 C.F.R. § 300.563 et seq.).

Amending Records

Parents also have the right to request that records be amended if they feel that they are incorrect or misleading. Specifically, the EHCA provides

> (a) A parent who believes that information in education records collected, maintained, or used under this part is inaccurate or misleading or violates the privacy or other rights of the child, may request the participating agency which maintains the information to amend the information.
>
> (b) The agency shall decide whether to amend the information in accordance with the request within a reasonable period of time of receipt of the request.
>
> (c) If the agency decides to refuse to amend the information in accordance with the request it shall inform the parent of the refusal, and advise the parent of a right to a hearing under [the EHCA]. (34 C.F.R. § 300.567)

If the request to amend the records is denied, the parents may contest the denial through a due process hearing. If the hearing results in a decision that the records do not need to be amended, the parents have the right to attach a statement commenting on the information contained in the records. That statement must be maintained in the records and included whenever the records are disseminated. Parental consent must be obtained before any information on a handicapped student is released to a third party (34 C.F.R. § 300.568 et seq.).

Students over 18 Years

As was mentioned a student over the age of 18 assumes the rights granted by FERPA. However, the EHCA provides that

> The State educational agency shall include policies and procedures in its annual program plan regarding the extent to which children are afforded rights of privacy similar to those afforded to parents, taking into consideration the age of the child and type or severity of disability. (34 C.F.R. § 300.574)

This regulation indicates that individual states are to develop their own policies regarding access to student records by the students themselves. Those policies must be consistent with FERPA but could grant access earlier than age 18. The regulation also indicates that the severity of a student's disability may be a factor in the development of state policy.

State Laws

Many states also have laws and regulations regarding the maintenance and use of student records. School administrators also need to become familiar with these policies.

NONDISCRIMINATORY TESTING AND EVALUATION

Even before the passage of the EHCA, the courts recognized the need for nondiscriminatory testing and evaluation procedures to ensure that students were not inappropriately placed in special education classes due to an inability to communicate in English. In *Diana* v. *State Board of Education* and *Larry P.* v. *Wilson Riles*, the courts invalidated the use of tests for placement purposes that were racially, culturally, or linguistically biased.

The EHCA also recognizes the need for nonbiased placement and testing procedures. Specifically, the act provides that

> Testing and evaluation materials and procedures used for the purposes of evaluation and placement of handicapped children must be selected and administered so as not to be racially or culturally discriminatory. (34 C.F.R. § 300.530(b))

Also, tests or other evaluation procedures must be administered in the child's native language unless it is obviously not feasible to do so (34 C.F.R. § 300.532(a)(1)).

The EHCA is very clear that when a school system evaluates a student whose native language is not English, evaluation procedures must be used that will not place the student at a disadvantage because of limited English proficiency. This means that the school system may have to make provisions to test the student in his native language. A native language evaluator, however, should be able to do more than just speak the language. The evaluator must also have an understanding of the student's culture including its customs and its own set of norms.

ATTORNEY FEES

Since the implementation of the EHCA, it has been the usual practice of both school boards and parents to engage the services of an attorney to represent their interests in any administrative hearings or court action brought under the act. The costs involved in doing so can quickly add up. Some parents who have prevailed in their due process action have attempted to recoup their expenses by suing the school board for the payment of their attorney fees.

Supreme Court Denies Award

The U.S. Supreme Court in *Smith* v. *Robinson* ruled in 1984, however, that an award of attorney fees was not available under the EHCA. The Court also indicated that parents could not seek an award of attorney fees under another piece of legislation, such as Section 504, because the EHCA was the exclusive avenue through which claims to a publicly financed special education could be brought.

Regarding the exclusivity of the EHCA, Mr. Justice Blackmun writing for the majority stated that the Court had little difficulty concluding that Congress intended the EHCA to be the exclusive avenue through which a handicapped student could assert a claim to a publicly financed education. The EHCA is a comprehensive scheme set up by Congress to assist the states in providing public education for handicapped children. The Court found that the provisions of the statute and its legislative history indicated that Congress intended for handicapped children with constitutional claims to a free appropriate public education to pursue those claims through the elaborate administrative and judicial mechanism set out in the act. To allow a plaintiff to circumvent the EHCA's administrative remedies would be inconsistent with Congress's carefully tailored scheme according to the Court. The Court determined that the legislative history gave no indication that Congress intended such a result but, rather, indicated that Congress perceived the EHCA to be the most effective vehicle for protecting the constitutional rights of a handicapped child to a public education. The Court concluded that where the EHCA is available to a handicapped child asserting a right to a free appropriate public education based on either the act or the Equal Protection Clause of the Fourteenth Amendment, the EHCA was the exclusive avenue through which the child and his or her parents or guardian could pursue their claim. Since the EHCA does not provide for an award of attorney fees and since the Court determined that other legislation could not be relied upon in a special education dispute, the parent's request for reimbursement of legal costs was denied.

Recent Legislation

In 1986 Congress passed the Handicapped Children's Protection Act (HCPA), which amended the EHCA to allow for the recovery of legal expenses to a prevailing parent in a special education suit. Under the terms of the HCPA the courts may award reasonable attorney's fees as part of the total settlement made to the parents or guardian of a handicapped child. The fees awarded under this legislation must be based on the rate customarily charged for similar services in the community where the action arose. No award may be made, however, for services performed after the school district made a written offer of settlement if that offer was not accepted by the parents and if the final relief obtained by the parents was not more favorable than that offer. This legislation was made retroactive to cover any proceedings that were pending on July 4, 1984, the day before the *Smith* decision was handed down.

REFERENCES

Aguilar v. *Felton*, 105 S.Ct. 3232 (1985).

Anderson v. *Banks*, 520 F.Supp. 472 (1981), mod. 540 F.Supp. 761 (1982).

Board of Education v. *Ambach*, 469 N.Y.S.2d 699 (1983).

Brookhart v. *Board of Education*, 697 F.2d 179 (1983).

Debra P. v. *Turlington*, 730 F.2d 1405 (1984).

Diana v. *State Board of Education,* Civ. No. C-70-37 RFP (1970 and 1973).

Larry P. v. *Wilson Riles,* 343 F.Supp. 1306, aff'd 502 F.2d 963 (1974).

Smith v. *Robinson,* 104 S.Ct. 3457 (1984).

Stock v. *Massachusetts Hospital School,* 476 N.E.2d 210 (1985).

Figure 8-1

LEADING CASES

Debra P. v. Turlington, 730 F.2d 1405 (1984)

Minimum competency testing must be a valid measure of the curriculum that has been taught to be a diploma requirement. Sufficient notice must also be given to the students who must pass the tests.

Aguilar v. Felton, 105 S.Ct. 3232 (1985)

Federal funds cannot be used to provide a remedial program to parochial school students staffed by public school personnel on parochial school premises as it violates the establishment clause. The supervisory system and administrative cooperation needed to maintain the program create an excessive entanglement between church and state.

Larry P. v. Wilson Riles, 502 F.2d 963 (1974)

Tests used for placement purposes may not be racially, culturally, or linguistically biased.

Smith v. Robinson, 104 S.Ct. 3457 (1984)

The EHCA is the exclusive avenue through which claims to a publicly financed special education can be brought. Since the EHCA does not provide for an award of attorney fees to the prevailing party, a successful litigant cannot rely on other legislation to seek an award of attorney fees.

(Note: This decision has been overturned by recent legislation.)

Figure 8-2

NOTICE OF MCT AS A GRADUATION REQUIREMENT

Date:_____

Parent:_____

Address:_____

_____

Dear_____:

    This is to inform you that as of _____, all students in the school district will be required to pass a minimum competency test to receive a standard high school diploma.

    Students will be expected to pass tests in reading, math, writing, and speaking skills. The tests will initially be administered in the junior year. Students who fail any portion of the tests may take the failed portion again in the senior year. Students who do not pass all sections of the test by their anticipated graduation date will receive a certificate of attendance.

    To pass the tests, students will be expected to demonstrate mastery of the educational objectives listed on the attached pages.

[Attach a general list of educational objectives that the test will cover.]

(Superintendent's Signature)

Figure 8-3

SAMPLE IEP STATEMENTS CONCERNING MCT

The evaluation team has determined that the student will not be required to take the minimum competency tests.

The evaluation team has determined that the student will not be required to take the math section of the minimum competency tests but will be required to take all other sections.

The evaluation team has determined that the student will be required to take all sections of the minimum competency tests with the following modifications: all tests will be administered in braille.

The evaluation team has determined that the student will be required to take all sections of the minimum competency tests.

Figure 8-4

LETTER TO PARENTS REGARDING SERVICES TO A PAROCHIAL SCHOOL STUDENT

Date: _____

Parents: _____

Address: _____

_____

Dear _____ :

The school district's evaluation team has recently determined that your child, _____, is in need of special education services. Since your child attends a parochial school and since federal law prohibits us from providing services on the premises of a parochial school, we must agree on an alternative method of providing services.

1. Your child could be enrolled in the public schools on a full-time basis. The advantages of this option are that your child would receive his or her total educational program at one location, coordination between regular and special education teachers would be improved, and the full complement of the school district's services would be available.

2. Your child could remain in the parochial school and come to the public schools for his or her special education services. The advantage of this option is that your child could remain at the school he or she has been attending.

Please contact this office at your earliest convenience so that we may discuss these options and develop a service delivery plan for your child.

(Special Education Administrator's Signature)

Figure 8-5

NOTICE TO PARENTS CONCERNING SCHOOL RECORDS

The school district regularly maintains records of an educational nature on your child. You have certain rights regarding those records.

1. You have the right to inspect your child's school records. Access to the records must be provided within two school days of the request.

2. You are entitled to copies of any portions of the school record. You may be charged a fee not to exceed the cost of reproduction.

3. You are entitled to have a school district representative interpret any portion of the records for you.

4. You may have the records inspected by a third party of your choosing.

5. No portion of your child's records may be released to a third party without your consent.

6. You may request that certain portions of the record be deleted or amended. A decision regarding the deletion or amendment of the record must be rendered by the school principal within one week of such a request. The school principal's decision may be appealed to the Superintendent of Schools, the School Board, to the State Department of Education, and eventually to the courts.

(Special Education Administrator's Signature)

Figure 8-6

RECORDS ACCESS LOG

Date	Party Receiving Access	Portion of Records Accessed	Purpose of Access	Released by

Figure 8-7

RELEASE OF INFORMATION

Student:_____ School:_____

Parents:_____ Grade:_____ D.O.B._____

Address:_____

     I hearby request that school records on my child be released to the following party:

Name:_____

Address:_____

_____

     Specifically, I request that the following portions of the record be released:

          _____ Complete file

          _____ Health record

          _____ Transcripts

          _____ Special education evaluation materials

          _____ Psychological reports

          _____ Standardized test results

     I am requesting the records be released for the following reasons:

_____   _____

Signature   Date

Figure 8-8

REQUEST FOR TRANSLATOR

To: Special Education Administrator

From: Evaluation Team Chairperson

Date:

I am requesting the services of a translator as indicated below:

Student: _____ School: _____

Parents: _____ Grade: _____ D.O.B. _____

Address: _____ Telephone: _____

Native Language of the Home: _____

Specific Dialect: _____

The translator's services are required on the following dates for the stated purposes:

Date	Time	Location	Purpose

Figure 8-9

REQUEST FOR NATIVE LANGUAGE TESTING

To: Special Education Administrator

From: Evaluation Team Chairperson

Date:

A referral has been received on the student listed below. The evaluation team has determined that due to the student's inability to understand and comprehend English fully, native language testing is required.

Student:_____ School:_____

Parents:_____ Grade:_____ D.O.B._____

Address:_____ Telephone:_____

Native Language:_____

Specific Dialect:_____

The following assessments must be completed in the child's native language:

All assessments must be completed by:_____

Figure 8-10

QUESTIONS ADMINISTRATORS OFTEN ASK

1. *Can a handicapped student be required to pass a minimum competency test to earn a regular high school diploma?*

Yes, minimum competency tests may be used as one criterion for earning a high school diploma as long as they are a valid measure of what has been taught and proper notice has been given. Modifications may be made to test procedures to accommodate a handicapped student, but handicapped students need not be exempted from the requirement.

2. *Are school districts required to provide special education services to parochial school students?*

Yes, the EHCA requires that handicapped parochial school students be provided with any needed special education and related services. However, those services should not be provided on the premises of the parochial school.

3. *What requirements exist concerning the educational records of handicapped students?*

Educational records for handicapped students must be maintained and administered according to the requirements of the Family Educational Rights and Privacy Act. Many of the provisions of FERPA have been reiterated in the EHCA.

4. *Do handicapped students have to be tested in their native language?*

The EHCA requires that any evaluations used for the identification and placement of handicapped students must not be racially, culturally, or linguistically biased. Provisions may have to be made to test a student of limited English proficiency in his or her native language.

Chapter 9

HOW DOES THE HANDICAPPED LAW AFFECT EDUCATIONAL POLICY AND DECISION MAKING?

> *The Act requires the state to treat each child as an individual, a human whose unique qualities and needs can be evaluated and served only by a plan designed with wisdom, care and educational expertise. Its grand design does not tolerate policies that impose a rigid pattern on the education of children. Each IEP must be prepared on the basis of an individual evaluation of a particular boy or girl. The child and his or her parents and guardians can exact no more. The state must provide no less.*
>
> **Circuit Judge Rubin**
> *Crawford v. Pittman*
> **708 F.2d 1028 at 1030 (1983)**

More than four million handicapped students in the United States currently receive special education services through the public schools. This was not always the case. When the public school system first came into being in colonial America, the handicapped were virtually excluded and any education or training they received was provided privately. In the nineteenth century special schools and classes for the handicapped were developed; however, these were substantially segregated from the mainstream and were often of poor quality. Handicapped students were generally not allowed to participate in the offerings of the regular public schools until well into the twentieth century.

The civil rights movement and the movement to gain equal educational opportunities for the poor, social minorities, and language minorities helped to open the doors of the public schools to the handicapped. In the late 1960s and early 1970s, advocates for the handicapped successfully turned to the courts to gain new educational rights for handicapped children. Many of the legal principles that had been previously applied by the courts in granting equal educational opportunities to minority students were consequently used to open those same doors to handicapped students.

FEDERAL LEGISLATION

In 1975 Congress passed, and President Gerald Ford signed into law, P.L. 94-142, the Education for All Handicapped Children Act (EHCA). The EHCA, which became effective on October 1, 1977, was basically an amendment to the Education of the Handicapped Amendments of 1974 (P.L. 93-380). The EHCA provided that recipients of federal funds were to assure all children a free appropriate public education designed to meet their unique needs.

The Education for All Handicapped Children Act and its implementing regulations provide specifically for the identification, evaluation, and placement of handicapped students. An Individualized Educational Program (IEP) that outlines the specific special education program developed for an identified handicapped child, a mandate that handicapped children be educated in the least restrictive environment possible, provisions for parental participation, and elaborate due process safeguards are among the act's major provisions. A companion law, Section 504 of the Rehabilitation Act of 1973, also prohibited the exclusion of handicapped students from programs receiving federal financial assistance. These laws provided that handicapped students were to receive an appropriate education in the least restrictive environment possible.

A COMMON LAW DEVELOPS

Although the EHCA and its implementing regulations are extremely comprehensive, they do not cover all possible situations. The courts have been left to interpret the act and determine how it should be applied to any given set of specific facts. A significant amount of litigation has arisen during the past few years over some of the gray areas of the EHCA. As a result, we now have a fair amount of case, or common, law regarding the education of handicapped children.

In a paper delivered before the 1979 annual convention of the National Organization on Legal Problems of Education (NOLPE), Thomas P. O'Donnell correctly predicted "that the law is only at the beginning of a history which may ultimately alter the scope and identity of our educational system" (p. 215). One year later Warren L. Kreunen, also in an address before the annual NOLPE convention, stated, "There has been literally an explosion of law in the area of education for the handicapped. . . . The future direction of the law in handicapped education will, in large measure, be determined by cases which are now being litigated" (p. 32). Although the litigation is certainly far from over, the courts clearly have begun to interpret the law and have provided guidelines for its implementation.

One commentator has noted that "The development of a 'common law' for decision making under the Act would eliminate much of the ambiguity of the current standards" (Harvard Note, p. 1127). Although these issues are still being litigated, we now have a sufficient number of decisions to provide school administrators with guidelines, based on a common law, to assist them in making program and placement decisions that will meet the EHCA's requirements.

CRITICAL DECISION MAKING

Special education administrators and regular school administrators must make critical decisions daily concerning the development of IEPs for handicapped students and the allocation of scarce resources. In making these decisions, administrators need to consider the legal requirements involved in providing an appropriate program of special education and related services. Also, since special requirements do exist for disciplining handicapped students, these must be considered in developing an IEP.

Court decisions in regard to the delivery of special education and related services under the EHCA have been examined in this handbook. The common law that has emerged from these decisions provides educational administrators with further guidance on how the EHCA is to be implemented. In that respect, the law is equally as important as the EHCA itself and its implementing regulations and should be referred to for additional insight before critical decisions are made. The purpose of this final chapter is to analyze the common law and to translate it into guidelines for educational administrators and special education personnel that will assist them in the decision-making process on a day-to-day basis.

APPROPRIATE EDUCATION DEFINED

One of the specific issues that has arisen in much of the litigation stems from the definition of the term "appropriate education." The EHCA mandates that each handicapped child is to be provided with an appropriate education, but it gives little guidance as to specifically what constitutes an appropriate education or precisely what components are contained therein.

The EHCA provides that any child who is suspected of being handicapped is to be given a comprehensive multidisciplinary evaluation to determine if the child is handicapped, the extent of the handicap, and the educational implications of that handicap. If it is determined that a handicapped child cannot be educated totally within the regular educational setting, but requires special services, an individualized educational program must be developed for that child. The courts have held that the program developed must be individually tailored to meet the specific unique educational needs of the child. An IEP that is developed according to what programs are readily available within the system, and tries to fit the child to one of those programs, is clearly unacceptable.

It has long been held that the term appropriate does not mean the best possible education but implies more than simple access to educational programs. Precisely where between these two extremes the definition of appropriate lies has been unclear. Although it is impossible to provide an accurate definition of the term that can be simply and easily applied to even a majority of circumstances, the U.S. Supreme Court has provided an interpretation that has substantially clarified the issue and has set the tone for all subsequent decisions. In the landmark *Rowley* case, the Supreme Court declared that an appropriate education was one that was developed in accordance with all the EHCA's procedural and substantive requirements and that was reasonably calculated to provide educational benefits to the handicapped student.

The court provided further guidance as to what would be considered a program that provided educational benefits. Such a program should include personalized or individualized instruction and, in the case of the student who is educated predominantly in the mainstream, should be designed so that the student has a reasonable chance of earning passing grades and of being promoted each year. However, a handicapped student who is promoted annually is not automatically receiving an appropriate education simply because he or she is being advanced from one grade to another.

In the case of the more severely handicapped student who is not educated primarily in the mainstream, however, the courts have held that the educational program developed should be one that is reasonably designed to allow the student to progress toward the goals of his or her educational plan. The courts have not, however, given much guidance as to what goals would be appropriate for such a student, except that the goals of self-sufficiency and independence should be included. As long as the student's educational goals were developed in accordance with the EHCA's procedures and were based on the results of a multidisciplinary evaluation, it is likely that they would legally be considered to be appropriate.

As it has been held that the appropriate education mandate does not require the provision of the best possible education, it has also been held that the existence of imperfections or flaws in a particular program do not render that program inappropriate. Even the existence and availability of a better program does not make a given program inappropriate. In this regard, educational administrators are generally allowed to use their own discretion in choosing among possible alternatives. As long as proper procedures are followed, the courts generally will not substitute their judgment for that of school officials. Although all a student's special needs must be addressed by his or her IEP, the courts have evaluated the appropriateness of an IEP by looking at it as a whole rather than by judging its individual components in isolation.

The EHCA also mandates that handicapped students are to be educated in the least restrictive environment possible. The courts have held that under this mandate, handicapped students may not be segregated or excluded from the mainstream without just cause and without appropriate due process. Handicapped students must be provided with access to any regular education programs, either academic or nonacademic, in which they are able to participate in and receive benefit from. Sometimes, however, school systems need to strike a balance between required services and mainstreaming. In such a situation the mainstreaming requirement becomes secondary and may not be used to prevent access to needed special education services.

Also in relation to the mainstreaming requirement, several courts have indicated that handicapped children should be educated in instructional groups that will provide each student with appropriate peer interaction. It has been held that an appropriate peer group would be one that has other students of the same age or developmental level and with similar educational needs. One court has also suggested that it is desirable, but not required, that both sexes be represented in an instructional group. It can be concluded that whether a handicapped child is educated in the mainstream or in a segregated setting, provisions should be made for peer interaction and socialization to the greatest extent possible. An appropriate peer group is especially important for a student with imitative tendencies. Such a student needs appropriate peers for modeling purposes.

The EHCA also provides that a handicapped child should be educated in the school that child would have attended if not handicapped unless other arrangements are required to implement the child's IEP. The courts have not interpreted this provision strictly but, rather, have held that it does not mean that handicapped children must be educated in their neighborhood school if an appropriate program can be provided within a reasonable distance. The courts, recognizing the fiscal constraints that have been placed on schools, have not required school systems to develop an appropriate program in a handicapped child's neighborhood school when an appropriate program exists nearby. The courts have indicated that the neighborhood school requirement is designed to encourage mainstreaming and that its purpose would be served as long as provisions for mainstreaming were made. The courts appear to find consolidation of special education programs acceptable as long as the purpose is to provide a greater scope of services and to utilize scarce resources better. Also, the courts have allowed school districts to transfer handicapped students to a school where they will receive a more appropriate education when evidence indicates that they are not progressing.

The EHCA has a regulation that indicates that handicapped children are to be provided with the same type of nonacademic and extracurricular programs that are provided to nonhandicapped children. This regulation has been invalidated by the Sixth Circuit Court of Appeals. Handicapped students should be provided with access to any regular extracurricular program that they qualify for. To exclude them because of their handicap alone would violate Section 504. Special extracurricular programs do not have to be developed specifically for a handicapped child unless such a program would be necessary for the child to benefit from the special education program.

The EHCA's mainstreaming requirement encourages school districts to develop appropriate programs within the public school setting. This does not mean that programs in separate facilities are automatically inappropriate. Many students require placement in a separate setting to receive an appropriate education. Handicapped children cannot be excluded from a public school placement when one is clearly warranted. The courts have held that handicapped students cannot be excluded because of physical disabilities or because they are carriers of hepatitis B. Although it has not yet been litigated, it may be assumed that handicapped students with AIDS also could not be excluded. As long as the risk to other students can be minimized through the use of proper prophylactic procedures, students who are health impaired must not be excluded.

By its own provisions, the EHCA applies to certain U.S. territories and possessions and Indian reservation schools as well as to state and local educational agencies. The courts have also held that students in government-operated overseas schools, state-operated schools, and eligible inmates in correctional facilities are also entitled to the services mandated by the law. Handicapped students are also entitled to receive more than the traditional 12 years of schooling if necessary. The EHCA and many state laws provide that handicapped students may receive special education and related services through the age of 21 if they have not earned a high school diploma.

In addition to the EHCA and its regulations each state also has a set of laws and regulations governing special education. Although the state laws must not conflict with the federal law, they may go beyond the federal standard. The federal law creates a basic floor of opportunity for handicapped children, but it establishes no ceiling. Some states have established standards of appropriateness that are much stricter than the EHCA's and provide for a greater degree of services. Those stricter standards are automatically incorporated into the EHCA and will be considered by the courts in determining the appropriateness of a given IEP. The standard in Massachusetts, for example, requires that the IEP provide a level of educational services that will help a handicapped child reach his maximum potential development. The services provided under that standard certainly must be more comprehensive than they would be under the federal "some educational benefit" standard.

REQUIREMENTS FOR PRIVATE PLACEMENTS

The placement of a handicapped child in a private day or residential school has been the subject of much controversy and litigation. The EHCA provides that school districts must have a continuum of programs available for possible placements, including private and residential schools. The EHCA further provides that such placements must be made with no cost to the parents. Most of the litigation has arisen when school districts have proposed programs within their own system and the handicapped child's parents have objected, feeling that those programs were not appropriate. Some litigation has arisen, however, over a school district's recommendation for private or residential placement with the parents objecting. The EHCA provides little guidance as to specifically when such a placement is required; however, the courts have once again provided further clarification.

Residential placements are required when the handicapped student needs 24-hour-per-day care or instruction or when the student needs full-time immersion in the program to remediate the student's disabilities. Twenty-four-hour instruction is generally considered to be necessary when the student's needs dictate that the approach used must be consistent in both the student's school and home environment. If the student's home environment cannot provide the needed consistency and follow-through, or if it does not provide the child with sufficient emotional support, a residential placement is required.

Private day and residential school placements are also required when the school district cannot provide an appropriate program within a public school setting. If the child has not been progressing, or if the evidence indicates that the child will not progress, in a public school placement, a more restrictive setting may be warranted. Private day or residential placements are also required if the student's needs require a highly structured, closely monitored, individualized program and such a program is unavailable or can't be provided in the public schools.

A student whose behavior has become so violent that it becomes a danger to the student and others or causes a substantial disruption to the educational process may require a more restrictive environment than the public schools. The Section 504 regulations indicate that where this happens, the needs of the handicapped child cannot be met in that environment. These regulations are also quoted in a comment to the EHCA's least restrictive environment regulations and indicate that school officials are justified in removing a disruptive handicapped student from a mainstream environment. The EHCA's due process safeguards must be invoked, however. The removal of handicapped students from the public schools for disciplinary purposes will be discussed later.

Students whose basic educational goals are to develop self-sufficiency and independence may also require a residential or private school placement. Such a placement may be needed to provide the student with the proper environment to learn and practice those skills needed for self-sufficiency and independence. Again, such a program would require consistency and close monitoring.

It is clear that school districts are required to pay all the costs of a residential placement that is made for purely educational reasons. What has not been as clear is if the school district is responsible for all costs when other noneducational factors also are considered in making the residential placement. When all the student's needs are so intertwined and interrelated that they can't be separated, the school district is responsible for providing the residential placement. When it is fairly clear, however, that the student's need for a residential placement does not arise out of the need to educate but, rather, arises out of other noneducational needs, the school district is not responsible for residential component costs. Parents also may not be required to surrender guardianship of the child to obtain a residential placement at no cost to themselves.

Under the least restrictive environment mandate, a residential or private school placement is not required if the child could be provided with an appropriate education in a less restrictive environment with the addition of other services. School districts should make every attempt possible to educate handicapped students within a public school setting, however, the least restrictive environment mandate may not be used to preclude a private school or residential placement when such a placement is warranted. In fact, a private placement may be a more appropriate alternative if a less restrictive placement with additional services is clearly not practical or is unreasonably expensive.

The *Rowley* decision has also helped to clarify the issue of whether or not a residential or private school placement is required. Under the *Rowley* standard, such a placement would not be required if the public schools had a program that would provide the handicapped student with some educational benefit. Also, once it has been determined that a public school program is appropriate, the school district has no duty to give further consideration to a private placement. *Rowley* also does not require that the residential school chosen be the best possible choice.

As with all placement decisions under the EHCA, the decision to place, or not to place, a handicapped child in a private day school or residential facility must be made on an individual basis and must be based on the results of a multidisciplinary evaluation. The state and local school districts may not have any policies or practices that preclude the consideration of private or residential placements.

TRANSFER FROM A PRIVATE TO A PUBLIC PROGRAM

The question also has arisen as to when it is appropriate to transfer a child from a private or residential facility to a public school program. Again, such a decision would have to be made on an individual basis. The student may be transferred to the public school program if that program is appropriate and if the student's needs no longer require the more restrictive environment. If any reasonable doubt exists as to whether or not the benefits of the public school program outweigh the risks of change, the student should remain in the private facility. If such a transfer is made, it would be best if the receiving teacher had some experience teaching students who were formerly in more restrictive settings. In the case of a student being transferred from a residential facility, the home environment must also be receptive for the transfer to take place. A handicapped student may be transferred to a public school setting as long as the public program is appropriate even though the methodology used may be different from that used in the private school.

ANNUAL DURATION OF SPECIAL EDUCATION

Another issue that has been widely litigated is whether or not school districts are required to provide educational programs for handicapped students beyond the traditional school year. Again, this is an area in which both the EHCA and its implementing regulations are silent.

It is fairly settled that extended school year programs must be an option available to handicapped students who may need them. The question then becomes: In what instances are such programs required? The *Armstrong* decision, that such a program is needed when the amount of regression the handicapped child suffers over the summer vacation and the time required for recoupment of those skills interfere with the attainment of educational goals, has become the accepted standard for such a determination. One court, however, has gone beyond that standard and has ordered school districts to also consider the nature of the handicap, the severity of the handicap, and the areas of learning that are crucial to the attainment of the goals of self-sufficiency and independence, in addition to the extent of the regression and the recoupment time. However, the regression/recoupment standard is generally accepted in most states.

Handicapped students who require residential placements, especially those who require such placements because they need 24-hour care and instruction, usually need the residential placement on a full-year basis. The courts have held that when year-round residential placements are necessary, they must be at public expense.

Summer school programs are often more on the nature of recreational or enrichment programs than academic programs. Such programs are often offered to nonhandicapped children, but handicapped children may benefit from them as well. Many handicapped children, because of their handicaps, are limited in recreational and enrichment activities. At least one court has held that such programs are required for handicapped children, especially if they are available to the nonhandicapped.

It is also fairly settled that extended school year programs are not required if the rate of regression and recoupment time required for the handicapped child is no greater than it is for a nonhandicapped child. Likewise, it has been held that extended school year programs are not required unless an irreparable loss of progress over the summer vacation period can be shown.

Again, the decision as to whether or not an extended school year program is required should be made on an individual basis using the results of a multidisciplinary evaluation. If such a program is determined to be appropriate, it should be written in as part of the student's IEP.

CHANGING A HANDICAPPED CHILD'S PLACEMENT

The EHCA provides that a handicapped child's educational placement cannot be changed unless that child is provided with certain due process safeguards, most important, notice and an opportunity to contest the proposed change in placement. The EHCA further provides that a child's placement cannot be changed while a due process action is pending, unless the parties agree otherwise. These provisions have been subject to much litigation.

During the past several years school systems throughout the country have had to make many adjustments and changes as a result of declining enrollments, fiscal constraints, and other external factors. These changes have affected all phases of the educational program, including special education. The courts have generally held that such overall changes that affect an entire group of students as opposed to a single student, do not constitute a change in placement as long as little change is made in educational programming. For example, the courts have held that the physical relocation of a special education program and even the complete termination of a program do not require the EHCA's due process safeguards. Generally, if a child's IEP can still be fully implemented after the change has taken place, a change in placement under the EHCA has not occurred. If a dispute arises as to whether or not the IEP can be implemented, the EHCA's complaint mechanism may be invoked to settle the dispute. If changes take place that do interfere with full implementation of the child's IEP, however, it may be held that a change in placement has occurred. Minor adjustments are usually allowable; however, a major change would not be acceptable. The determining factor most often will be the effect the change has on the child's learning.

The courts have been reluctant to interfere with school officials' decision-making authority in regard to the change in placement issue. As long as programmatic changes have not negatively impacted the amount, type, or general quality of special education services offered, the courts have upheld the changes. Changes that have been made to improve the educational offering have also been upheld.

The courts have also held that the expulsion of a handicapped child is a change in placement sufficient to invoke the EHCA's due process safeguards. This will be discussed later.

The graduation of a handicapped child, with its consequent termination of special education services is also a change in placement under the EHCA. When the decision is made to graduate a handicapped student, full due process must be provided just as with any other placement change. The first step in that process would be to indicate on the last IEP developed prior to the graduation date that it is anticipated that the student will graduate. Furthermore, any requirement that the student must meet to graduate should also be clearly spelled out in that IEP. The student and his or her parents should also be notified that they have the same rights concerning the proposed graduation as they would have with any other change in placement.

The student and his or her parents may contest the graduation proposal through an impartial due process hearing if they disagree with it. School administrators should note that if, in fact, the proposed graduation is contested, the student is entitled to remain in his or her then current educational program until the issue is finally resolved. In other words the school district cannot graduate the student as long as due process appeals are pending. Since these appeals often take several years to reach a final settlement, the question could become moot if the student reached the upper age limit of eligibility for special education services while appeals were still in progress.

STATUS QUO PENDING APPEALS

Most of the litigation in this area has arisen over a change in placement that has occurred during the pendency of an appeals action. In some cases the student was unable, or it was inadvisable for the student, to remain in the then current placement as required by the EHCA during the pendency of the appeals, and the parties were unable to agree on an alternative. In many cases the parents have unilaterally transferred the student and later sought to recover the costs they incurred in doing so.

Generally, the status quo should be maintained until a final administrative hearing decision is handed down. The parents of a handicapped child may rely on such a decision in placing their child without fear of later being sued for recovery of the costs of that placement if the decision is overturned by the courts. Also, the courts may be called upon to use their traditional powers of equity to determine an interim placement pending the resolution of appeals. In such an instance the party seeking to modify the status quo would bear the burden of proof before the court.

It is clear from the foregoing that school systems may change the location of a special education program or make other changes that do not affect the types or quantity of special education services provided without having to provide full due process. If, however, the changes affect the types or quantity of services provided, in any way alter the scope of the student's IEPs, or preclude full implementation of the IEPs, school districts should provide due process safeguards. If in doubt, remember that it is always better to provide more due process than is required.

UNILATERAL PLACEMENT CHANGES

The parents of handicapped children, feeling that the public school program was inappropriate, have often unilaterally, changed their child's placement to a private facility before exhausting all appeals. If they eventually prevail in having the private school declared to be the appropriate placement, they may later seek to recover all the funds they expended in making the unilateral placement. Whether or not they are entitled under the EHCA to be reimbursed for those costs has been the most controversial issue litigated since the passage of P.L. 94-142.

Initially, the courts almost unanimously declared that reimbursement was not available to parents who violated the status quo provision unless exceptional circumstances existed to warrant such action. However, the U.S. Supreme Court has overturned those rulings in its *Burlington* decision by declaring that parents who are successful in their due process action are entitled to be reimbursed for private school tuition expenses. However, the high court warned that parents who violate the status quo do so at their own financial risk since they will not be reimbursed if the school district can prove that it proposed and had the capacity to implement an appropriate IEP.

THE PROVISION OF RELATED SERVICES

Litigation has often come before the courts over the EHCA's requirement that certain related, or supportive, services must be provided to handicapped students if they are needed for the students to benefit from their special education programs. Virtually any service that would allow a handicapped student to benefit from the special education program could be considered a related service, except for medical services which are expressly excluded. The EHCA's regulations list 13 specific related services but indicate that this list is not exhaustive.

The exempted medical services have been considered in much of this litigation. Several medically related services are specifically listed as required related services and the courts have been called upon to determine whether certain services fall within the realm of exempted medical services or are required related services. The courts have basically held that services that must legally be performed only by a licensed physician are medical services whereas services that can be performed by other trained personnel are related services. Since state laws vary in this regard, what is and is not an exempted medical service may only be determined on a state-by-state basis.

Psychotherapy is one such issue. In some states, psychotherapy, by law, may only be provided by a licensed psychiatrist. Psychotherapy, in those states, would fall within the medical services exemption. Other states, however, allow psychologists, trained counselors, or social workers to provide psychotherapy. In those states psychotherapy could be considered a required related service if it is needed by the student to benefit from special education. Some students with emotional handicaps, for example, may need psychotherapy because the effort to educate may depend on the resolution of emotional issues. The courts have held that psychotherapy must be provided as a related service in cases such as this. If the need for psychotherapy, however, has little to do with the effort to educate, it is unlikely that it would be found to be a related service. A school district may also be required to pay for psychotherapy if it is provided as part of a total therapeutic program and is needed for the student to benefit from that program.

The courts have also held that health services that can be performed by the school nurse, a health aide, or even a trained layperson may be considered required related services. Again, state medical laws may dictate who may and may not provide medically related services. The courts have held that school systems must provide health services to a student with a tracheotomy tube and catheterization to students needing it. Without these services, the students would not be able to attend school and could not, therefore, benefit from special education programs.

One court indicated, however, that such services would be required only if they had to be provided during school hours. In another case, the court held that the school department was required to air condition the classroom of a physically handicapped student who was unable to regulate his own body temperature. Again, without the air conditioning, the student would be unable to attend school.

Although services that normally must be provided by a physician are exempted from the related services mandate, services that by law may be performed by a nonphysician, but are provided by a physician are not exempted. However, the school system is responsible only for costs no greater than the fees normally charged by a nonphysician provider.

Parents may also be required to use their private medical insurance to pay for diagnostic evaluations as long as such use would not incur a financial cost to them. The school district would be responsible for any excess costs not covered by the insurance.

School systems may also be required to provide training and counseling for the parents of handicapped students. Many severely handicapped students require consistency and follow through in the home of what has been taught in the school. Without this consistency and follow-through they would derive little or no benefit from their special education programs. For some students a residential placement may be the only way of obtaining the necessary consistency, but for others it can be obtained by training the student's parents in proper techniques. This would enable the student to be educated in a less restrictive environment.

The EHCA also requires that handicapped students be provided with recreational activities. These activities are especially important for handicapped students whose opportunities for such activities may be limited. These activities may help a handicapped student develop better socialization and peer interaction skills. Such skills are often included in the overall goals of a student's IEP. In such a case the provision of recreational activities would assist the student in benefiting from the special education program. Although such programs would not be required for all handicapped students, they could be required if they would help the student attain his or her educational goals. School systems may also be required, particularly under Section 504, to provide such programs to handicapped students if they are provided to nonhandicapped students.

The EHCA specifically requires that handicapped students are to be provided with transportation if needed for the child to gain access to the special education program. The term "transportation" has been held to include transporting the child from the building to the vehicle. The term does not, however, encompass therapeutic trips home for a residential school student. The transportation plan developed must be appropriate and minor changes to that plan would not constitute a change in placement.

The *Rowley* decision by the U.S. Supreme Court also has implications for the provision of related services, since the parents' requested service, a sign language interpreter, was denied. The high court found that the student was able to achieve satisfactorily without the provision of this service. Although none of these related services decisions relied on the *Rowley* standard, it is reasonable to assume that a specific related service would not be required if the student were able to make satisfactory progress toward the goals of his or her IEP, and therefore derive educational benefit from the special education program, without the related service. This is consistent with the EHCA's definition of related services being such supportive services that are required to assist the handicapped child in benefiting from special education. If the student is already benefiting from special education, under the *Rowley* standard no additional supportive services would be required. The courts have not required that school systems provide each and every special education service that would be helpful to a handicapped child, and it is unlikely that they would require each and every related service that would be beneficial.

The high court has also declared in the *Tatro* decision that related services need not be provided to a nonspecial education student and only services that are necessary to aid a handicapped child to benefit from special education must be provided. Also, only life support services that must be administered during the school day need be provided.

The EHCA also requires school districts to provide speech pathology, audiology, physical therapy, and occupational therapy when needed by handicapped students as related services. However, these provisions have not been litigated to date.

The determination of whether or not a specific related service is needed can be made in a similar manner as the decision of whether or not special education services are needed. In fact, it is best to make the determination at the same time. It is reasonable to assume that related services are not required if the student is able to make satisfactory progress toward the goals of his or her IEP, and thus derive educational benefit, without the related service.

DISCIPLINING A DISRUPTIVE HANDICAPPED STUDENT

One of the more controversial issues that has emerged since the implementation of the EHCA concerns the discipline of handicapped students. This issue is not directly addressed by either the EHCA or its implementing regulations; however, many of their provisions have implications for the application of disciplinary procedures to handicapped children. The issue has been very delicate since the courts have recognized that the authority of school officials to maintain order and discipline should not be undermined; however, the provisions of the EHCA also should not be circumvented through disciplinary policies. The common law that has emerged very definitely strikes that balance between the needs of school authorities to maintain discipline and the rights of behaviorally disordered students to obtain an appropriate education.

The common law, as it stands at this writing, in regard to disciplining handicapped students is best exemplified by the court of appeals decision in *Turlington*. According to that standard, a handicapped student cannot be expelled if his or her behavior is a manifestation of his or her handicap. That determination can only be made by a group of knowledgeable persons, such as the school's evaluation team. The handicapped student can, however, be temporarily suspended or transferred to a more restrictive environment if his or her presence in the school poses a risk to himself or herself or to other students or substantially disrupts the educational process for others. A transfer to a more restrictive environment may be made involuntarily. In fact, disruptive behavior may be an indication that a more restrictive setting is needed.

If the offensive behavior is determined to not be a manifestation of the student's handicap, the student may be expelled. However, a complete cessation of educational services would not be allowed, so the school system would be required to provide some type of alternate educational arrangement such as homebound instruction. School officials must assume the burden of making the determination as to whether or not a student's disruptive behavior is a manifestation of his or her handicap.

The foregoing scheme does not undermine the authority of school officials to maintain order and discipline and still affords handicapped students their full rights to an appropriate education under the EHCA. The *Turlington* standard simply requires that when a handicapped student is disciplined, school officials must employ procedures that are consistent with the EHCA rather than the normal *Goss* procedures. When a handicapped student is disruptive, school officials may take action to curb the disruption and restore order. The school system has the right, and even the responsibility, to bar a student that it determines is dangerous, even if the student is handicapped. If the school's evaluation team determines that a more restrictive placement is needed, and that finding is rejected by the student's parents, the school may bar the student during the appeals process if it determines that he is dangerous.

If a handicapped student becomes disruptive or dangerous, school officials may take swift action just as they would with a nonhandicapped student. Emergency procedures may be employed whether the student is handicapped or not. If the student is handicapped, the school's evaluation team should be notified immediately. The team should convene as soon as possible, preferably within five days, to make a determination as to whether or not the student's handicap caused his or her behavior and to make a decision regarding the appropriate course of action.

School officials may also develop a disciplinary policy as part of a student's IEP. That policy should spell out what is expected of the student and what will happen if those expectations are not realized. That policy may be similar to the school's disciplinary policies for nonhandicapped children as long as it meets the student's individual needs. If a disciplinary policy is written into a student's IEP, there should be no question as to what action should be taken if the student becomes disruptive and no legal problems after that action is taken.

Some disagreement has arisen concerning how students referred for an evaluation but not yet determined to be handicapped should be treated. One court approved a consent decree that stipulated that such students would be treated in the same manner as handicapped students while another court specifically stated that the EHCA requires that they be treated as if they were not handicapped. Since a consent decree is binding only on the parties who agree to it, the decision of the latter court is more persuasive. Absent any contrary agreement, state statute, or local policy, school officials should assume that a student is not handicapped until such time as a student is determined to be handicapped. Such a student could, therefore, be disciplined as a nonhandicapped student. The disciplinary process could not, however, interfere with, or stop the evaluation process. If the student is subsequently determined to be handicapped, any prior disciplinary measures, such as an expulsion, cannot be used to deny the student an appropriate education.

School officials should also take steps to evaluate a nonhandicapped student who is persistently disruptive. Such behavior may be a manifestation of an unidentified handicap. Under the EHCA school districts have an affirmative duty to identify and serve all handicapped children.

MINIMUM COMPETENCY TESTS

School officials must often decide whether or not to administer minimum competency tests (MCTs) to handicapped students. This question becomes more critical if the awarding of a high school diploma is contingent on passing the tests. School districts do have the right to set minimum standards for earning a diploma, and those may include passing an MCT, as long as proper notice has been provided and the tests are a valid reflection of the curriculum that has been taught.

Handicapped students may be required to meet the same standards as other students to receive a standard diploma. However, the MCTs may have to be administered in a modified fashion to accommodate the student's handicap. No modification is required on test content, however.

HANDICAPPED PAROCHIAL SCHOOL STUDENTS

The EHCA specifically mandates that needed special education services must also be provided to handicapped parochial school students. However, in view of many Establishment Clause cases that have been decided by the federal courts, care must be taken so that the method of service provision does not violate the U.S. Constitution.

To avoid charges of excessive entanglement between the public and parochial schools, it would be best to provide all services within the public school facilities. Contact between public and parochial school officials should be limited to that which is necessary to ensure that the special education program will result in educational benefit. It is also unlikely that school systems would be required to transport a parochial student to the public school building for that student to receive special education services.

RECORD KEEPING

The EHCA provides some very specific guidelines regarding the maintenance of handicapped student records. These regulations provide that the student's parents have the right to inspect the records and may request that the records be amended. The regulations also limit the release of these records to a third party. Basically, the requirements of the EHCA on student records are consistent with those of the Family Educational Rights and Privacy Act that apply to all students.

NATIVE LANGUAGE TESTING

The EHCA requires that non-English–speaking students are to be tested and evaluated in their native language. All diagnostic and placement procedures used must not be culturally or linguistically biased so that the student is not placed at a disadvantage because of limited English proficiency. This means that tests used must be administered in the child's native language and should also be normed according to the child's culture.

PAYMENT OF ATTORNEYS' FEES

The due process procedures of the EHCA can prove to be expensive for both the school system and the handicapped child's parents, especially if the case reaches the court level. In the *Smith* opinion, the U.S. Supreme Court found that since the EHCA does not specifically provide for the awarding of attorney fees to the prevailing party in a special education dispute, the parents of a handicapped child cannot be awarded reimbursement of their legal costs even if they win their suit. This has all changed, however, as Congress recently amended the EHCA to allow the courts to award attorneys' fees to prevailing parents.

STATE LEGISLATION

This book has focused on the courts' interpretations of the EHCA in regard to the provision of special education and related services. The EHCA is not the only special education law in the nation, however. Each of the states, the District of Columbia, and the possessions and territories have special education laws and codes of their own. Although state laws must be consistent with the federal law, differences do exist. School administrators should, therefore, also be familiar with state law provisions before making any decisions regarding the provision of special education and related services.

CONCLUSION

The overriding theme of the EHCA is that all placement and programming decisions on handicapped students must be made on an individual basis and must be made on the basis of information gathered from a variety of sources. If an administrator makes a decision on those bases, follows the procedures mandated by the EHCA, and makes the decision in good faith with the best interests of the child and school system in mind, that decision has a reasonable chance of being upheld.

REFERENCES

Armstrong v. *Kline*, 476 F.Supp. 583 (1979).

Board of Education v. *Rowley*, 102 S.Ct. 3034 (1982).

Burlington School Committee v. *Department of Education*, 105 S.Ct. 1996 (1985).

Crawford v. *Pittman*, 708 F2d 1028 (1983).

Goss v. *Lopez*, 419 U.S. 565 (1975).

Harvard Note, "Enforcing the Right to an 'Appropriate' Education: The Education for All Handicapped Children Act of 1975," 92 *Harvard Law Review* 1003 (1979).

Irving I.S.D. v. *Tatro*, 104 S.Ct. 3371 (1984).

Kreunen, W. L., "The Law and the Handicapped Student," *School Law for a New Decade*, NOLPE (1981).

O'Donnell, T. P., "The Education of the Handicapped Act: Some Recent Case Developments," *School Law in Contemporary Society*, NOLPE (1980).

S-1 v. *Turlington*, 635 F.2d 342 (1981).

Smith v. *Robinson*, 104 S.Ct. 3457 (1984).

Appendix A

GLOSSARY OF COMMONLY USED TERMS

Administrative appeals   Quasi-judicial proceedings before impartial hearing officers as mandated by the due process requirements of the EHCA (20 U.S.C. §1415).

Affirm   To uphold the lower court's decision in an appeal.

Annual review   A review of a child's progress in a special education program and an examination of his or her future special educational needs held at least once every year. An annual review may repeat some of the original assessments, but is generally not as thorough as the original evaluation. The student's IEP is revised and updated at the annual review meeting.

Appellant   The party who appeals a decision of one court to a higher court.

Appellee   The party against whom an appeal is made to a higher court.

Certiorari   A writ issued by an appeals court (most commonly the U.S. Supreme Court) indicating that it will review the lower court's decision.

Consent Decree   An agreement by the parties to a lawsuit and sanctioned by the court that basically settles the dispute between those parties by mutual consent.

Decree   The judgment of a court that outlines the legal consequences of the facts of the case.

Defendant   The party against whom a lawsuit is brought.

Dicta   Statements in a court's opinion that go beyond the facts of the case and are not binding on future cases.

EHCA   The Education for All Handicapped Children Act of 1975, P.L. 94-142, codified as 20 U.S.C. § 1401 et seq.

Evaluation team   A group of individuals who perform certain assessments of the child to determine if the child is handicapped, and if so, what educational services will be required by the child. The evaluation team may be composed of classroom teachers, special education teachers, administrators, psychologists, the parents of the child (or the child), and other specialists.

Handicapped children   "Mentally retarded, hard of hearing, deaf, speech impaired, visually handicapped, seriously emotionally disturbed, orthopedically impaired, or other health impaired children, or children with specific learning disabilities, who by reason thereof require special education and related services" (20 U.S.C. § 1401(1)).

Handicapping conditions   See *Handicapped children*. Terms referring to specific handicapping conditions are used as they are defined in the law and regulations (20 U.S.C. § 1401 and 34 C.F.R. § 300.5).

IEP   Individualized Education Plan (or Program). A document outlining the specific program of special education and related services to be provided to a handicapped child.

Injunction   An order issued by the court forbidding a party to take some contemplated action, or restraining the party from continuing an action.

Plaintiff   The party bringing a lawsuit to court.

Reevaluation   The EHCA requires that at least every three years a complete reevaluation of a handicapped child take place. The reevaluation generally is similar to the original evaluation, but may include additional assessments if warranted.

Regulations   The regulations for the implementation of P.L. 94-142, codified as 34 C.F.R. § 300 et seq., originally published in the *Federal Register* on August 23, 1977.

Remand   To send a case back to the lower court, usually with specific instructions for further action.

Reverse   To revoke the lower court's decision in an appeal.

Section 504   Section 504 of The Rehabilitation act of 1973, codified as 29 U.S.C. § 794.

Vacate   To set aside the lower court's decision in an appeal.

Appendix B

KEY TO LEGAL CITATIONS

A	*Atlantic Reporter*
Cal. Rptr.	*California Reporter*
C.F.R.	*Code of Federal Regulations*
Ed. Law	*Education Law Reporter*
EHLR	*Education of the Handicapped Law Reports*
F.2d	*Federal Reporter,* Second Series
F.Supp.	*Federal Supplement*
Ill.Dec.	*Illinois Decisions*
L.Ed.	*Lawyer's Edition*
N.E.	*North Eastern Reporter*
N.W.	*North Western Reporter*
N.Y.Supp.	*New York Supplement*
P	*Pacific Reporter*
S	*Southern Reporter*
S.Ct.	*Supreme Court Reporter*
S.E.	*South Eastern Reporter*
S.W.	*South Western Reporter*
U.S.	*United States Reports*
U.S.C.	*United States Code*

Appendix C

THE LAW AND REGULATIONS

Copies of the Education for All Handicapped Children Act and its implementing regulations can be obtained from

Superintendent of Documents
U.S. Government Printing Office
Washington, D.C. 20402
Telephone: (202) 783-3238

Copies are also available through federal government bookstores located in many major cities.

The law itself (P.L. 94-142) is contained in the *United States Code,* Vol. 20, Pts. 1401–1485. The implementing regulations are contained in the *Code of Federal Regulations,* Vol. 34, Pt. 300.

Index

A

B

C

D

M

Mainstreaming, *see* Least restrictive environment
Manifestation of handicap, 160–62, 211–12
Maximization of potential, 34, 36, 39
Medical service, 69, 134–39, 142–43, 209
Minimum competency tests, 178–80, 213
More restrictive environment, 22, 36, 157, 166–67, 204, 212

N

Native language testing, 185, 214
Neighborhood school, 21–22, 202
Neurological exams, 142–43
Nonacademic services, 23, 139–40, 202–3
Non-discriminatory evaluations, 4–5, 185, 214
Non-educational placements, 67–69
Nursing services, *see* Health services

O

Obligation to maintain placement, 76
Otherwise qualified, *see* Section 504
Overseas schools, 24, 66, 203

P

Parent training and counseling, 71, 135 210
Parochial schools, 180–82, 213
Peer group, 29–30, 65, 202
Physical education, 95, 140
Physicians, *see* Medical services

Placement, *see* Appropriate placement
Placement pending appeals, *see* Status quo
Preponderance of the evidence, 13
Preschool, 25
Private schools, 59–77, 203–5
Procedural safeguards, *see* Due process
Programmatic changes, 106
Promotion, 35, 201
Psychological services, 132–33
Psychotherapy, 131–35, 209

R

Records, *see* Student records
Recreation programs, 23, 94–95, 139–40, 210
Regression, 91–92, 116, 206
Regulations, 217, 219
Rehabilitation Act, 12, *see also* Section 504
Reimbursement, 113–20, 140–41, 208–9
Related services, 71–72, 130–43, 209–11
Relocation of programs, 104–5
Residential schools, *see* Private schools
Return to public schools, 74–76, 205

S

School closings, 104–7
Section 504, 12, 17, 24, 104, 137, 140, 157–58, 161, 166, 179–80, 185, 199, 204, 210
Self-sufficiency, 64, 201
Separate facilities, 37–38, 203
Sign language interpreter, 32–33
Social work services, 131–32
Special education, defined, 25
State operated schools, 24
State standards, 9, 25, 28, 33, 37, 39, 203, 214
Status quo, 109–13, 208

T

U